The Harmony Guide to

ARAN AND

FAIR ISLE

KNITTING

The Harmony Guide to

ARAN AND

FAIR ISLE

KNITTING

Debra Mountford, Editor

Crown Trade Paperbacks
New York

Published by Crown Trade Paperbacks, 201 East 50th Street, New York, New York 10022. Member of the Crown Publishing Group.

Portions of this book were previously published in *The Harmony Guide to Aran Knitting* by Lyric Books Limited in 1991.

Random House, Inc. New York, Toronto, London, Sydney, Auckland

Crown Trade Paperbacks and colophon are trade marks of Crown Publishers, Inc.

Manufactured in Spain

Library of Congress Cataloging-in-Publication Data available upon request

ISBN 0-517-88405-4

10 9 8 7 6 5 4 3 2 1

First Edition

Contents

INTRODUCTION

The Harmony Guide to Aran and Far Isle Knitting is a comprehensive guide on the two most popular traditional knitting styles. Not only does it give a complete collection of stitches, patterns and techniques, but it also gives clear and easy to follow illustrations and diagrams for the beginner and the more advanced knitter.

The book is designed to stimulate and inspire as well as instruct and provide problem solving answers. Stitch patterns are shown in photographs, as pattern charts and are explained as detailed written instructions. Techniques are illustrated with clear step by step diagrams with the use of colour to add clarity.

The Aran section of the book represents one of the most comprehensive stitch collections ever compiled. The stitches are simply displayed and explained. It shows the incredible range of cables, twists, bobbles and clusters and the way in which Aran combinations can be worked and developed to create individual designs. It is to be studied and enjoyed as an inspiration to originality. The crofters in the Isles of Aran used the stitches to demonstrate their creativity. Today's knitter can now use this guide to express a personality with their own mixture of panels and cables. No two Aran designs need be alike!

Fair Isle knitting has a long and fascinating history. Influences from the central plains of Europe, the Baltic Sea and Scandinavia arrived on the windswept isles of the Shetlands through a combination of invasion by the Norwegians, trade and the North Sea fishing fleets. We have tried to indicate the nature of Fair Isle knitting through its design and colour combinations. As the book developed we became fascinated by the way in which a single diagram could vary and change by using colours as if in a kaleidoscope. We have taken single patterns, created repeats, both vertically and horizontally, and played with the colour combinations to demonstrate the individuality of Fair Isle design.

This book is a textbook to individuality and self expression. Its aim is to inspire hand knitters to be original at their craft. Aran and Fair Isle knitting stitches and techniques are a means of flexible expression where the individual chooses the combinations and is in control of the result.

ARAN

KNITTING

ARAN KNITTING

This detailed Harmony Guide has been compiled to provide the most comprehensive range of Aran designs and patterns. The step by step instructions and diagrams explain and illustrate particular Aran techniques, from the basic cables and twists to bobbles and clusters.

To describe the individual stitch patterns, we have given the precise written pattern, the stitch chart and a detailed photograph.

Aran knitting is a dynamic form of knitting. It involves the combination of traditional stitch patterns to create variety and individuality. The original stitch patterns could often be linked to a family, village or region. They were not written down, merely learnt by example. They are thought to have had religious interpretations, as with Trinity Stitch, or occupatioal significance such as the cables and netting designs which symbolize boats, the sea and specifically fishing. Each stitch pattern had its own meaning and connotation.

We have illustrated many combinations to show the unique and personal designs that can be achieved. These indicate the unlimited ways in which the sample panels, ribs and borders can be used in various designs with either simple or extremely complicated repeats.

The Aran style is exemplified in the patterns we have chosen. First, there is the Lady's Cable Sweater. Then we have designed a traditional His and Her Sweater incorporating many of the most recognised cables and panels. Lastly, there is a selection of accessories for women and children, which are simple and easy to finish. All are illustrated in full colour have clear instructions.

Aran Knitting

Origins of Aran Knitting

The Isles of Aran lie off the west coast of Ireland in the mouth of Galway Bay. There are three main islands, Inishmore, Inishmaan and Inisheer. Irish Gaelic is still spoken by the peoples of these islands and they remain one of the few outposts of Celtic culture.

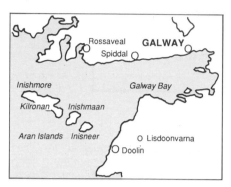

The islands are cut off from the mainland by the Atlantic Ocean. The grey limestone that makes up the islands was scoured by the Ice Age glaciers leaving only a scanty covering of soil which is difficult to cultivate. People have lived on the islands for almost 4,000 years and have until recently made a living from subsistence farming and fishing. Much labour was required to grow basic crops and rear a few hardy varieties of cattle and sheep. The seaweed that surrounds the islands was used as fertilizer and in some cases, turf was cut from the mainland and brought over to form fields. Dry stone walls were built to protect these precious resources. The unpredictable and often inhospitable Atlantic had to be braved in small canoes made of canvas known as 'Currachs'. These were used for fishing and also to retain a link with the mainland. Today the Aran fishermen still use the small frail looking Currachs.

Outdoor work in this harsh environment created a need for warm, protective and practical clothing. This need was crucial to the development of the traditional Aran Sweater. Contrary to the popular opinion that knitting is a womanly craft, the men of the Aran Isles believed that spinning the yarn was women's duty while they reserved the privilege of knitting for themselves. As seamen they were adept at ropemaking. This involved twisting, braiding and folding strands of hemp and they developed these shapes when working the ropes and plaits used in Aran knitting.

There is much speculation as to the origins of the distinctive patterns used on the Aran Sweaters. The patterns seem to reflect elements of Celtic Art. In the early centuries AD following invasions by the Romans, Angles and Saxons, the Celtic language and culture were pushed to the remote peripheries of the British Isles, (Wales, Scotland, Cornwall and Ireland including the Islands of Aran).

The distinctive form of art practised by the Celts consisted of complex mathematically based interlacings and knots. Examples of this art have survived in the Stone Crosses of Ireland and East Scotland, the Lindisfarne Gospels, the Book of Kells and perhaps Aran Knitting. It is impossible to know for certain the meanings of these intricate designs but they are generally used within a religious context, therefore it is likely that they symbolize religious themes. A single unbroken line is thought to be a symbol of eternity or continuity. Many Aran patterns have traditional interpretations usually of religious significance. For example, Trinity Stitch (page 25), made by working three stitches from one and one stitch from three, is thought to signify the Holy Trinity (Father, Son and Holy Ghost).

Originally patterns were not written down. They could only be learnt by example and were passed on from generation to generation within a family. It is said that an islander can often tell from the patterns used in a genuine Aran sweater what family the knitter belongs to. Early examples of Aran knitting were often worked in a seemingly careless way with many mistakes, possibly due to the way the patterns were worked from memory. Strangely, the more complex designs were often knitted perfectly.

Only when patterns were written down could they be preserved and used more widely. A suitable method of notation for knitting remains important for the development of patterns. The modern method of charting has allowed more complex Aran patterns to be designed and worked.

Despite being famous for knitting, the islanders have never earned a living from it. Remuneration from hand knitting is small in relation to the skill and time needed to produce a garment. The inhabitants of Aran have profited indirectly from the islands' fame as it has helped establish a thriving tourist industry. The Aran Isles offer much to visitors interested in Celtic history or wanting to escape from the stress of modern day life. They can now be reached by regular ferry service and the two larger islands can also be reached by air.

Today Aran knitting is known throughout the world. Aran sweaters, as well as being practical workwear, have become fashion garments. The patterns and garment shapes have been recorded so that competent knitters everywhere can produce 'authentic' Aran sweaters.

Yarn

Aran garments are traditionally knitted in thickish, creamy white wool called 'Bainin' (pronounced 'Bawneen') which means milky white in Gaelic. Wool has many properties that help make garments excellent for outdoor wear. It is a very good insulator and has the ability to absorb moisture without feeling wet, thus helping to keep the wearer warm and dry. Originally sweaters were knitted using unscoured wool that retained its natural greases thus making garments more waterproof. Wool is also very malleable allowing it to be steamed into shape. This is important for some of the more intricate Aran patterns as they require a light steam in order to lie flat. For this reason synthetic yarns that do not possess this quality are sometimes unsuitable for Aran work. However Aran sweaters can take on a whole new look if knitted in non-traditional yarns such as mohair or cotton or if colour is used.

Cables

The basis of many Aran patterns is the simple cable. A cable needle is used to move one stitch or a group of stitches over or behind another. When knitted on a plain background this resembles rope.

Cables

Cables are achieved by moving one group of knit stitches over another. Here the cable panel consist of four stitches in stocking stitch against a reverse stocking stitch background.

 C4B (Cable 4 Back)

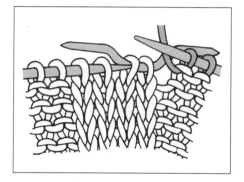

1. On a right side row, work to the position of the cable panel and slip the next two stitches onto the cable needle.

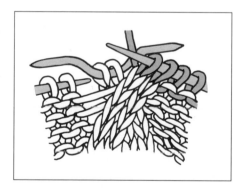

2. With the stitches on the cable needle held at the back of the work, knit the next two stitches from the left-hand needle.

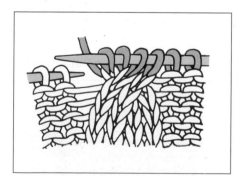

3. Now knit the two stitches from the cable needle to produce the crossover.

Leaving the first set of stitches at the back of the work produces a cable that crosses to the right.

 C4F (Cable 4 Front)

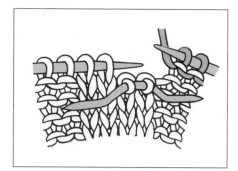

1. On a right side row, work to the position of the cable panel and slip the next two stitches onto the cable needle, leaving it at the front of the work.

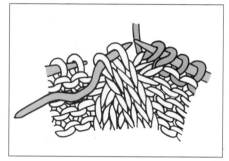

2. Working behind the cable needle, knit the next two stitches from the left-hand needle.

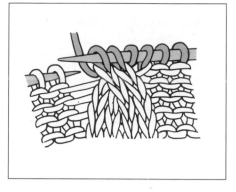

3. Now knit the two stitches from the cable needle to produce the crossover.

Leaving the first set of stitches at the front of the work produces a cable that crosses to the left.

The number of stitches crossed can vary to make larger and smaller cables. The photograph below shows different sized cables on a reverse stocking stitch background. The stitch abbreviation and its reference number in this book are given below each example. To find the written and charted instruction for any stitch refer to the index on pages 174 and 174. The number of rows between each cable can also vary (see page 17).

Once the basic cable technique has been mastered it can be used to produce many variations of the simple rope pattern.

2.1/C2B 2.2/C2F 4.3/C4B 4.2/C4F 6.1/C6B 6.2/C6F 8.2/C8B 8.3/C8F 10.3/C10B 10.2/C10F

Stitch No./Abbreviation

Twist and Cross Stitches

Twisting Stitches

Lattice effects and more complicated cable patterns can be worked by using twist stitches. These are similar to cables but the effect is achieved using knit and purl stitches, not just knit stitches.

Here two stitches are moved in a diagonal direction across a background of reverse st st.

 T3B (Twist 3 Back)

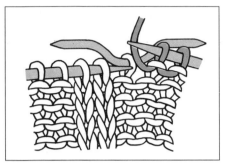

1. On a right side row, work to one stitch before the two knit stitches. Slip the next stitch onto a cable needle and leave it at the back of the work.

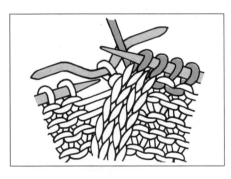

2. Knit the next two stitches from the left-hand needle.

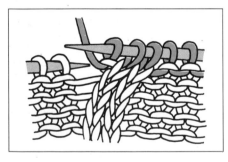

3. Now purl the stitch from the cable needle to produce a twist to the right.

 T3F (Twist 3 Front)

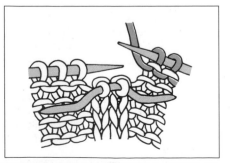

1. On a right side row, work to the two knit stitches. Slip these two stitches onto a cable needle and leave them at the front of the work.

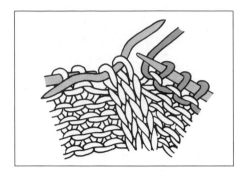

2. Purl the next stitch from the left-hand needle.

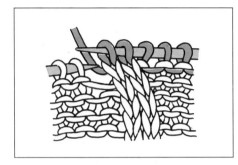

3. Knit the two stitches from the cable needle to produce a twist to the left.

The examples given show two stitches twisted to the right (T3B) and left (T3F) over a background of reverse stocking stitch (8.12, 8.15, 12.17 and 12.18, on pages 33 and 40 show diagonals produced using this technique). Like cables the number of stitches within a twist can vary. Also twist stitches can be worked over a variety of background stitches, usually stocking stitch or reverse stocking stitch.

Stitches can be cabled and twisted in countless knit and purl combinations. However, the basic principle is always the same. Do not be put off by the complicated sounding abbreviation names as they are required to differentiate all the variations. Just follow the instructions step by step and they will become easy. The more unusual abbreviations are given with each pattern while the more common ones have been grouped together on pages 20 and 21.

Cross Stitches

These are very small cables involving only 2 stitches. They can be done either with or without a cable needle. It is well worth experimenting with both methods to discover which method suits you best. Instructions for cable needle methods are given on page 20.

Crossing Stitches Without a Cable Needle.

 C2B (Cross 2 Back)

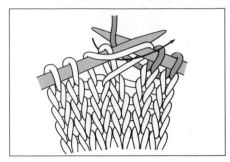

1. Miss the first stitch on the left-hand needle and knit the second stitch, working through the front of the loop only.

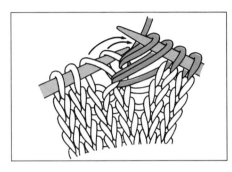

2. Do not slip the worked stitch off the needle, but twist the needle back and knit the missed stitch through the front of the loop, then slip both stitches off the needle together.

 C2F (Cross 2 Front)

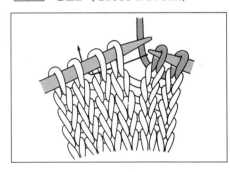

Work as given for C2B but knit the second stitch on the left-hand needle through the back of the loop working behind the first stitch.

 T2B (Twist 2 Back)

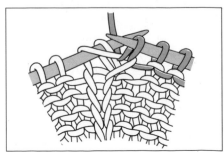

1. Miss the first stitch, then knit the second stitch through the front of the loop.

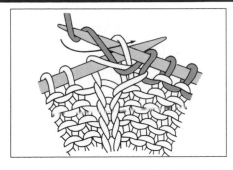

2. Without slipping the worked stitch off the needle, bring the yarn to the front and purl the missed stitch through the front of the loop, then slip both stitches off the needle at the same time.

L= T2F (Twist 2 Front)

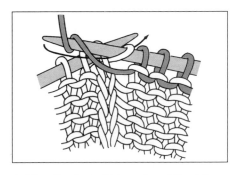

1. Miss the first stitch and purl the following stitch through the back of the loop working behind the first stitch.

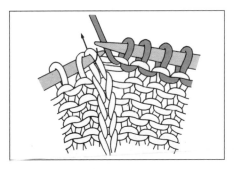

2. Without slipping the purled stitch off the needle, bring the needle to the front of the work, take the yarn back and knit the missed stitch then slip both stitches off the needle at the same time.

For crossing stitches without a cable needle on wrong side rows see instructions on page 20.

Knit or Purl into Back of Stitch

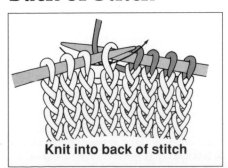

Knit into back of stitch

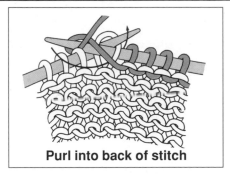

Purl into back of stitch

Knitting or purling into the back of a loop twists the stitch, making it firmer and more distinct. This technique is often combined with crossing stitches to make the resulting patterns stronger (see 24.22 on page 75)

Bobbles

Bobbles can be an important feature of Aran knitting. They can add texture and emphasize designs. Although they are fairly slow to work, the effort can be worthwhile. There are many ways of working bobbles. Shown below are fourteen different bobbles. They vary in size from a small 'popcorn' bobble (MB#1) to a large bobble worked over 5 rows (MB#14) and can be worked in either stocking stitch or reverse stocking stitch. Full instructions for each bobble are given with the general abbreviations on page 21.

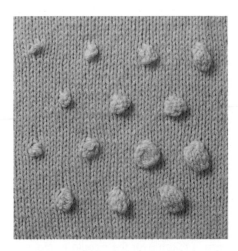

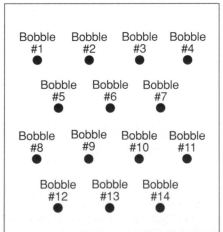

Bobble #1	Bobble #2	Bobble #3	Bobble #4
●	●	●	●
	Bobble #5	Bobble #6	Bobble #7
	●	●	●
Bobble #8	Bobble #9	Bobble #10	Bobble #11
●	●	●	●
	Bobble #12	Bobble #13	Bobble #14
	●	●	●

The following more detailed instructions are for a bobble that is used quite often in this book. It is worked in stocking stitch against a reverse stocking stitch background and involves making four stitches out of one. It is referred to as:

● MB#3 (Make Bobble number three)

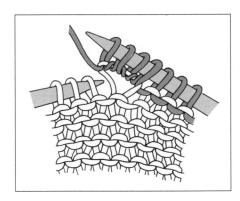

1. On a right side row work to the position of the bobble. Work [k1, p1] twice all into next stitch. Slip the stitch off the left-hand needle so that the four new stitches are on the right-hand needle.

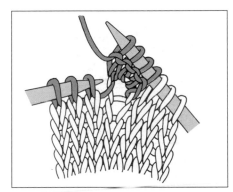

2. Turn the work so that the wrong side is facing and purl the four bobble stitches, then turn again and knit them. Turn and purl these 4 stitches again, thus making three rows in stocking stitch worked over the bobble stitches.

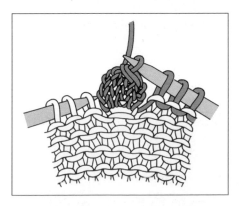

3. Turn the work so that the right side is facing. Slip the first two bobble stitches onto the right-hand needle, knit the next two together, then pass the two slipped stitches over the stitch resulting from the knit two together.

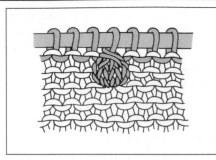

4. One stitch remains and you continue to work the remainder of the row as required. Any small gap in the fabric is hidden by the bobble when you continue knitting.

Cluster and Bound Stitches

These are methods of grouping or bunching stitches together. Generally the Cluster technique is used to group a large number of stitches together (see 8.18 on page 34) and the binding technique is used when only 2 or 3 stitches are involved (see 24.9 and 24.14 on pages 69 and 71).

The following example shows a basic cluster stitch. Here six rib stitches are bunched together.

 **Cluster 6**

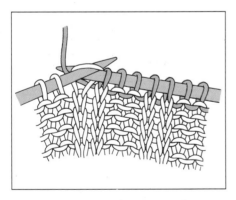

1. K2, p2, k2 from left-hand needle.

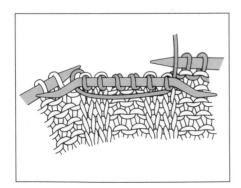

2. Slip these 6 stitches onto a cable needle. Wrap yarn from front to back (anti- clockwise) twice around the stitches on the cable needle.

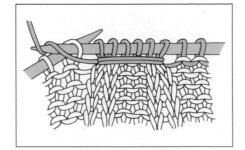

3. Slip stitches back onto right-hand needle. Pull yarn to bunch stitches together.

The stitches that make up a cluster can be worked in various combinations of knit and purl. How tightly the yarn is wrapped around the stitches on the cable needle and the number of times it is wrapped can alter the appearance of a cluster.

The following method is used to bind three stitches together.

 Bind 3

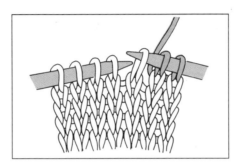

1. Slip one stitch to right-hand needle keeping yarn at back of work.

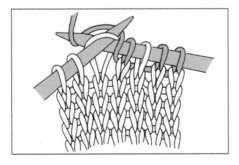

2. Knit one stitch, then bring yarn forward so that when the next stitch is worked the yarn is taken over the needle to make a stitch.

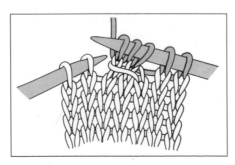

3. With tip of left-hand needle, lift slipped stitch over the k1, yf, k1, thus binding the stitches together. The total number of stitches remains the same.

Miscellaneous Techniques

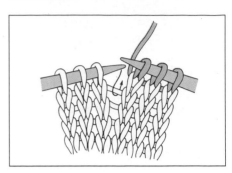 **M1K (Make 1 stitch knitwise)**

1. Insert the right-hand needle from front to back under the horizontal strand which runs between the stitches on the right and left-hand needles.

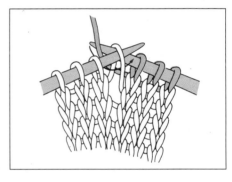

2. Place the strand on left-hand needle and knit into back of it.

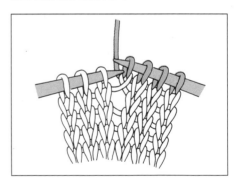

3. The new stitch is twisted to prevent a hole that would otherwise form.

M1P (Make 1 stitch purlwise)

Work as for M1K, but purling into back of strand.

 **Work 5tog (Work 5 stitches together)**

There are several methods of working five stitches together. The following method is fairly unusual but it is deceptively simple to work and it gives a very pleasing result.

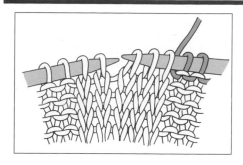

1. Keeping yarn at back of work slip first three stitches of the 5 onto right-hand needle.

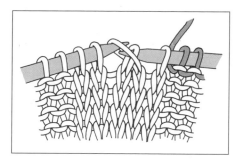

2. Pass second stitch on right-hand needle over 3rd stitch, which is the centre stitch of the 5.

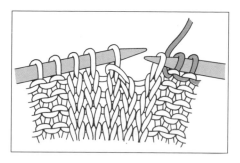

3. Slip centre stitch back onto left-hand needle.

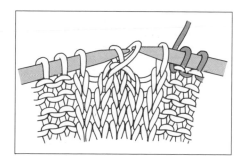

4. Pass second stitch on left-hand needle over central stitch.

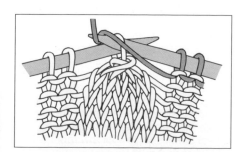

5. Slip centre stitch back onto right-hand needle then repeat steps 2, 3 and 4. One stitch remains on left-hand needle. This stitch can be knitted or purled as required.

Stitch Charts

Most knitters have already used charts to knit fairisle or intarsia patterns. We have given all the aran patterns in this book both written and charted directions in the hope that you will discover how useful charts can be for Aran patterns. A chart also gives a visual impression of how the finished pattern will appear, enabling instructions for long and complicated patterns to be given in a clear and concise way. This can also be very useful when learning a new stitch or altering the row repeat of a panel to enable it to fit better with other panels (see page 17)

How to Read Charts

Charts are read exactly as the knitting is worked - from the bottom to the top. After the last row at the top has been worked repeat the sequence from row 1.

Each symbol represents an instruction. Symbols have been designed as far as possible to resemble the actual appearance of the knitting. However it is not always possible to be exact, therefore it is vital that you **always** refer to the detailed description of each symbol.

Before starting to knit look up all the symbols on your chosen chart so that you are familiar with the techniques involved. These are either shown with the pattern as a special abbreviation or on pages 20 and 21. A reminder of the more common abbreviations that are not shown as special abbreviations is given at the bottom of each page. (Refer to pages 20 and 21 for more detailed descriptions).

Each square represents a stitch and each horizontal line a row. Place a ruler above the line you are working and work the symbols one by one. If you are new to

chart reading you may find it helpful to compare the charted instructions with the written ones.

Some patterns and panels that have increases and decreases do not have the same number of stitches on each row. These charts have blank spaces on them so that the total number of stitches in any row is still represented by the number of squares on the chart.

For knitters who wish to follow the written directions it is still a good idea to look at the chart before starting, to see what the repeat looks like and how the pattern has been balanced.

Make sure you understand the difference between working similar symbols on a right side row and a wrong side row.

Right Side and Wrong Side Rows.

'Right side rows' are rows where the right side of the fabric is facing you when you work and 'wrong side rows' are rows where the wrong side of the fabric is facing you when you work. Row numbers are shown at the side of the charts **at the beginning of the row**. Right side rows are always read from right to left. Wrong side rows are always read from left to right.

Symbols on the charts are shown as they appear from the right side of the work. For example, a horizontal dash stands for a purl 'bump' on the right side regardless of whether it was achieved by purling on a right side row or knitting on a wrong side row. To make charts clearer symbols on right side rows are slightly darker than those on wrong side rows.

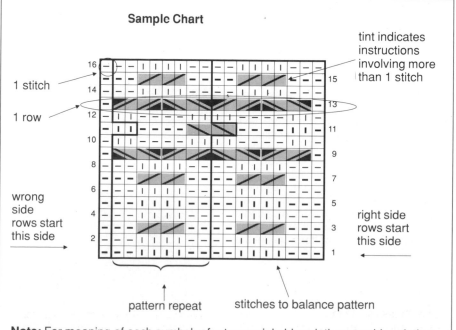

Sample Chart

1 stitch

1 row

tint indicates instructions involving more than 1 stitch

wrong side rows start this side

right side rows start this side

pattern repeat

stitches to balance pattern

Note: For meaning of each symbol refer to special abbreviations or abbreviations on pages 20 and 21.

Aran Design

Pattern Panels and All-over Patterns

Aran designs are usually made up of combinations of pattern panels and all-over patterns.

Panels

A pattern panel is worked across a given number of stitches on a background of a contrasting stitch. A simple rope or cable is a common example of a pattern panel.

All the cable and twist panels in this book have been worked on a suggested background stitch. On the charts this is indicated by two stitches at either side of the panel. To work any of the panels you must cast on enough stitches to work the panel plus the required number of background stitches each side.

All-over Patterns

An all-over pattern is one where the number of stitches given as a multiple is repeated and can be knitted across as narrow or wide a piece of the knitting as required.

The 'Multiple' of each all-over pattern is given with each set of instructions, for example:- **'Multiple of 7 sts + 4'**. This means that you can cast on any number of stitches which is a multiple of 7 plus 4 stitches; for instance 14 + 4 sts, 21 + 4 sts, 28 + 4 sts etc.

In the written instructions the 7 stitches are shown in parentheses or brackets or follow an asterisk (*), and these stitches are repeated across the row the required number of times. In charted instructions the multiple is indicated by a bracket at the bottom of the chart and heavier vertical lines. The extra stitches not included in the multiple are there to 'balance' the row or make it symmetrical and are only worked once.

Tension or Gauge

Knitting tension/gauge refers to the number of stitches and rows in a given area. Patterns containing cables and twist stitches are denser than flat patterns such as stocking stitch and therefore have relatively high tensions. When knitting an Aran garment from a commercial pattern the tension/gauge is frequently given over stocking stitch (for example: 22 sts and 30 rows = 10 cms [4 ins] square measured over stocking stitch). If you obtain this tension/gauge with a particular needle size it is likely that you will achieve the correct tension over pattern using the same needles.

Altering an Existing Pattern

Knitters with only a limited amount of experience should be able to add a cable panel from this book to a favourite stocking stitch pattern. The extra stitches required for the panel should be calculated as follows:

1. Knit a swatch in the background stitch and measure the tension/gauge.

2. Knit a piece of the cable panel with a few stitches extra in the background fabric at either side. The swatch should be a minimum of 5 cm (2 ins) in length, or at least one complete pattern repeat, whichever is the greater.

3. Mark the edges of the cable panel with pins (inside the extra background stitches) and measure the distance between the pins without stretching.

4. Calculate how many stitches in the background fabric would be required to produce the same width as the cable panel. Subtract this number from the number of stitches in the cable panel to find the number of stitches to be increased. For example, a cable panel contains 36 sts and measures 15 cm (6 ins). The background stitch is stocking stitch with a tension of 18 sts to 10 cm (4 ins). To produce 15 cm (6 ins) of stocking stitch, 27 sts would be required. The cable panel has 9 sts more than this, therefore an extra 9 sts would have to be increased to allow for the cable panel and maintain the same width. These stitches should be increased above the ribbing across the position of the stitches to be used for the panel.

Aran Design

Arans are usually knitted with two needles, in separate pieces which are subsequently sewn together.

Ribbed Edgings

The borders, neckbands and cuffs of Aran garments need to be elastic so that they can stretch and then contract to fit snugly in wear.

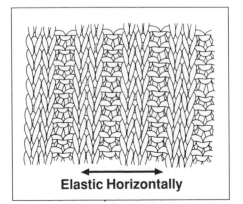

Elastic Horizontally

Ribs are formed by alternately knitting then purling a stitch or stitches to give unbroken vertical lines on both right and wrong sides. Rib patterns produce a horizontally elastic fabric.

The most common rib patterns used for edgings are 1x1, 2x2 and 3x3 rib. These are easy to work and produce a very effective elastic fabric. Fancy ribs are generally less elastic than the more common ribs and are therefore less practical. However, some of the most attractive Arans have fancy rib patterns as edgings. 4.22 and 4.23 on pages 25 and 29 are examples of fancy ribs.

Ribs are usually worked on a smaller size needle than the main body of the garment to keep them firm. Because many Aran patterns have a relatively high stitch tension/gauge, (a high number of stitches per cm/inch), quite a large increase row usually follows the rib. When knitting an Aran with a fancy welt the finished appearance is enhanced if the increases are worked so that elements of the pattern in the rib continue up into the main body of the garment.

Texture and Background Patterns

These are patterns with small multiples and small row repeats. They form the backgrounds on which cables and more elaborate Aran panels are worked. Texture patterns can also be incorporated within larger diamond and lattice panels. Because cables and lattices are generally worked in stocking stitch, the most frequently used background stitch is reverse stocking stitch as this makes the patterns stand out boldly and is also easy to work. Moss stitch, Double Moss stitch, Rice stitch and Trinity stitch are all texture patterns that are also used frequently within Aran knitting.

Row Repeats

You will see that the patterns in this book are divided into chapters under headings giving the number of rows required to complete one 'repeat' of the pattern. This has been done to make it easier to work combinations of pattern panels or all-over patterns that fit into a similar repeat. Aran designs are complicated enough without the added difficulty of trying to remember where you are while working one 28 row repeat panel next to a 24 row repeat! The first 24 rows would be simple enough but the further you progressed the more difficult it would be to keep a record of your position (see combination B, on page 19, which has incompatible row repeats).

For your convenience we have added the following table to give compatible row repeats 'at a glance'.

Compatible Row Repeats	Largest Row Repeat
2, 4, 8	8
2, 4, 6, 12	12
2, 4, 8, 16	16
2, 6, 18	18
2,4,10,20	20
2, 4, 6, 8, 12, 24	24
2, 4, 14, 28	28
2, 6, 10, 30	30
2, 4, 8, 16, 32	32
2, 4, 6, 12, 18, 36	36
2, 4, 8, 10, 20, 40	40
2, 4, 22, 44	44
2, 4, 6, 8, 12, 24, 48	48

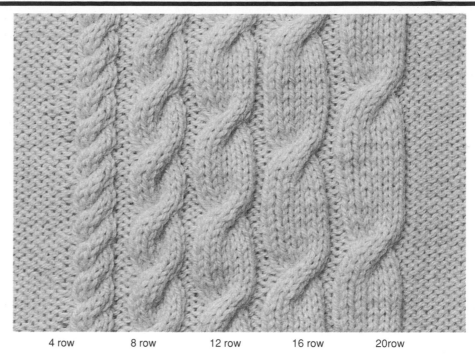

4 row   8 row   12 row   16 row   20row

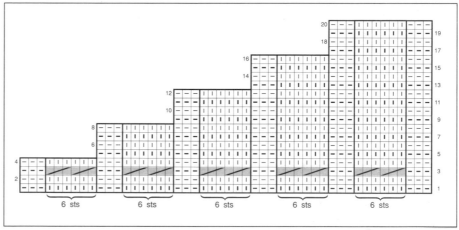

Altering Row Repeats

In some cases it is possible to reduce or increase the number of rows in a panel. It is useful to be able to tailor a panel in this way to make it compatible with other patterns and panels.

The photograph and corresponding chart on right show five simple panels. They are all 6 stitch cables crossed to the right (C6B) but the number of stocking stitch rows between crossings varies from 3 to 19. Note how the appearance of the panel changes from the firm 4 row repeat to the loose 20 row repeat. Many simple panels can be altered by adding or subtracting stocking stitch rows in this way. If you become familiar with working from charts, alterations of this sort are easier as it is possible to visualize where rows could be added or left out.

Traditional Combinations

The backs and fronts of Traditional Aran sweaters are characterised by a large central panel surrounded by varying numbers of side panels with a texture or background stitch at either side and between panels. Designs are usually symmetrical each side of the central panel. For example, a cable panel is often crossed to the right on one side of the central panel and to the left on the other. Also zig-zag panels should be started on different rows at either side of the central panel (see combination V on page 108) so that they are staggered. To make panels stand out they are usually spaced by a few stitches of reverse stocking stitch and often accompanied by a single knit stitch or KB1 each side (see combination A on following page). The side edges are

usually worked in a texture stitch as elaborate Aran patterns would not be seen under the arm and would also be bulky, making the garment uncomfortable for the wearer. The same principle applies for sleeves. However, because of size restrictions a smaller central panel and fewer side panels may be used.

Working Patterns as Panels

Many patterns work very well over a restricted number of stitches within a traditional Aran combination. Honeycomb and Diamond patterns are particularly

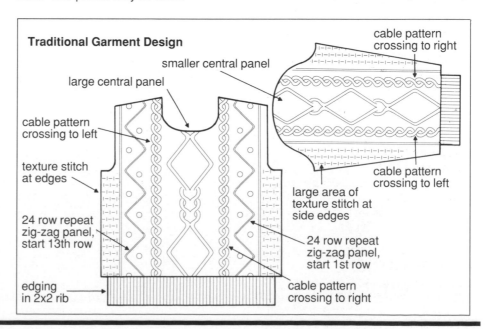

Traditional Garment Design

cable pattern crossing to right

smaller central panel

large central panel

cable pattern crossing to left

texture stitch at edges

24 row repeat zig-zag panel, start 13th row

edging in 2x2 rib

large area of texture stitch at side edges

cable pattern crossing to left

24 row repeat zig-zag panel, start 1st row

cable pattern crossing to right

Aran Design

suitable as central panels. Patterns with smaller stitch repeats can be incorporated between side panels.

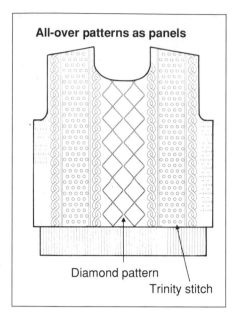

All-over patterns as panels

Diamond pattern

Trinity stitch

How to Work Aran Combination Examples

In addition to showing individual stitches we have included some photographs showing a few ways of combining different patterns and panels. These combinations could be used as a basis for garment design. By studying them we hope you will see some of the ways that intricate Aran Designs can be built up.

To avoid duplication of information combination details are given in the form of a table (see opposite). These tables contain all the information you will need to knit the samples as shown. Where extra information is required this is given clearly with each table.

Use the index on pages 174 and 175 to locate all panels and pattern stitches used in the combination. Note any special instructions that may apply (for example 'start 13th row'). Then make yourself familiar with any of the symbols that are used on the combination chart. The most frequently used symbol is ★ = reverse stocking stitch. Sometimes it has been necessary to give instructions for panels and patterns that are not used elsewhere. These are given as a symbol on the combination chart and the instructions should be followed in the usual way. Finally check how many stitches and rows make up each part of the combination.

You will need an appropriate number of stitches including a chosen number of background stitches at either side of the combination. Just like the pattern charts combination tables should be read as follows: right side rows from right to left and wrong side rows from left to right.

Each combination starts with a right side row, therefore starting at the right of table, work your chosen number of background stitches, then work each part of combination panel and finish with chosen number of background stitches. Work second row in the same way starting at left side of chart. The pattern has now been established. Continue working in this way keeping all panels and patterns correct.

If you prefer working from charts it may help to draw out the pattern stitches, that make up the combination, on graph paper as we have done with combination A on page 19.

The combinations have been given to show you some of the ways to use Aran stitches. However, the possibilities are unlimited and we hope these will just be a starting point for you to develop your own unique combinations.

Non-Traditional Designs

Aran techniques lend themselves to be used in many ways. Garments do not have to be designed along traditional lines. Instead of building up a design by combining panels, patterns can be repeated over the entire surface of the garment. All the patterns given with a repeat in this book can be used in this way to produce garments with an Aran appearance. Also many of the panels can be repeated with or without spacing stitches to give an all-over effect. Where panels are thought to have been particularly suited to this, a note has been given with the instructions.

Combination A. Panel of 100 sts worked on a background of double moss stitch (4.21).

Table for Combination A

2	2	8	2	8	2	4	2	8	2	8	2	2	Rows
	3	12	9	12	3	22	3	12	9	12	3		Sts
4.21	✿	8.7	✳	8.7	✿	4.17	✿	8.7	✳	8.7	✿	4.21	

100 sts

✳ = **1st row** (right side): P1, [KB1, p2] twice, KB1, p1.
2nd row: K1, [p1, k2] twice, p1, k1.
Rep these 2 rows.

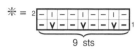
9 sts

✿ = **1st row** (right side): P1, KB1, p1.
2nd row: K1, p1, k1.
Rep these 2 rows.

3 sts

Combination A drawn out in chart form

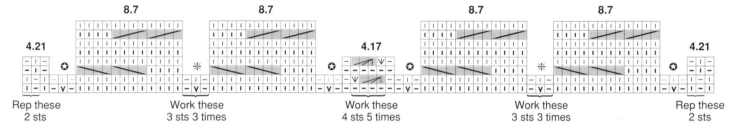

Combination B. Panel of 74 sts on a background of double moss st (4.21).

Note: This combination contains panels with incompatible row repeats (2,4,16,18,24 rows) making it more difficult to work.

4	2	18	2	16	2	24	2	16	2	18	2	2	Rows
	2	12	2	8	2	22	2	8	2	12	2		Sts
4.21	★	18.5	★	16.5	★	24.15	★	16.5	★	18.5	★	4.21	

74 sts

★ = reverse st st.

Abbreviations and Symbols

Abbreviations

Alt = alternate; **beg** = beginning; **cm** = centimetres; **dec** = decrease; **inc** = increase; **ins** = inches; **k** = knit; **KB1** = knit into back of stitch; **m** = metres; **mm** = millimetres; **p** = purl; **PB1** = purl into back of stitch; **psso** = pass slipped stitch over; **p2sso** = pass 2 slipped stitches over; **p3sso** = pass 3 slipped stitches over; **rep** = repeat; **sl** = slip; **st(s)** = stitch(es); **st st** = stocking stitch (1 row knit, 1 row purl); **tog** = together; **tbl** through back of loops; **yb** = yarn back; **yf** = yarn forward; **yfrn** = yarn forward and round needle; **yon** = yarn over needle; **yrn** = yarn round needle.

Note

Symbols are dark on right side rows and light on wrong side rows.

Basic Symbols

I	**K** knit on right side rows
−	**K** knit on wrong side rows
−	**P** purl on right side rows
I	**P** purl on wrong side rows

Common Abbreviations and Symbols

These techniques are used regularly throughout the book. If the pattern you are working contains an abbreviation or symbol that is not given as a special abbreviation it will be found here. At the foot of each page the abbreviation for any 'common' symbol used on that particular page is given.

KB1 knit into back of st on right side rows

PB1 purl into back of st on wrong side rows

sl 1 slip one st with yarn at back (wrong side) of work

k2tog

sl 1, k1, psso

p2tog

p3tog

p3tog on wrong side

sl 2tog knitwise, k1, p2sso

sl 1, k2tog, psso

yf, yfrn, yon, yrn (to make a st)

M1K (Make 1 st Knitwise) = pick up strand of yarn lying between last st worked and next st and knit into back of it.

M1P (Make 1 st Purlwise) = pick up strand of yarn lying between last st worked and next st and purl into back of it.

M3 (Make 3 sts) = [k1, p1, k1] all into next st.

M3 (Make 3 sts) = [k1, p1, k1] all into next st on wrong side rows.

C2B (Cross 2 Back) = slip next st onto cable needle and hold at back of work, knit next st from left-hand needle, then knit st from cable needle.

Or without a cable needle:
C2B = knit into front of 2nd st on needle, then knit first st slipping both sts off needle at the same time (see page 12).

C2F (Cross 2 Front) = slip next st onto cable needle and hold at front of work, knit next st from left-hand needle, then knit st from cable needle.

Or without a cable needle:
C2F = knit into back of 2nd st on needle then knit first st slipping both sts off needle at the same time (see page 12).

C2BW (Cross 2 Back on Wrong Side) = slip next st onto cable needle and hold at back (right side) of work, purl next st from left-hand needle, then purl st from cable needle.

Or without a cable needle:
C2BW = purl into front of 2nd st on needle, then purl first st slipping both sts off needle at the same time.

C2FW (Cross 2 Front on Wrong Side) = slip next st onto cable needle and hold at front (wrong side) of work, purl next st from left-hand needle, then purl st from cable needle.

Or without a cable needle:
C2FW = purl into back of 2nd st on needle, then purl first st slipping both sts off needle at the same time.

T2B (Twist 2 Back) = slip next st onto cable needle and hold at back of work, knit next st from left-hand needle, then purl st from cable needle.

Or without a cable needle:
T2B = knit into front of 2nd st on needle then purl first st slipping both sts off needle at the same time (see page 12).

For North American Readers

English terms are used throughout this book. Please note the equivalent American terms:

Tension - Gauge

Cast Off - Bind Off

Stocking Stitch - Stockinette Stitch

Yf, Yfrn, Yon and Yrn (to make a st) - Yarn Over

T2F (Twist 2 Front) = slip next st onto cable needle and hold at front of work, purl next st from left-hand needle, then knit st from cable needle.

Or without a cable needle:
T2F = purl into back of 2nd st on needle then knit first st slipping both sts off needle at the same time (see page 12).

T2BW (Twist 2 Back on Wrong side) = slip next st onto cable needle and hold at back (right side) of work, knit next st from left-hand needle, then purl st from cable needle.

Or without a cable needle:
T2BW = knit into front of 2nd st on needle, then purl first st slipping both sts off needle at the same time.

T2FW (Twist 2 Front on Wrong side) = slip next st onto cable needle and hold at front (wrong side) of work, purl next st from left-hand needle, then knit st from cable needle.

Or without a cable needle:
T2FW = purl into back of 2nd st on needle, then knit first st slipping both sts off needle at the same time.

C3B (Cable 3 Back) = slip next st onto cable needle and hold at back of work, knit next 2 sts from left-hand needle, then knit st from cable needle.

C3F (Cable 3 Front) = slip next 2 sts onto cable needle and hold at front of work, knit next st from left-hand needle, then knit sts from cable needle.

C3R (Cable 3 Right) = slip next 2 sts onto cable needle and hold at back of work, knit next st from left-hand needle, then knit sts from cable needle.

C3L (Cable 3 Left) = slip next st onto cable needle and hold at front of work, knit next 2 sts from left-hand needle, then knit st from cable needle.

T3B (Twist 3 Back) = slip next st onto cable needle and hold at back of work, knit next 2 sts from left-hand needle, then purl st from cable needle.

T3F (Twist 3 Front) = slip next 2 sts onto cable needle and hold at front of work, purl next st from left-hand needle, then knit sts from cable needle.

C4B (Cable 4 Back) = slip next 2 sts onto cable needle and hold at back of work, knit next 2 sts from left-hand needle, then knit sts from cable needle.

C4F (Cable 4 Front) = slip next 2 sts onto cable needle and hold at front of work, knit next 2 sts from left-hand needle, then knit sts from cable needle.

C4R (Cable 4 Right) = slip next st onto cable needle and hold at back of work, knit next 3 sts from left-hand needle, then knit st from cable needle.

Abbreviations and Symbols

C4L (Cable 4 Left) = slip next 3 sts onto cable needle and hold at front of work, knit next st from left-hand needle, then knit sts from cable needle.

T4B (Twist 4 Back) = slip next 2 sts onto cable needle and hold at back of work, knit next 2 sts from left-hand needle, then purl sts from cable needle.

T4F (Twist 4 Front) = slip next 2 sts onto cable needle and hold at front of work, purl next 2 sts from left-hand needle, then knit sts from cable needle.

T4R (Twist 4 Right) = slip next st onto cable needle and hold at back of work, knit next 3 sts from left-hand needle, then purl st from cable needle.

T4L (Twist 4 Left) = slip next 3 sts onto cable needle and hold at front of work, purl next st from left-hand needle, then knit sts from cable needle.

T4BP (Twist 4 Back Purl) = slip next 2 sts onto cable needle and hold at back of work, knit next 2 sts from left-hand needle, then p1, k1 from cable needle.

T4FP (Twist 4 Front Purl) = slip next 2 sts onto cable needle and hold at front of work, k1, p1 from left-hand needle, then knit sts from cable needle.

C5B (Cable 5 Back) = slip next 3 sts onto cable needle and hold at back of work, knit next 2 sts from left-hand needle, then knit sts from cable needle.

C5F (Cable 5 Front) = slip next 2 sts onto cable needle and hold at front of work, knit next 3 sts from left-hand needle, then knit sts from cable needle.

T5B (Twist 5 Back) = slip next 3 sts onto cable needle and hold at back of work, knit next 2 sts from left-hand needle, then purl sts from cable needle.

T5F (Twist 5 Front) = slip next 2 sts onto cable needle and hold at front of work, purl next 3 sts from left-hand needle, then knit sts from cable needle.

T5R (Twist 5 Right) = slip next 2 sts onto cable needle and hold at back of work, knit next 3 sts from left-hand needle, then purl sts from cable needle.

T5L (Twist 5 Left) = slip next 3 sts onto cable needle and hold at front of work, purl next 2 sts from left-hand needle, then knit sts from cable needle.

T5BP (Twist 5 Back Purl) = slip next 3 sts onto cable needle and hold at back of work, knit next 2 sts from left-hand needle, then p1, k2 from cable needle.

C6B (Cable 6 Back) = slip next 3 sts onto cable needle and hold at back of work, knit next 3 sts from left-hand needle, then knit sts from cable needle.

C6F (Cable 6 Front) = slip next 3 sts onto cable needle and hold at front of work, knit next 3 sts from left-hand needle, then knit sts from cable needle.

T6B (Twist 6 Back) = slip next 3 sts onto cable needle and hold at back of work, knit next 3 sts from left-hand needle, then purl sts from cable needle.

T6F (Twist 6 Front) = slip next 3 sts onto cable needle and hold at front of work, purl next 3 sts from left-hand needle, then knit sts from cable needle.

C7B (Cable 7 Back) = slip next 4 sts onto cable needle and hold at back of work, knit next 3 sts from left-hand needle, then knit sts from cable needle.

C8B (Cable 8 Back) = slip next 4 sts onto cable needle and hold at back of work, knit next 4 sts from left-hand needle, then knit sts from cable needle.

C8F (Cable 8 Front) = slip next 4 sts onto cable needle and hold at front of work, knit next 4 sts from left-hand needle, then knit sts from cable needle.

C10B (Cable 10 Back) = slip next 5 sts onto cable needle and hold at back of work, knit next 5 sts from left-hand needle, then knit sts from cable needle.

C10F (Cable 10 Front) = slip next 5 sts onto cable needle and hold at front of work, knit next 5 sts from left-hand needle, then knit sts from cable needle.

C12B (Cable 12 Back) = slip next 6 sts onto cable needle and hold at back of work, knit next 6 sts from left-hand needle, then knit sts from cable needle.

C12F (Cable 12 Front) = slip next 6 sts onto cable needle and hold at front of work, knit next 6 sts from left-hand needle, then knit sts from cable needle.

● Bobbles

MB#1 = (Make Bobble number 1). (K1, p1) twice all into next st, pass 2nd, then 3rd and 4th sts over first st and off needle (bobble completed).

MB#2 = (Make Bobble number 2). (K1, p1) twice all into next st, turn and p4, turn and sl 2, k2tog, p2sso (bobble completed).

MB#3 = (Make Bobble number 3). (K1, p1) twice all into next st, turn and p4, turn and k4, turn and p4, turn and sl 2, k2tog, p2sso (bobble completed).

MB#4 = (Make Bobble number 4). (K1, p1) twice all into next st (turn and p4, turn and k4) twice, turn and p4, turn and sl 2, k2tog, p2sso (bobble completed).

MB#5 = (Make Bobble number 5). (K1, p1) twice all into next st, turn and k4, turn and sl 2, k2tog, p2sso (bobble completed).

MB#6 = (Make Bobble number 6). (K1, p1) twice all into next st, turn and k4, turn and p4, turn and k4, turn and sl 2, k2tog, p2sso (bobble completed).

MB#7 = (Make Bobble number 7). (K1, p1) twice all into next st, (turn and k4, turn and p4) twice, turn and k4, turn and sl 2, k2tog, p2sso (bobble completed).

MB#8 = (Make Bobble number 8). (K1, p1) three times all into next st, pass 2nd, then 3rd, 4th, 5th and 6th sts over first st and off needle (bobble completed).

MB#9 = (Make Bobble number 9). (K1, p1) three times all into next st, turn and p6, turn and sl 3, k3tog, p3sso st resulting from k3tog (bobble completed).

MB#10 = (Make Bobble number 10). (K1, p1) three times all into next st, turn and p6, turn and k6, turn and p6, turn and sl 3, k3tog, p3sso st resulting from k3tog (bobble completed).

MB#11 = (Make Bobble number 11). (K1, p1) three times all into next st, (turn and p6, turn and k6) twice, turn and p6, turn and sl 3, k3tog, p3sso st resulting from k3tog (bobble completed).

MB#12 = (Make Bobble number 12). (K1, p1) three times all into next st, turn and k6, turn and sl 3, k3tog, p3sso st resulting from k3tog (bobble completed).

MB#13 = (Make Bobble number 13). (K1, p1) three times all into next st, turn and k6, turn and p6, turn and k6, turn and sl 3, k3tog, p3sso st resulting from k3tog (bobble completed).

MB#14 = (Make Bobble number 14). (K1, p1) three times all into next st, (turn and k6, turn and p6) twice, turn and k6, turn and sl 3, k3tog, p3sso st resulting from k3tog (bobble completed).

2 Row Repeats

2.1 - 2.2

2.1 (on left of photograph)
Panel of 2 sts on a background of reverse st st.

1st row (right side): C2B.
2nd row: P2.
Rep these 2 rows.

2 sts

2.2 (on right of photograph)
Panel of 2 sts on a background of reverse st st.

1st row (right side): C2F.
2nd row: P2.
Rep these 2 rows.

2 sts

2.3 - 2.4

2.3 (on right of photograph)
Panel of 5 sts on a background of reverse st st.

1st row (right side): C2B, k1, C2F.
2nd row: P5.
Rep these 2 rows.

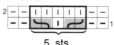

5 sts

2.4 (on left of photograph)
Work as given for 2.3 **but** working C2F in place of C2B, and C2B in place of C2F.

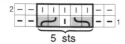

5 sts

2.5 - 2.6

2.5 (on left of photograph)
Panel of 3 sts on a background of reverse st st.

1st row (right side): K1, C2F.
2nd row: P1, C2BW.
Rep these 2 rows.

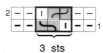

3 sts

2.7

Panel of 4 sts on a background of reverse st st.

1st row (right side): C2B, C2F.
2nd row: P4.
Rep these 2 rows.

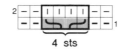

4 sts

2.8 Moss Stitch

2.6 (on right of photograph)
Work as given for 2.5 **but** working C2B in place of C2F, and C2FW in place of C2BW.

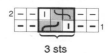

3 sts

2.9

Panel of 5 sts on a background of reverse st st.

1st row (right side): K1, [C2F] twice.
2nd row: P1, [C2BW] twice.
Rep these 2 rows.

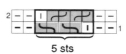

5 sts

2.10 Rice Stitch

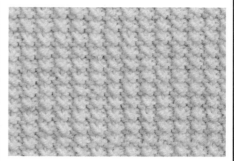

Multiple of 2 sts + 1.
1st row (right side): P1, *KB1, p1; rep from * to end.
2nd row: Knit.
Rep these 2 rows.

Rep these 2 sts

Multiple of 2 sts + 1.
1st row (right side): K1, *p1, k1; rep from * to end.
2nd row: K1, *p1, k1; rep from * to end.
Rep these 2 rows.

Rep these 2 sts

 = KB1. = yb, sl 1 purlwise. = C2B. = C2F. = C2BW. = C2FW. = C4B. = C4F.

2.11

Multiple of 3 sts + 2.
1st row (right side): P2, *yb, sl 1 purlwise, yf, p2; rep from * to end.
2nd row: K2, *p1, k2; rep from * to end.
Rep these 2 rows.

Rep these 3 sts

2.12

Multiple of 5 sts + 2.
1st row (right side): P2, *k3, p2; rep from * to end.
2nd row: K2, *p1, k1, p1, k2; rep from * to end.
Rep these 2 rows.

Rep these 5 sts

4.1

4.2 - 4.3

4.2 (on left of photograph)
Panel of 4 sts on a background of reverse st st.
1st row (right side): K4.
2nd row: P4.
3rd row: C4F.
4th row: P4.
Rep these 4 rows.

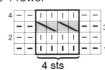

4 sts

4.4

Panel of 8 sts on a background of reverse st st.
1st row (right side): K8.
2nd row: P8.
3rd row: C4B, C4F.
4th row: P8.
Rep these 4 rows.

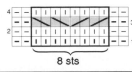

8 sts

Panel of 2 sts on a background of reverse st st.
1st row (right side): C2B.
2nd row: P2.
3rd row: C2F.
4th row: P2.
Rep these 4 rows.

2 sts

4.3 (on right of photograph)
Work as given for 4.2 **but** working C4B in place of C4F.

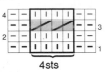

4 sts

4.5

Panel of 6 sts on a background of reverse st st.
1st row (right side): K1, C2B, C2F, k1.
2nd row: P6.
3rd row: C2B, k2, C2F.
4th row: P6.
Rep these 4 rows.

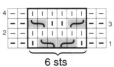

6 sts

4.6

Panel of 4 sts on a background of reverse st st.
1st row (right side): C2B, C2F.
2nd row: P4.
3rd row: C2F, C2B.
4th row: P4.
Rep these 4 rows.

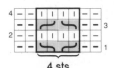

4 sts

4 Row Repeats

4.7 - 4.8

4.7 (on left of photograph)
Panel of 7 sts on a background of reverse st st.
1st row (right side): K7.
2nd row: P7.
3rd row: C3R, k1, C3L.
4th row: P7.
Rep these 4 rows.

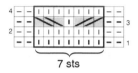

7 sts

4.8 (on right of photograph)
Work as given for 4.7 **but** working C3L in place of C3R and C3R in place of C3L.

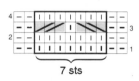

7 sts

4.10 - 4.11

4.10 (on left of photograph)
Panel of 6 sts on a background of reverse st st.
1st row (right side): K2, C4F.
2nd row: P6.
3rd row: C4B, k2.
4th row: P6.
Rep these 4 rows.

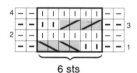

6 sts

4.11 (on right of photograph)
Work as given for 4.10 **but** working C4B in place of C4F, and C4F in place of C4B.

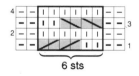

6 sts

4.14 - 4.15

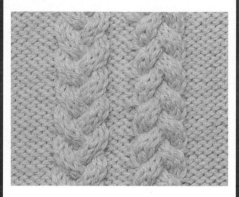

4.14 (on left of photograph)
Panel of 9 sts on a background of reverse st st.
1st row (right side): K3, C6F.
2nd row: P9.
3rd row: C6B, k3.
4th row: P9.
Rep these 4 rows.

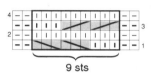

9 sts

4.15 (on right of photograph)
Work as given for 4.14 **but** working C6B in place of C6F, and C6F in place of C6B.

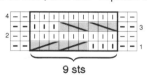

9 sts

4.9

Panel with a multiple of 4 sts + 6.
Example shown is worked over 10 sts on a background of reverse st st.
1st row (right side): K2, *C4F; rep from * to end.
2nd row: Purl.
3rd row: *C4B; rep from * to last 2 sts, k2.
4th row: Purl.
Rep these 4 rows.

4.12 - 4.13

4.12 (on left of photograph)
Panel of 6 sts on a background of reverse st st.
1st row (right side): K6.
2nd row: P6.
3rd row: C6B.
4th row: P6.
Rep these 4 rows.

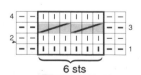

6 sts

4.13 (on right of photograph)
Work as given for 4.12 **but** working C6F in place of C6B.

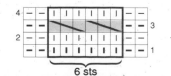

6 sts

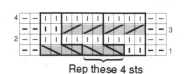

Rep these 4 sts

$\boxed{V}$ = M3. = p3tog. = C2B. = C2F. = C2BW. = C2FW. = T2B.

4.16

Multiple of 4 sts + 6.
1st row (right side): P1, *T2F, T2B; rep from * to last st, p1.
2nd row: K2, *C2BW, k2; rep from * to end.
3rd row: P1, *T2B, T2F; rep from * to last st, p1.
4th row: K1, p1, k2, *C2FW, k2; rep from * to last 2 sts, p1, k1.
Rep these 4 rows.

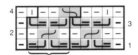

Rep these 4 sts

4.17 Trinity Stitch

Trinity Stitch is thought to have been so named because the pattern is formed by working three stitches from one and one stitch from three, signifying the Holy Trinity.

Multiple of 4 sts + 2.
1st row (right side): Purl.
2nd row: K1, *M3, p3tog; rep from * to last st, k1.
3rd row: Purl.
4th row: K1, *p3tog, M3; rep from * to last st, k1.
Rep these 4 rows.

Rep these 4 sts

4.18 Box Stitch

Multiple of 4 sts + 2.
1st row (right side): K2, *p2, k2; rep from * to end.
2nd row: P2, *k2, p2; rep from * to end.
3rd row: P2, *k2, p2; rep from * to end.
4th row: K2, *p2, k2; rep from * to end.
Rep these 4 rows.

Rep these 4 sts

4.19

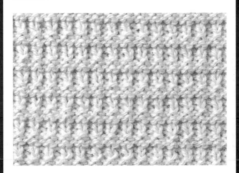

Multiple of 2 sts + 1.
1st row (right side): Purl.
2nd row: Knit.
3rd row: K1, *p1, k1; rep from * to end.
4th row: P1, *k1, p1; rep from * to end.
Rep these 4 rows.

...

Rep these 2 sts

4.20

4.21 Double Moss Stitch

Multiple of 2 sts + 1.
1st row (right side): K1, *p1, k1; rep from * to end.
2nd row: P1, *k1, p1; rep from * to end.
3rd row: P1, *k1, p1; rep from * to end.
4th row: K1, *p1, k1; rep from * to end.
Rep these 4 rows.

Rep these 2 sts

4.22

Multiple of 3 sts + 1.
1st row (right side): P1, *C2B, p1; rep from * to end.
2nd row: K1, *p2, k1; rep from * to end.
3rd row: P1, *C2F, p1; rep from * to end.
4th row: As 2nd row.
Rep these 4 rows.

Rep these 3 sts

Multiple of 6 sts + 4.
1st row (right side): Knit.
2nd row: P4, *k2, p4; rep from * to end.
3rd row: Knit.
4th row: P1, k2, *p4, k2; rep from * to last st, p1.
Rep these 4 rows.

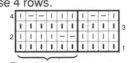

Rep these 6 sts

= T2F.　= C3R.　= C3L.　= C4B.　= C4F.　= C6B.　= C6F.

4-6 Row Repeats

4.23

Multiple of 9 sts + 5.

1st row (right side): P2, KB1, p2, *k4, p2, KB1, p2; rep from * to end.

2nd row: K2, PB1, k2, *p4, k2, PB1, k2; rep from * to end.

3rd row: P2, KB1, p2, *C4B, p2, KB1, p2; rep from * to end.

4th row: As 2nd row.

Rep these 4 rows.

Rep these 9 sts

4.24

Multiple of 5 sts + 2.

Special Abbreviation

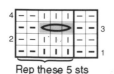 **Bind 3** = slip 1 st purlwise with yarn at back of work, k1, yf, k1, pass slipped st over the k1, yf, k1.

1st row (right side): P2, *k3, p2; rep from * to end.

2nd row: K2, *p3, k2; rep from * to end.

3rd row: P2, *bind 3, p2; rep from * to end.

4th row: As 2nd row.

Rep these 4 rows.

Rep these 5 sts

4.25

Multiple of 6 sts + 2.

1st row (right side): P2, *C2B, C2F, p2; rep from * to end.

2nd row: K2, *p4, k2; rep from * to end.

3rd row: P2, *C2F, C2B, p2; rep from * to end.

4th row: As 2nd row.

Rep these 4 rows.

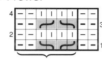

Rep these 6 sts

6.1 - 6.2

6.1 (on right of photograph)
Panel of 6 sts on a background of reverse st st.

1st row (right side): K6.

2nd row: P6.

3rd row: C6B.

4th row: P6.

5th and 6th rows: As 1st and 2nd rows.

Rep these 6 rows.

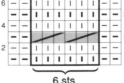

6 sts

6.2 (on left of photograph)
Work as given for 6.1 **but** working C6F in place of C6B.

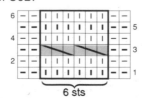

6 sts

4.26

Multiple of 6 sts + 2.

1st row (right side): P2, *k4, p2; rep from * to end.

2nd row: K2, *p4, k2; rep from * to end.

3rd row: P2, *C4B, p2; rep from * to end.

4th row: As 2nd row.

Rep these 4 rows.

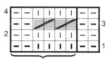

Rep these 6 sts

6.3

Panel of 3 sts on a background of reverse st st.

Special Abbreviation

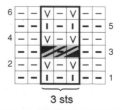 **T3RP (Twist 3 Right Purl)** = slip next 2 sts onto cable needle and hold at back of work, knit next st from left-hand needle, then p1, k1 from cable needle.

1st row (right side): K1, p1, k1.

2nd row: PB1, k1, PB1.

3rd row: T3RP.

4th row: PB1, k1, PB1.

5th and 6th rows: As 1st and 2nd rows.

Rep these 6 rows.

3 sts

V = KB1.   v = PB1.   = C2B.   = C2F.   = T2B.   = T2F.   = C4B.   = C4F.

6.4

Panel of 12 sts on a background of reverse st st.

1st row (right side): K12.
2nd row: P12.
3rd row: C6B, C6F.
4th row: P12.
5th and 6th rows: As 1st and 2nd rows.
Rep these 6 rows.

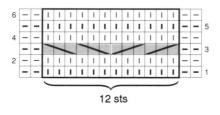

12 sts

6.5

Panel of 16 sts on a background of reverse st st.

1st row (right side): K4, C4B, C4F, k4.
2nd row: P16.
3rd row: K2, C4B, k4, C4F, k2.
4th row: P16.
5th row: C4B, k8, C4F.
6th row: P16.
Rep these 6 rows.

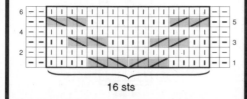

16 sts

6.6 - 6.7

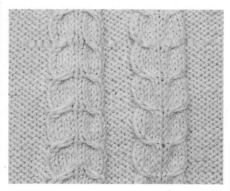

6.6 (on left of photograph)
Panel of 9 sts on a background of reverse st st.

Special Abbreviations

RC4 (Right Cable 4) = slip next 3 sts onto cable needle and hold at back of work, knit next st from left-hand needle, then knit sts from cable needle.

LC4 (Left Cable 4) = slip next st onto cable needle and hold at front of work, knit next 3 sts from left-hand needle, then knit st from cable needle.

1st row (right side): K9.
2nd row: P9.
3rd row: LC4, k1, RC4.
4th row: P9.
5th and 6th rows: As 1st and 2nd rows.
Rep these 6 rows.

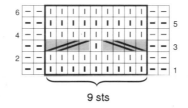

9 sts

6.8

Multiple of 6 sts + 7.
1st row (right side): K3, p1, *k5, p1; rep from * to last 3 sts, k3.
2nd row: P2, k1, p1, k1, *p3, k1, p1, k1; rep from * to last 2 sts, p2.

6.7 (on right of photograph)
Work as given for 6.6 **but** working RC4 in place of LC4, and LC4 in place of RC4

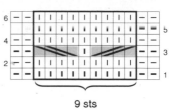

9 sts

6.9

Multiple of 12 sts + 3.

1st row (right side): K3, *p2, T2B, k1, T2F, p2, k3; rep from * to end.
2nd row: P3, *k2, p1, [k1, p1] twice, k2, p3; rep from * to end.
3rd row: K3, *p1, T2B, p1, k1, p1, T2F, p1, k3; rep from * to end.
4th row: P3, *k1, p1, [k2, p1] twice, k1, p3; rep from * to end.
5th row: K3, *T2B, p2, k1, p2, T2F, k3; rep from * to end.
6th row: P3, *k4, p1, k4, p3; rep from * to end.
Rep these 6 rows.

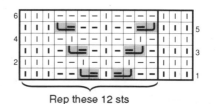

Rep these 12 sts

3rd row: K1, *p1, k3, p1, k1; rep from * to end.
4th row: K1, *p5, k1; rep from * to end.
5th row: As 3rd row.
6th row: As 2nd row.
Rep these 6 rows.

Rep these 6 sts

= C6B.   = C6F.

6-8 Row Repeats

6.10

Multiple of 13 sts + 1.

1st row (right side): P1, [k1, p1] twice, T2B, T2F, *p1, [k1, p1] 4 times, T2B, T2F; rep from * to last 5 sts, p1, [k1, p1] twice.

2nd row: [K1, p1] 3 times, k2, *p1, [k1, p1] 5 times, k2; rep from * to last 6 sts, [p1, k1] 3 times.

3rd row: P1, [k1, p1] twice, T2F, T2B, *p1, [k1, p1] 4 times, T2F, T2B; rep from * to last 5 sts, p1, [k1, p1] twice.

4th row: [K1, p1] twice, k2, p2, k2, *p1, [k1, p1] 3 times, k2, p2, k2; rep from * to last 4 sts, [p1, k1] twice.

5th row: [P1, k1] twice, p2, C2B, p2, *k1, [p1, k1] 3 times, p2, C2B, p2; rep from * to last 4 sts, [k1, p1] twice.

6th row: As 4th row.

Rep these 6 rows.

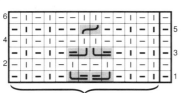

Rep these 13 sts

8.1

Panel of 4 sts on a background of reverse st st.

1st row (right side): C2B, C2F.

2nd row: P4.

3rd and 4th rows: Rep the last 2 rows once more.

5th row: C2F, C2B.

8.2 - 8.3

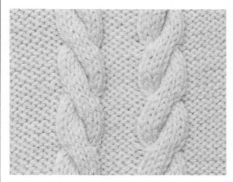

8.2 (on right of photograph)
Panel of 8 sts on a background of reverse st st.

1st row (right side): K8.

2nd row: P8.

3rd row: C8B.

4th row: P8.

5th to 8th rows: Rep 1st and 2nd rows twice.

Rep these 8 rows.

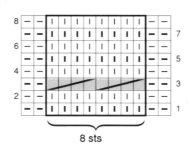

8 sts

8.3 (on left of photograph)
Work as given for 8.2 **but** working C8F in place of C8B.

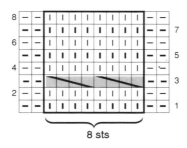

8 sts

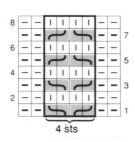

4 sts

6th row: P4.

7th and 8th rows: Rep the last 2 rows once more.

Rep these 8 rows.

8.4

Panel of 8 sts on a background of reverse st st.

1st row (right side): K8.

2nd and every alt row: P8.

3rd row: C4B, C4F.

5th row: K8.

7th row: C4F, C4B.

8th row: P8.

Rep these 8 rows.

8 sts

8.5

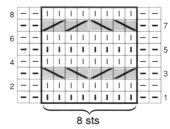

Panel of 4 sts on a background of reverse st st.

1st row (right side): K4.

2nd and every alt row: P4.

3rd row: C4B.

5th row: K4.

7th row: C4F.

8th row: P4.

Rep these 8 rows.

4 sts

 = C2B.   = C2F.   = T2B. = T2F. = C3B. = C3F. = T3B. = T3F.   = C4B.

8.6 - 8.7

8.6 (on right of photograph)
Panel of 12 sts on a background of reverse st st.
1st row (right side): K12.
2nd row: P12.
3rd row: K4, C8B.
4th row: P12.
5th and 6th rows: As 1st and 2nd rows.
7th row: C8F, k4.
8th row: P12.
Rep these 8 rows.

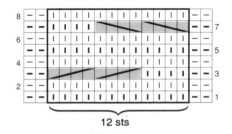

12 sts

8.7 (on left of photograph)
Work as given for 8.6 **but** working C8F in place of C8B, and C8B in place of C8F.

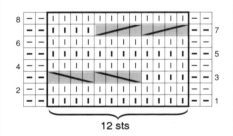

12 sts

8.8

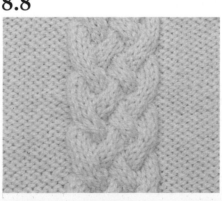

8.9

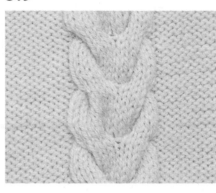

8.10

Panel of 12 sts on a background of reverse st st.
1st row (right side): P3, C3B, C3F, p3.
2nd row: K3, p6, k3.
3rd row: P2, C3B, k2, C3F, p2.
4th row: K2, p8, k2.
5th row: P1, T3B, k4, T3F, p1.
6th row: K1, p2, k1, p4, k1, p2, k1.
7th row: T3B, p1, C4B, p1, T3F.
8th row: P2, k2, p4, k2, p2.
Rep these 8 rows.

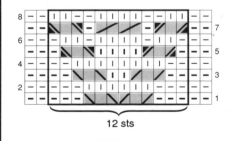

12 sts

Panel with a multiple of 6 sts + 9.
Example shown is worked over 15 sts on a background of reverse st st.
1st row (right side): Knit.
2nd row: Purl.
3rd row: K3, *C6F; rep from * to end.
4th row: Purl.
5th and 6th rows: As 1st and 2nd rows.
7th row: *C6B; rep from * to last 3 sts, k3.
8th row: Purl.
Rep these 8 rows.

16 sts

Panel of 16 sts on a background of reverse st st.
1st row (right side): K16.
2nd row: P16.
3rd row: C8B, C8F.
4th row: P16.
5th to 8th rows: Rep 1st and 2nd rows twice.
Rep these 8 rows.

8.11

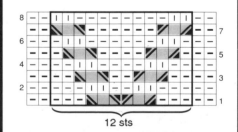

Panel of 12 sts on a background of reverse st st.
1st row (right side): P3, T3B, T3F, p3.
2nd row: K3, p2, k2, p2, k3.
3rd row: P2, T3B, p2, T3F, p2.
4th row: K2, p2, k4, p2, k2.
5th row: P1, T3B, p4, T3F, p1.
6th row: K1, p2, k6, p2, k1.
7th row: T3B, p6, T3F.
8th row: P2, k8, p2.
Rep these 8 rows.

12 sts

Rep these 6 sts

= C4F.　　= C6B.　　= C6F.　　= C8B.　　= C8F.

8 Row Repeats

8.12

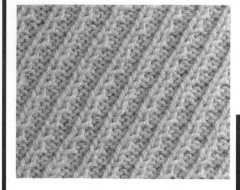

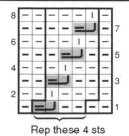

Rep these 4 sts

Multiple of 4 sts + 3.

1st row (right side): P4, T2B, *p2, T2B; rep from * to last st, p1.

2nd row: K2, p1, *k3, p1; rep from * to last 4 sts, k4.

3rd row: P3, *T2B, p2; rep from * to end.

4th row: K3, *p1, k3; rep from * to end.

5th row: *P2, T2B; rep from * to last 3 sts, p3.

6th row: K4, p1, *k3, p1; rep from * to last 2 sts, k2.

7th row: P1, T2B, *p2, T2B; rep from * to last 4 sts, p4.

8th row: K5, p1, *k3, p1; rep from * to last st, k1.

Rep these 8 rows.

8.13

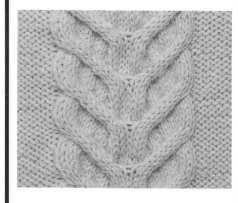

Panel of 30 sts on a background of reverse st st.

1st row (right side): K9, C6B, C6F, k9.

2nd and every alt row: P30.

3rd row: K6, C6B, k6, C6F, k6.

5th row: K3, C6B, k12, C6F, k3.

7th row: C6B, k18, C6F.

8th row: P30.

Rep these 8 rows.

8.14

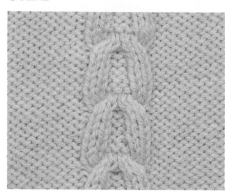

Panel of 8 sts on a background of reverse st st.

1st row (right side): K2, p4, k2.

2nd row: P2, k4, p2.

3rd row: C4F, C4B.

4th row: P8.

5th to 8th rows: Rep 1st and 2nd rows twice.

Rep these 8 rows.

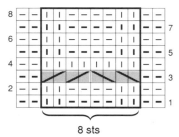

8 sts

8.15

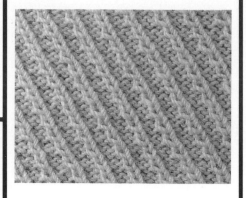

Multiple of 4 sts + 3.

1st row (right side): P1, T2F, *p2, T2F; rep from * to last 4 sts, p4.

2nd row: K4, p1, *k3, p1; rep from * to last 2 sts, k2.

3rd row: *P2, T2F; rep from * to last 3 sts, p3.

4th row: K3, *p1, k3; rep from * to end.

5th row: P3, *T2F, p2; rep from * to end.

6th row: K2, p1, *k3, p1; rep from * to last 4 sts, k4.

7th row: P4, T2F, *p2, T2F; rep from * to last st, p1.

8th row: K1, p1, *k3, p1; rep from * to last 5 sts, k5.

Rep these 8 rows.

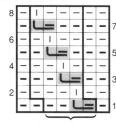

Rep these 4 sts

8.16

Panel of 24 sts on a background of reverse st st.

1st row (right side): K2, p4, T4F, p1, C2B, p1, T4B, p4, k2.

2nd row: P2, k6, [p2, k1] twice, p2, k6, p2.

3rd row: T4F, p4, T4F, T4B, p4, T4B.

4th row: K2, p2, k6, p4, k6, p2, k2.

5th row: P2, C4F, p4, T2F, T2B, p4, C4B, p2.

6th row: K2, p4, k5, p2, k5, p4, k2.

7th row: T4B, T4F, p3, C2B, p3, T4B, T4F.

8th row: P2, k4, [p2, k3] twice, p2, k4, p2.

Rep these 8 rows.

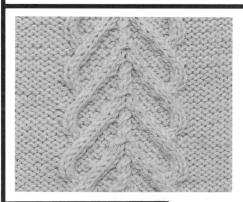

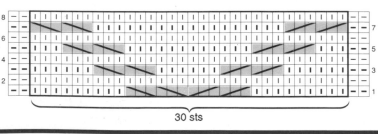

30 sts

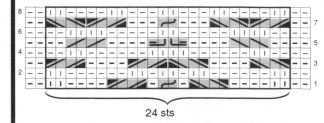

24 sts

◢ = C2B. ◢= T2B. ◣ = T2F. ◣◣ = C4B. ◥◥ = C4F.

8.17

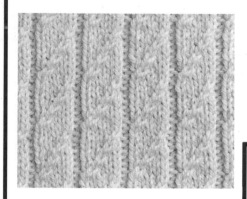

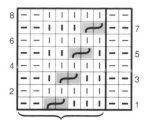

Rep these 7 sts

Multiple of 7 sts + 2.

1st row (right side): P2, *k3, C2B, p2; rep from * to end.

2nd and every alt row: K2, *p5, k2; rep from * to end.

3rd row: P2, *k2, C2B, k1, p2; rep from * to end.

5th row: P2, *k1, C2B, k2, p2; rep from * to end.

7th row: P2, *C2B, k3, p2; rep from * to end.

8th row: As 2nd row.

Rep these 8 rows.

8.18

Multiple of 8 sts + 10.

Special Abbreviation

Cluster 6 = k2, p2, k2 from left-hand needle, slip these 6 sts onto a cable needle. Wrap yarn twice anticlockwise round these 6 sts. Slip sts back onto right-hand needle.

1st row (right side): P2, *k2, p2; rep from * to end.

2nd and every alt row: K2, *p2, k2; rep from * to end.

3rd row: P2, *cluster 6, p2; rep from * to end.

5th row: As 1st row.

7th row: P2, k2, p2, *cluster 6, p2; rep from * to last 4 sts, k2, p2.

8.19

Multiple of 8 sts + 5.

1st row (right side): K5, *p3, k5; rep from * to end.

2nd row: P5, *k3, p5; rep from * to end.

3rd and 4th rows: Rep the last 2 rows once more.

5th row: K1, p3, *k5, p3; rep from * to last st, k1.

6th row: P1, k3, *p5, k3; rep from * to last st, p1.

7th and 8th rows: Rep the last 2 rows once more.

Rep these 8 rows.

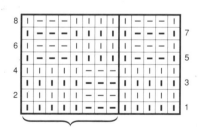

Rep these 8 sts

8th row: As 2nd row.

Rep these 8 rows.

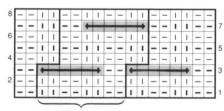

Rep these 8 sts

8.20

Multiple of 4 sts + 2.

1st row (right side): Knit.

2nd row: Purl.

3rd row: K2, *p2, k2; rep from * to end.

4th row: P2, *k2, p2; rep from * to end.

5th and 6th rows: As 1st and 2nd rows.

7th row: P2, *k2, p2; rep from * to end.

8th row: K2, *p2, k2; rep from * to end.

Rep these 8 rows.

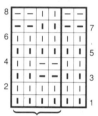

Rep these 4 sts

8.21

Multiple of 4 sts + 3.

1st row (right side): Knit.

2nd row: K3, *p1, k3; rep from * to end.

3rd and 4th rows: Rep the last 2 rows once more.

5th row: Knit.

6th row: K1, p1, *k3, p1; rep from * to last st, k1.

7th and 8th rows: Rep the last 2 rows once more.

Rep these 8 rows.

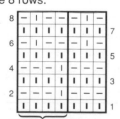

Rep these 4 sts

= T4B. = T4F. = C6B. = C6F.

8 Row Repeats

8.22

Multiple of 6 sts + 2.

1st row (right side): P2, *k4, p2; rep from * to end.

2nd and every alt row: K2, *p4, k2; rep from * to end.

3rd row: P2, *C4B, p2; rep from * to end.

5th row: As 1st row.

7th row: P2, *C4F, p2; rep from * to end.

8th row: As 2nd row.

Rep these 8 rows.

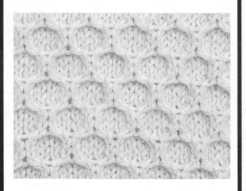

Rep these 6 sts

8.23

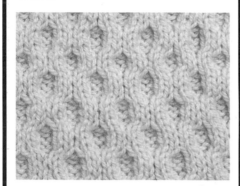

Multiple of 8 sts + 2.

1st row (right side): P3, k4, *p4, k4; rep from * to last 3 sts, k3.

2nd row: K3, p4 *k4, p4; rep from * to last 3 sts, k3.

3rd row: P1, *T4B, T4F; rep from * to last st, p1.

4th row: K1, p2, *k4, p4; rep from * to last 3 sts, p2, k1.

5th row: P1, k2, p4, *k4, p4; rep from * to last 3 sts, k2, p1.

6th row: As 4th row.

7th row: P1, *T4F, T4B; rep from * to last st, p1.

8th row: As 2nd row.

Rep these 8 rows.

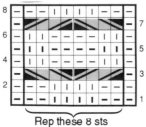

Rep these 8 sts

8.24

Multiple of 8 sts + 2.

1st row (right side): Knit.

2nd row: Purl.

3rd row: K1, *C4B, C4F; rep from * to last st, k1.

4th row: Purl.

5th and 6th rows: As 1st and 2nd rows.

7th row: K1, *C4F, C4B; rep from * to last st, k1.

8th row: Purl.

Rep these 8 rows.

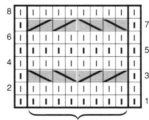

Rep these 8 sts

Note: This stitch is also very effective when worked as a panel with a multiple of 8 sts on a background of reverse st st (see 8.4 on page 28).

8.25

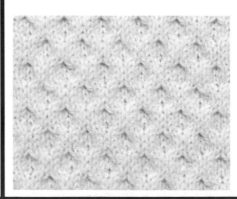

8.26

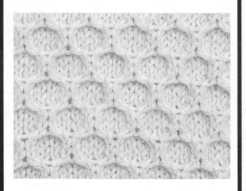

Multiple of 6 sts + 2.

1st row (right side): Knit.

2nd row: Purl.

3rd row: K1, *C3R, C3L; rep from * to last st, k1.

4th row: Purl.

5th and 6th rows: As 1st and 2nd rows.

7th row: K1, *C3L, C3R; rep from * to last st, k1.

8th row: Purl.

Rep these 8 rows.

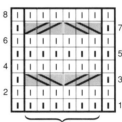

Rep these 6 sts

Note: This stitch is also very effective when worked as a panel with a multiple of 6 sts on a background of reverse st st.

Multiple of 6 sts + 2.

1st row (right side): Knit.

2nd and every alt row: Purl.

3rd row: K1, *C3B, C3F; rep from * to last st, k1.

5th row: Knit.

7th row: K1, *C3F, C3B; rep from * to last st, k1.

8th row: Purl.

Rep these 8 rows.

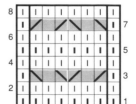

Rep these 6 sts

Note: This stitch is also very effective when worked as a panel with a multiple of 6 sts on a background of reverse st st.

= C3B.   = C3F.   = C3L.   = C3R.   = C4B.   = C4F.

8.27

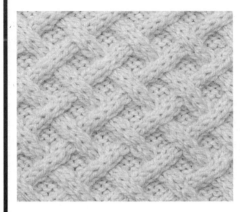

Multiple of 8 sts + 10.

1st row (right side): P3, C4B, *p4, C4B; rep from * to last 3 sts, p3.

2nd row: K3, p4, *k4, p4; rep from * to last 3 sts, k3.

3rd row: P1, *T4B, T4F; rep from * to last st, p1.

4th row: K1, p2, k4, *p4, k4; rep from * to last 3 sts, p2, k1.

5th row: P1, k2, p4, *C4B, p4; rep from * to last 3 sts, k2, p1.

6th row: As 4th row.

7th row: P1, *T4F, T4B; rep from * to last st, p1.

8th row: As 2nd row.

Rep these 8 rows.

8.28

Multiple of 12 sts + 2.

1st row (right side): Knit.

2nd and every alt row: Purl.

3rd row: K1, *C4B, k4, C4F; rep from * to last st, k1.

5th row: Knit.

7th row: K3, C4F, C4B, *k4, C4F, C4B; rep from * to last 3 sts, k3.

8th row: Purl.

Rep these 8 rows.

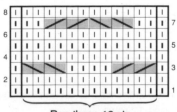

Rep these 12 sts

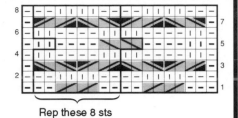

Rep these 8 sts

8.29

Multiple of 8 sts + 10.

1st row (right side): P3, C4B, *p4, C4B; rep from * to last 3 sts, p3.

2nd row: K3, p4, *k4, p4; rep from * to last 3 sts, k3.

3rd row: P1, *T4B, T4F; rep from * to last st, p1.

4th row: K1, p2, k4, *p4, k4; rep from * to last 3 sts, p2, k1.

5th row: P1, k2, p4, *C4F, p4; rep from * to last 3 sts, k2, p1.

6th row: As 4th row.

7th row: P1, *T4F, T4B; rep from * to last st, p1.

8th row: As 2nd row.

Rep these 8 rows.

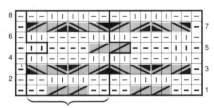

Rep these 8 sts

10.2 (on left of photograph)

Panel of 10 sts on a background of reverse st st.

1st row (right side): K10.

2nd row: P10.

3rd row: C10F.

4th row: P10.

5th to 10th rows: Rep 1st and 2nd rows 3 times.

Rep these 10 rows.

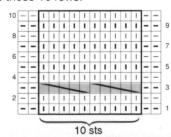

10 sts

10.1

Panel of 7 sts on a background of reverse st st.

Special Abbreviation

T7B rib (Twist 7 Back rib) = slip next 4 sts onto cable needle and hold at back of work, k1, p1, k1 from left-hand needle, then [p1, k1] twice from cable needle.

1st row (right side): K1, [p1, k1] 3 times.

2nd row: PB1, [k1, PB1] 3 times.

3rd row: T7B rib.

4th row: As 2nd row.

5th to 10th rows: Rep 1st and 2nd rows 3 times.

Rep these 10 rows.

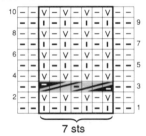

7 sts

10.2 - 10.3

10.3 (on right of photograph)

Work as given for 10.2 **but** working C10B in place of C10F.

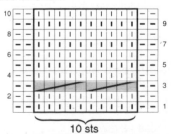

10 sts

= T4B. = T4F. = C10B. = C10F.

12 Row Repeats

12.1

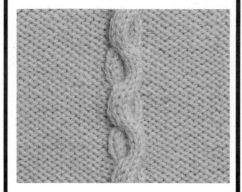

Panel of 6 sts on a background of reverse st st.

1st row (right side): K6.
2nd row: P6.
3rd row: C6B.
4th row: P6.
5th to 8th rows: Rep 1st and 2nd rows twice.
9th row: C6F.
10th row: P6.
11th and 12th rows: As 1st and 2nd rows.
Rep these 12 rows.

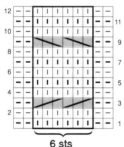

6 sts

12.2

Panel of 4 sts on a background of reverse st st.

1st row (right side): K4.
2nd row: P4.
3rd row: C4B.
4th row: P4.
5th to 8th rows: Rep these 4 rows once more.
9th to 12th rows: Rep 1st and 2nd rows twice.
Rep these 12 rows.

12.3 - 12.4

12.3 (on right of photograph)
Panel of 12 sts on a background of reverse st st.

1st row (right side): K12.
2nd row: P12.
3rd row: C12B.
4th row: P12.
5th to 12th rows: Rep 1st and 2nd rows 4 times.
Rep these 12 rows.

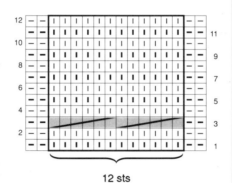

12 sts

12.4 (on left of photograph)
Work as given for 12.3 **but** working C12F in place of C12B.

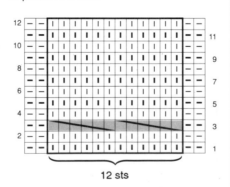

12 sts

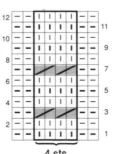

4 sts

12.5

Panel of 6 sts on a background of reverse st st.

1st row (right side): K2, C4F.
2nd row: P6.
3rd row: K6.
4th row: P6.
5th and 6th rows: As 1st and 2nd rows.
7th row: C4B, k2.
8th row: P6.
9th and 10th rows: As 3rd and 4th rows.
11th and 12th rows: As 7th and 8th rows.
Rep these 12 rows.

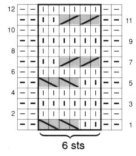

6 sts

12.6

Panel of 20 sts on a background of reverse st st.

1st row (right side): K20.
2nd row: P20.
3rd row: K4, [C8F] twice.
4th row: P20.
5th to 8th rows: Rep 1st and 2nd rows twice.
9th row: [C8B] twice, k4.
10th row: P20.
11th and 12th rows: As 1st and 2nd rows.
Rep these 12 rows.

= T3B. = T3F. = C4B. = C4F. = C6B. = C6F. = C8B. = C8F.

12.7

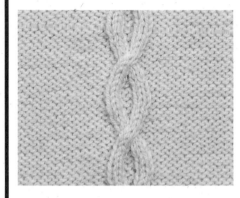

Panel of 8 sts on a background of reverse st st.

1st row (right side): P2, C4B, p2.
2nd row: K2, p4, k2.
3rd row: P1, T3B, T3F, p1.
4th row: K1, p2, k2, p2, k1.
5th row: T3B, p2, T3F.
6th row: P2, k4, p2.
7th row: K2, p4, k2.
8th row: P2, k4, p2.
9th row: T3F, p2, T3B.
10th row: K1, p2, k2, p2, k1.
11th row: P1, T3F, T3B, p1.
12th row: K2, p4, k2.
Rep these 12 rows.

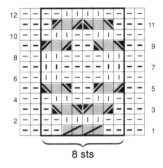

8 sts

12.8

Panel of 12 sts on a background of reverse st st.

1st row (right side): K12.
2nd row: P12.
3rd row: C6B, C6F.
4th row: P12.
5th to 8th rows: Rep 1st and 2nd rows twice.
9th row: C6F, C6B.
10th row: P12.
11th and 12th rows: As 1st and 2nd rows.
Rep these 12 rows.

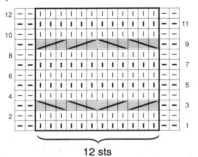

12 sts

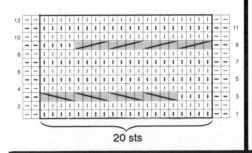

20 sts

12.9

Panel of 6 sts on a background of reverse st st.

1st row (right side): K6.
2nd row: P6.
3rd row: C6B.
4th row: P6.
5th and 6th rows: As 1st and 2nd rows.
7th row: K1, C4B, k1.
8th row: P6.
9th to 12th rows: Rep the last 4 rows once more.
Rep these 12 rows.

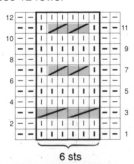

6 sts

12.10

Panel of 8 sts on a background of reverse st st.

1st row (right side): K8.
2nd row: P8.
3rd row: C8B.
4th row: P8.
5th and 6th rows: As 1st and 2nd rows.
7th row: K2, C4B, k2.
8th row: P8.
9th to 12th rows: Rep the last 4 rows once more.
Rep these 12 rows.

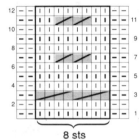

8 sts

12.11

Panel of 20 sts on a background of reverse st st.

1st row (right side): K20.
2nd row: P20.
3rd row: C10B, C10F.
4th row: P20.
5th to 12th rows: Rep 1st and 2nd rows 4 times.
Rep these 12 rows.

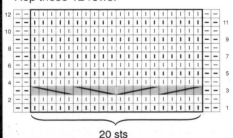

20 sts

= C10B.　　= C10F.　　= C12B.　　= C12F.

Lady's Cable Sweater

To Fit

Bust/Chest sizes

85/90	95/100	105/110	cm
34/36	38/40	42/44	ins

Finished measurement

104	115	127	cm
41¹/2	46	51	ins

Length to Shoulder

64	68	72	cm
25¹/4	26³/4	28¹/4	ins

Sleeve length

45	47	48	cm
17³/4	18¹/2	19	ins

Materials

Aran type (Worsted Weight) knitting yarn	800	1000	1150	grams
	29	36	41	ounces

Pair needles each size 5mm (No.6) and 4mm (No.8)
Cable needle.

The quantities of yarn stated are based on average requirements and are therefore approximate.

For abbreviations see pages 20 and 21.

Instructions are given for the smallest size; larger sizes are given in ( )s. Figures or instructions given in [ ]s should be repeated as stated after the brackets. Where only one figure is given this applies to all sizes.

Tension

19 sts and 26 rows = 10 cm [4 ins] square measured over double moss stitch using larger needles.

Special Abbreviations

Inc 2 = work (p1, k1, p1) all into next st.

Slip marker = make a slip knot in a short length of contrasting yarn and place on needle where indicated. On following rows slip marker from one needle to the other until pattern is established.

Cable Panel

(worked across 22 sts between markers)
1st row: P2, [k8, p2] twice.
2nd and every alt row: K2, [p8, k2] twice.
3rd row: P2, [C4B, C4F, p2] twice.
5th row: As 1st row.
7th row: As 3rd row.
9th row: As 1st row.
11th row: P2, [C4F, C4B, p2] twice.
13th row: As 1st row.
15th row: As 11th row.
16th row: As 2nd row.
These 16 rows form the pattern panel.

Back

Using smaller needles cast on 85(95-105) sts.
1st row (right side): K1, *p1, k1; rep from * to end.
2nd row: P1, *k1, p1; rep from * to end.
Rep the last 2 rows until rib measures 8 cm [3 ins] ending with a right side row ★.
Next row (increase): Rib 2, Inc 2 [rib 3(5-7), Inc 2] twice, rib 2, [inc in next st, rib 1] 6 times, inc in next st, rib 8, Inc 2 [rib 13(15-13), Inc 2] 3(3-4) times, rib 8(8-6). 106(116-128) sts.
Change to larger needles and commence pattern.
1st row: [P1, k1] 33(36-40) times, slip marker, work 1st row of Cable Panel across next 22 sts, slip marker, [k1, p1] 9(11-13) times.
2nd row: [K1, p1] 9(11-13) times, work 2nd row of Cable Panel, [p1, k1] 33(36-40) times.
3rd row: [K1, p1] 33(36-40) times, work 3rd row of Cable Panel, [p1, k1] 9(11-13) times.
4th row: [P1, k1] 9(11-13) times, work 4th row of Cable Panel, [k1, p1] 33(36-40) times.
These 4 rows form double moss stitch pattern at either side of Cable Panel.
Keeping 16 rows of Cable Panel correct on sts between markers, continue in pattern until Back measures 64(68-72) cm [25¹/4 (26³/4-28¹/4) ins] or required length to shoulder ending with a wrong side row.

Shape Shoulders

Next row: Cast off 35(39-44) sts, work

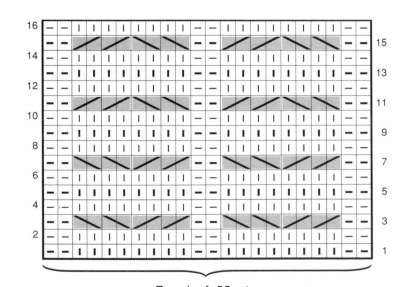

Panel of 22 sts

▨▨▨ = C4F	▨▨▨ = C4B

Lady's Cable Sweater

until there are 29(31-33) sts on right-hand needle, cast off remaining 42(46-51) sts. Slip remaining 29(31-33) sts on to a holder for neckband.

Front

Work as given for Back to ★.

Next row (increase): Rib 8(8-6), [Inc 2, rib 13(15-13)] 3(3-4) times, Inc 2, rib 8 [inc in next st, rib 1] 6 times, inc in next st, rib 2, [Inc 2, rib 3(5-7)] twice, Inc 2 rib 2. 106(116-128) sts.

Change to larger needles and commence pattern.

1st row: [P1, k1] 9(11-13) times, slip marker, work 1st row of Cable Panel across next 22 sts, slip marker, [k1,p1] 33(36-40) times.

2nd row: [K1, p1] 33(36-40) times, work 2nd row of Cable Panel, [k1, p1] 9(11-13) times.

3rd row: [K1, p1] 9(11-13) times, work 3rd row of Cable Panel, [k1, p1] 33(36-40) times.

4th row: [P1, k1] 33(36-40) times, work 4th row of Cable Panel, [p1, k1] 9(11-13) times.

Keeping 16 rows of Cable Panel correct on sts between markers, continue in pattern until front is 23(27-31) rows shorter than back to shoulder, thus ending with a right side row.

Shape Neck

Next row: Work 43(48-54) sts, turn and complete this side first.

Keeping pattern correct dec 1 st at neck edge on next 5 rows, then following 3(4-5) alt rows. 35(39-44) sts remain.

Work 11(13-15) rows straight thus ending with a wrong side row. Cast off.

Slip next 13 sts at centre on to a holder for neckband. With wrong side facing rejoin yarn to neck edge of remaining 43(48-54) sts and work to end. Dec 1 st at neck edge on next 5 rows, then following 3(4-5) alt rows. 35(39-44) sts remain.

Work 11(13-15) rows straight thus ending with a wrong side row. Cast off.

Sleeves

Using smaller needles cast on 41(47-51) sts and work 8 cm [3 ins] in k1, p1 rib as given for Back ending with a right side row.

Next row (increase): Rib 4(2-4), *Inc 2, rib 7(9-9); rep from * to last 5(5-7) sts, Inc 2, rib to end. 51(57-61) sts.

Change to larger needles and work 4 rows in double moss stitch as given for Back.

Bringing extra sts into double moss stitch, inc 1 st at each end of next and every following 4th row until there are 63(77-107) sts.

1st (2nd) sizes only: Inc 1 st at each end of every following 5th row until there are 87(97) sts.

All sizes: Work straight until sleeve measures 45(47-48) cm [17³/4(18¹/2-19) ins] or required length ending with a wrong side row. Cast off.

Finishing and Neckband

Press pieces according to instructions on ball band. Join left shoulder seam.

Neckband

Using smaller needles and with right side facing, knit across sts on holder at back neck decreasing 1 st at centre, pick up and k20(23-26) sts down left front slope, knit across sts on holder at front neck and pick up and k20(23-26) sts up right front slope. 81(89-97) sts.

Starting with a 2nd row, work 8 cm [3 ins] in k1, p1 rib as given for Back. Slip sts on to a length of yarn.

Join right shoulder seam and ends of neckband. Fold neckband in half to inside and slip stitch loosely in place, allowing for stretch and taking care to catch every stitch.

Fold sleeves in half lengthways and mark centre of cast off edge. Sew sleeve to side edge placing centre at shoulder seam.

Note: Armhole should measure approximately 23(25-28) cm [9(10-11¹/4) ins]. Join side and sleeve seams. Press seams if required.

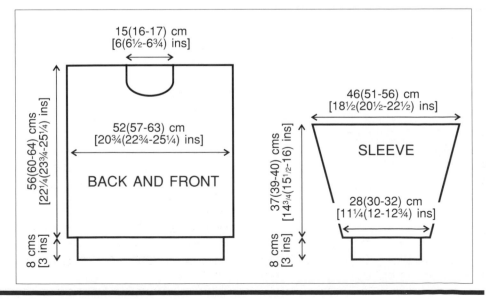

12.12

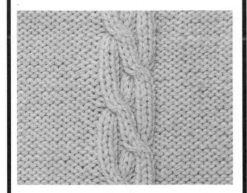

Panel of 10 sts on a background of reverse st st.

Special Abbreviation

T6L rib (Twist 6 Left rib) = slip next 4 sts onto cable needle and hold at front of work, knit next 2 sts from left-hand needle, slip the 2 purl sts from cable needle back to left-hand needle and purl them, then knit 2 sts from cable needle.

1st row (right side): K2, [p2, k2] twice.
2nd row: P2, [k2, p2] twice.
3rd row: T6L rib, p2, k2.
4th row: As 2nd row.
5th to 8th rows: Rep 1st and 2nd rows twice.
9th row: K2, p2, T6L rib.
10th row: As 2nd row.
11th and 12th rows: As 1st and 2nd rows.
Rep these 12 rows.

10 sts

12.14

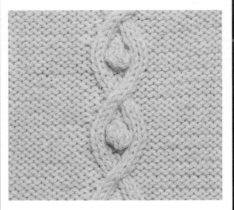

Panel of 9 sts on a background of reverse st st.

Special Abbreviation

● **MB#4 (Make Bobble number 4)** see page 21

1st row (right side): P1, T3B, p1, T3F, p1.
2nd row: K1, p2, k3, p2, k1.
3rd row: T3B, p3, T3F.
4th row: P2, k5, p2.
5th row: K2, p2, MB#4, p2, k2.
6th row: P2, k5, p2.
7th row: T3F, p3, T3B.
8th row: As 2nd row.
9th row: P1, T3F, p1, T3B, p1.
10th row: K2, p5, k2.
11th row: P2, T5BP, p2.
12th row: K2, p5, k2.
Rep these 12 rows.

9 sts

12.15

Panel of 16 sts on a background of reverse st st.

Special Abbreviations

T8B rib (Twist 8 Back rib) = slip next 4 sts onto cable needle and hold at back of work, k1, p2, k1 from left-hand needle, then k1, p2, k1 from cable needle.

T8F rib (Twist 8 Front rib) = slip next 4 sts onto cable needle and hold at front of work, k1, p2, k1 from left-hand needle, then k1, p2, k1 from cable needle.

1st row (right side): K1, p2, [k2, p2] 3 times, k1.
2nd row: P1, k2, [p2, k2] 3 times, p1.
3rd row: T8B rib, T8F rib.
4th row: As 2nd row.
5th to 12th rows: Rep 1st and 2nd rows 4 times.
Rep these 12 rows.

16 sts

12.13

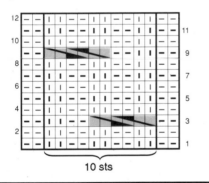

Multiple of 4 sts + 2.
1st row (right side): P3, T2B, *p2, T2B; rep from * to last st, p1.
2nd row: K2, *p1, k3; rep from * to end.
3rd row: P2, *T2B, p2; rep from * to end.
4th row: *K3, p1; rep from * to last 2 sts, k2.
5th row: P1, T2B, *p2, T2B; rep from * to last 3 sts, p3.
6th row: K4, p1, *k3, p1; rep from * to last st, k1.
7th row: P1, T2F, *p2, T2F; rep from * to last 3 sts, p3.
8th row: As 4th row.
9th row: P2, *T2F, p2; rep from * to end.
10th row: As 2nd row.
11th row: P3, T2F, *p2, T2F; rep from * to last st, p1.

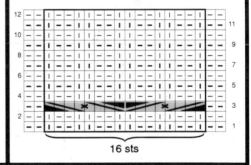

Rep these 4 sts

12th row: K1, p1, *k3, p1; rep from * to last 4 sts, k4.
Rep these 12 rows.

Note: This stitch is also very effective when worked as a panel of 4 sts on a background of reverse st st.

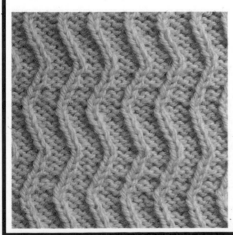

= T2B. = T2F. = T3B. = T3F. = T5BP.

12 Row Repeats

12.16

Multiple of 28 sts + 18.

1st row (right side): P6, k6, *p4, [k2, p4] 3 times, k6; rep from * to last 6 sts, p6.

2nd row: K6, p6, *k4, p14, k4, p6; rep from * to last 6 sts, k6.

3rd row: P4, T4B, k2, *[T4F, p2] twice, k2, [p2, T4B] twice, k2; rep from * to last 8 sts, T4F, p4.

4th row: K4, *p10, k4; rep from * to end.

5th row: P2, T4B, p2, k2, *[p2, T4F] twice, k2, [T4B, p2] twice, k2; rep from * to last 8 sts, p2, T4F, p2.

6th row: K2, p14, *k4, p6, k4, p14; rep from * to last 2 sts, k2.

7th row: P2, *[k2, p4] 3 times, k6, p4; rep from * to last 16 sts, k2, [p4, k2] twice, p2.

8th row: As 6th row.

9th row: P2, T4F, p2, k2, *[p2, T4B] twice, k2, [T4F, p2] twice, k2; rep from * to last 8 sts, p2, T4B, p2.

10th row: As 4th row.

11th row: P4, T4F, k2, *[T4B, p2] twice, k2, [p2, T4F] twice, k2; rep from * to last 8 sts, T4B, p4.

12th row: As 2nd row.

Rep these 12 rows.

Note: This stitch is also be very effective worked as a panel of 46 sts, (28 + 18 = 46) on a background of reverse st st.

12.17

Multiple of 6 sts + 4.

1st row (right side): P1, *T3F, p3; rep from * to last 3 sts, p3.

2nd row: K6, p2, *k4, p2; rep from * to last 2 sts, k2.

3rd row: P2, *T3F, p3; rep from * to last 2 sts, p2.

4th row: K5, p2, *k4, p2; rep from * to last 3 sts, k3.

5th row: *P3, T3F; rep from * to last 4 sts, p4.

6th row: K4, *p2, k4; rep from * to end.

7th row: P4, *T3F, p3; rep from * to end.

8th row: K3, *p2, k4; rep from * to last st, k1.

9th row: P5, T3F, *p3, T3F; rep from * to last 2 sts, p2.

10th row: K2, *p2, k4; rep from * to last 2 sts, k2.

11th row: P6, T3F, *p3, T3F; rep from * to last st, p1.

12th row: K1, *p2, k4; rep from * to last 3 sts, k3.

Rep these 12 rows.

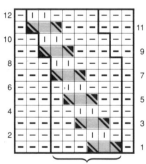

Rep these 6 sts

12.18

Multiple of 6 sts + 4.

1st row (right side): P6, T3B, *p3, T3B; rep from * to last st, p1.

2nd row: K2, *p2, k4; rep from * to last 2 sts, k2.

3rd row: P5, T3B, *p3, T3B; rep from * to last 2 sts, p2.

4th row: K3, *p2, k4; rep from * to last st, k1.

5th row: P4, *T3B, p3; rep from * to end.

6th row: K4, *p2, k4; rep from * to end.

7th row: *P3, T3B; rep from * to last 4 sts, p4.

8th row: K5, p2, *k4, p2; rep from * to last 3 sts, k3.

9th row: P2, *T3B, p3; rep from * to last 2 sts, p2.

10th row: K6, p2, *k4, p2; rep from * to last 2 sts, k2.

11th row: P1, *T3B, p3; rep from * to last 3 sts, p3.

12th row: K7, p2, *k4, p2; rep from * to last st, k1.

Rep these 12 rows.

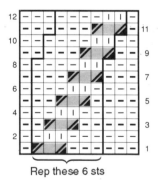

Rep these 6 sts

Rep these 28 sts

= T3B. = T3F. = C4B. = C4F. = T4B. = T4F.

12.19

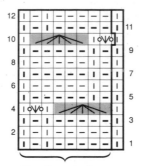

Rep these 8 sts

Multiple of 8 sts + 1.

Special Abbreviations

Work 5tog (Work 5 sts together) = with yarn at front (wrong side), slip 3 sts purlwise, k2tog, p3sso.

M1K, M3, M1K (see abbreviations on pages 20 and 21).

1st row (right side): K1, *p5, k1, p1, k1; rep from * to end.

2nd row: P1, *k1, p1, k5, p1; rep from * to end.

3rd row: As 1st row.

4th row: P1, *M1K, M3, M1K, p1, work 5tog, p1; rep from * to end.

5th row: K1, *p1, k1, p5, k1; rep from * to end.

6th row: P1, *k5, p1, k1, p1; rep from * to end.

Rep the last 2 rows once more, then 5th row again.

10th row: P1, *work 5tog, p1, M1K, M3, M1K, p1; rep from * to end.

11th and 12th rows: As 1st and 2nd rows.

Rep these 12 rows.

12.20

12.21

Multiple of 12 sts + 14.

1st row (right side): P3, T4B, T4F, *p4, T4B, T4F; rep from * to last 3 sts, p3.

2nd row: K3, p2, *k4, p2; rep from * to last 3 sts, k3.

3rd row: P1, *T4B, p4, T4F; rep from * to last st, p1.

4th row: K1, p2, k8, *p4, k8; rep from * to last 3 sts, p2, k1.

5th row: P1, k2, p8, *C4B, p8; rep from * to last 3 sts, k2, p1.

6th row: As 4th row.

7th row: P1, *T4F, p4, T4B; rep from * to last st, p1.

8th row: As 2nd row.

9th row: P3, T4F, T4B, *p4, T4F, T4B; rep from * to last 3 sts, p3.

10th row: K5, p4, *k8, p4; rep from * to last 5 sts, k5.

11th row: P5, C4F, *p8, C4F; rep from * to last 5 sts, p5.

12th row: As 10th row.

Rep these 12 rows.

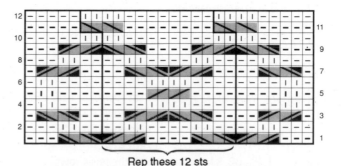

Rep these 12 sts

Multiple of 12 sts + 2.

Special Abbreviations

T6R rib (Twist 6 Right rib) = slip next 4 sts onto cable needle and hold at back of work, knit next 2 sts from left-hand needle, slip the 2 purl sts from cable needle back to left-hand needle and purl them, then knit 2 sts from cable needle.

T6L rib (Twist 6 Left rib) = slip next 4 sts onto cable needle and hold at front of work, knit next 2 sts from left-hand needle, slip the 2 purl sts from cable needle back to left-hand needle and purl them, then knit 2 sts from cable needle.

1st row (right side): P2, *k2, p2; rep from * to end.

2nd and every alt row: K2, *p2, k2; rep from * to end.

3rd row: P2, *T6R rib, p2, k2, p2; rep from * to end.

5th and 7th rows: As 1st row.

9th row: P2, *k2, p2, T6L rib, p2; rep from * to end.

11th row: As 1st row.

12th row: As 2nd row.

Rep these 12 rows.

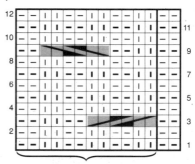

Rep these 12 sts

14-16 Row Repeats

14.1

Panel of 11 sts on a background of reverse st st.

Special Abbreviation

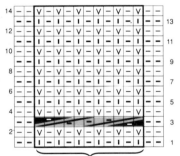 **T11B rib (Twist 11 Back rib)** = slip next 6 sts onto cable needle and hold at back of work, k1, [p1, k1] twice from left-hand needle, then [p1, k1] 3 times from cable needle.

1st row (right side): K1, [p1, k1] 5 times.
2nd row: PB1, [k1, PB1] 5 times.
3rd row: T11B rib.
4th row: As 2nd row.
5th to 14th rows: Rep 1st and 2nd rows 5 times.
Rep these 14 rows.

[chart: Rep these 11 sts]

14.2

Panel of 9 sts on a background of reverse st st.

1st row (right side): P2, T2B, KB1, T2F, p2.
2nd row: K2, p1, [k1, p1] twice, k2.
3rd row: P1, C2B, p1, KB1, p1, C2F, p1.
4th row: K1, p2, k1, p1, k1, p2, k1.

16.1 - 16.2

16.1 (on left of photograph)

Panel of 18 sts on a background of reverse st st.

1st row (right side): K18.
2nd row: P18.
3rd row: K6, C12F.
4th row: P18.
5th to 10th rows: Rep 1st and 2nd rows 3 times.
11th row: C12B, k6.
12th row: P18.
13th to 16th rows: Rep 1st and 2nd rows twice.
Rep these 16 rows.

[chart: 18 sts]

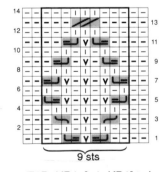

5th row: T2B, KB1, [p1, KB1] twice, T2F.
6th row: P1, [k1, p1] 4 times.
7th row: T2F, KB1, [p1, KB1] twice, T2B.
8th row: As 4th row.
9th row: P1, T2F, p1, KB1, p1, T2B, p1.
10th row: As 2nd row.
11th row: P2, T2F, KB1, T2B, p2.
12th row: K3, p3, k3.
13th row: P3, C3R, p3.
14th row: K3, p3, k3.
Rep these 14 rows.

[chart: 9 sts]

16.2 (on right of photograph)

Work as given for 16.1 **but** working C12B in place of C12F, and C12F in place of C12B.

[chart: 18 sts]

16.3

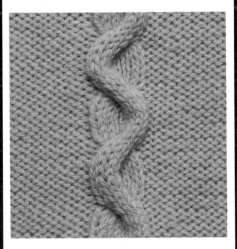

Panel of 8 sts on a background of reverse st st.

1st row (right side): K8.
2nd row: P8.
3rd row: C8B.
4th row: P8.
5th to 10th rows: Rep 1st and 2nd rows 3 times.
11th row: C8F.
12th row: P8.
13th to 16th rows: Rep 1st and 2nd rows twice.
Rep these 16 rows.

[chart: 8 sts]

 = KB1.   = PB1.   = T2B.   = T2F. = C2B. = C2F. = C3B. = C3F. = T3B. = T3F.   = C4B.

16.4

Panel of 16 sts on a background of reverse st st.

1st row (right side): K16.
2nd row: P16.
3rd row: C8B, C8F.
4th row: P16.
5th to 10th rows: Rep 1st and 2nd rows 3 times.
11th row: C8F, C8B.
12th row: P16.
13th to 16th rows: Rep 1st and 2nd rows twice.
Rep these 16 rows

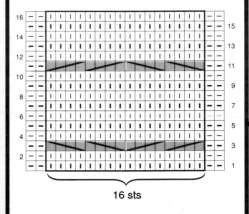

16 sts

16.5

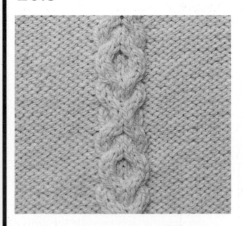

Panel of 8 sts on a background of reverse st st.

16.6

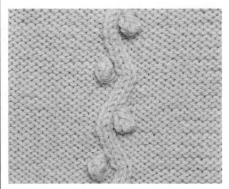

Panel of 6 sts on a background of reverse st st.

Special Abbreviation

⬤ **MB#2 (Make Bobble number 2)** see page 21.

1st row (right side): P1, MB#2, p1, T3B.
2nd row: K1, p2, k3.
3rd row: P2, T3B, p1.
4th row: K2, p2, k2.
5th row: P1, T3B, p2.
6th row: K3, p2, k1.
7th row: T3B, p3.
8th row: K4, p2.
9th row: T3F, p1, MB#2, p1.
10th row: K3, p2, k1.
11th row: P1, T3F, p2.
12th row: K2, p2, k2.
13th row: P2, T3F, p1.
14th row: K1, p2, k3.
15th row: P3, T3F.
16th row: P2, k4.
Rep these 16 rows.

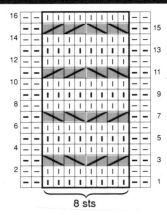

8 sts

1st row (right side): K8.
2nd row: P8.
3rd row: C4B, C4F.
4th row: P8.
5th to 10th rows: Rep these 4 rows once more, then 1st and 2nd rows again.
11th row: C4F, C4B.
12th row: P8.
13th and 14th rows: As 1st and 2nd rows.
15th and 16th rows: As 11th and 12th rows.
Rep these 16 rows.

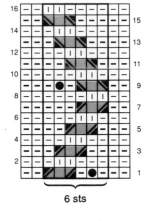

6 sts

16.7

Panel of 11 sts on a background of reverse st st.

1st row (right side): P2, C3B, p1, C3F, p2.
2nd row: K2, p3, k1, p3, k2.
3rd row: P1, C3B, p1, k1, p1, C3F, p1.
4th row: K1, p3, k1, p1, k1, p3, k1.
5th row: C3B, p1, [k1, p1] twice, C3F.
6th row: P3, k1, [p1, k1] twice, p3.
7th row: K2, p1, [k1, p1] 3 times, k2.
8th row: P2, k1, [p1, k1] 3 times, p2.
9th row: T3F, p1, [k1, p1] twice, T3B.
10th row: K1, p2, k1, [p1, k1] twice, p2, k1.
11th row: P1, T3F, p1, k1, p1, T3B, p1.
12th row: K2, p2, k1, p1, k1, p2, k2.
13th row: P2, T3F, p1, T3B, p2.
14th row: K3, p2, k1, p2, k3.
15th row: P3, C5B, p3.
16th row: K3, p5, k3.
Rep these 16 rows.

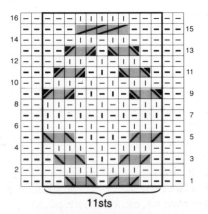

11sts

16 Row Repeats

16.8

Panel of 10 sts on a background of reverse st st.

1st row (right side): P1, k8, p1.
2nd row: K1, p8, k1.
3rd row: P1, C4B, C4F, p1.
4th row: As 2nd row.
5th and 6th rows: As 1st and 2nd rows.

7th row: P1, T4B, T4F, p1.
8th row: K1, p2, k4, p2, k1.
9th row: T3B, p4, T3F.
10th row: P2, k6, p2.
11th row: K2, p6, k2.
12th row: P2, k6, p2.
13th row: T3F, p4, T3B.
14th row: As 8th row.
15th row: P1, C4F, C4B, p1.
16th row: K1, p8, k1.
Rep these 16 rows.

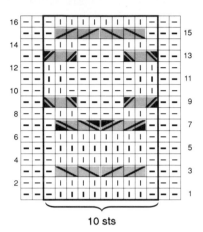

10 sts

16.9

Panel of 17 sts on a background of reverse st st.

1st row (right side): K2, p4, k2, p1, k2, p4, k2.

2nd row: K6, p2, k1, p2, k6.
3rd row: P6, T5BP, p6.
4th row: As 2nd row.
5th row: P5, T3B, k1, T3F, p5.
6th row: K5, p2, k1, p1, k1, p2, k5.
7th row: P4, T3B, k1, p1, k1, T3F, p4.
8th row: K4, p2, k1, [p1, k1] twice, p2, k4.
9th row: P3, T3B, k1, [p1, k1] twice, T3F, p3.
10th row: K3, p2, k1, [p1, k1] 3 times, p2, k3.
11th row: P2, T3B, k1, [p1, k1] 3 times, T3F, p2.
12th row: K2, p2, k1, [p1, k1] 4 times, p2, k2.
13th row: P1, T3B, k1, [p1, k1] 4 times, T3F, p1.
14th row: K1, p2, k1, [p1, k1] 5 times, p2, k1.
15th row: T3B, k1, [p1, k1] 5 times, T3F.
16th row: P2, k1, [p1, k1] 6 times, p2.
Rep these 16 rows.

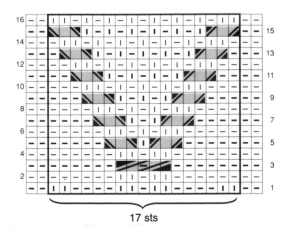

17 sts

16.10

Panel of 11 sts on a background of reverse st st.

Special Abbreviation

● **MB#3 (Make Bobble number 3)** see page 21.

1st row (right side): P11.
2nd row: K11.
3rd row: P5, MB#3, p5.
4th row: K5, PB1, k5.
5th row: P2, MB#3, p2, KB1, p2, MB#3, p2.
6th row: K2, [PB1, k2] 3 times.
7th row: MB#3, p1, T2F, p1, KB1, p1, T2B, p1, MB#3.
8th row: PB1, k2, PB1, [k1, PB1] twice, k2, PB1.
9th row: T2F, p1, T2F, KB1, T2B, p1, T2B.
10th row: K1, T2BW, k1, [PB1] 3 times, k1, T2FW, k1.
11th row: P2, T2F, M1P, sl 1, k2tog, psso, M1P, T2B, p2.
12th row: K3, T2BW, PB1, T2FW, k3.
13th row: P4, M1P, sl 1, k2tog, psso, M1P, p4.
14th row: K5, PB1, k5.
15th row: P11.
16th row: K11.
Rep these 16 rows.

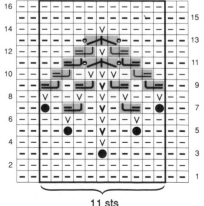

11 sts

V = KB1. V = PB1. ● = M1P. ⩜ = sl 1, k2tog, psso. ⊐⏌ = T2B. ⊏⎿ = T2F. ⊐⏌ = T2BW. ⊏⎿ = T2FW. ⧄⧄ = T3B. ⧅⧅ = T3F.

16.11

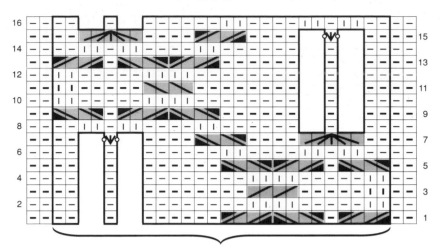

22 sts

Panel of 22 sts on a background of reverse st st.

Special Abbreviations

Work 5tog (Work 5 sts together) = with yarn at back of work, slip 3 sts purlwise, *pass 2nd st on right-hand needle over 1st (centre) st, slip centre st back to left-hand needle, pass 2nd st on left-hand needle over*, slip centre st back to right-hand needle; rep from * to * once more, purl centre st. (**Note:** Stitch referred to as 'centre st' is centre one of 5 sts).

M1K, M3, M1K (see abbreviations on pages 20 and 21)

1st row (right side): T4B, p1, T4F, T4B, p9.
2nd row: K11, p4, k5, p2.
3rd row: K2, p5, C4B, p11.
4th row: As 2nd row.
5th row: T4F, p1, T4B, T4F, p9.
6th row: K9, p2, k4, p2, k1, p2, k2.
7th row: P2, work 5tog, p4, T4F, p4, M1K, M3, M1K, p2.
8th row: K2, p2, k1, p2, k4, p2, k9.

9th row: P9, T4F, T4B, p1, T4F.
10th row: P2, k5, p4, k11.
11th row: P11, C4F, p5, k2.
12th row: As 10th row.
13th row: P9, T4B, T4F, p1, T4B.
14th row: As 8th row.
15th row: P2, M1K, M3, M1K, p4, T4B, p4, work 5tog, p2.
16th row: As 6th row.
Rep these 16 rows.

16.12

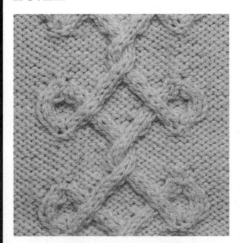

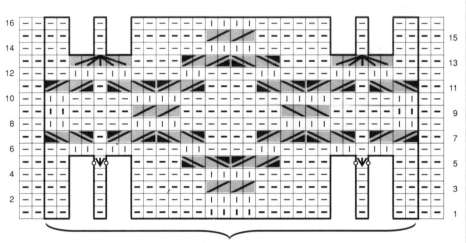

Start with 22 sts

Panel starts with 22 sts and is worked on a background of reverse st st. The number of sts within the panel varies there work between markers.

Special Abbreviations

Work 5tog (Work 5 sts together) = with yarn at back of work, slip 3 sts purlwise, *pass 2nd st on right-hand needle over 1st (centre) st, slip centre st back to left-hand needle, pass 2nd st on left-hand needle over*, slip centre st back to right-hand needle; rep from * to * once more, purl centre st. (**Note:** Stitch referred to as 'centre st' is centre one of 5 sts).

M1K, M3, M1K (see abbreviations on pages 20 and 21)

1st row (right side): P9, k4, p9.
2nd row: K9, p4, k9.
3rd row: P9, C4B, p9.
4th row: K9, p4, k9.
5th row: P2, M1K, M3, M1K, p4, T4B,

T4F, p4, M1K, M3, M1K, p2. 30 sts
6th row: K2, p2, k1, [p2, k4] 3 times, p2, k1, p2, k2.
7th row: T4B, p1, T4F, T4B, p4, T4F, T4B, p1, T4F.
8th row: P2, k5, p4, k8, p4, k5, p2.
9th row: K2, p5, C4F, p8, C4B, p5, k2.
10th row: As 8th row.
11th row: T4F, p1, T4B, T4F, p4, T4B, T4F, p1, T4B.
12th row: As 6th row.
13th row: P2, work 5tog, p4, T4F, T4B, p4, work 5tog, p2. 22 sts.
14th to 16th rows: As 2nd to 4th rows.
Rep these 16 rows.

16 Row Repeats

16.13

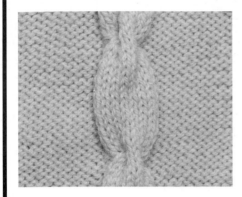

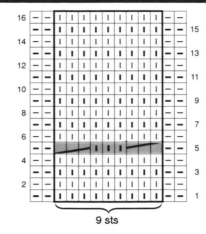

9 sts

Panel of 9 sts on a background of reverse st st.

Special Abbreviation

C9X (Cable 9X) = slip next 3 sts onto a cable needle and hold at back of work, slip following 3 sts onto 2nd cable needle and hold at front of work, knit next 3 sts from left-hand needle, knit the 3 sts from 2nd cable needle, then the 3 sts from 1st cable needle.

1st row (right side): K9.
2nd row: P9.
Rep the last 2 rows once more.
5th row: C9X.
6th row: P9.
7th to 16th rows: Rep 1st and 2nd rows 5 times.
Rep these 16 rows.

Panel of 24 sts on a background of reverse st st.
1st row (right side): P2, C4B, [p4, C4B] twice, p2.
2nd row: K2, p4, [k4, p4] twice, k2.
3rd row: P1, T3B, [T4F, T4B] twice, T3F, p1.
4th row: K1, p2, k3, p4, k4, p4, k3, p2, k1.
5th row: T3B, p3, C4F, p4, C4F, p3, T3F.
6th row: P2, k4, [p4, k4] twice, p2.
7th row: K2, p3, T3B, T4F, T4B, T3F, p3, k2.
8th row: [P2, k3] twice, p4, [k3, p2] twice.
9th row: [K2, p3] twice, C4B, [p3, k2] twice.
10th row: As 8th row.
11th row: K2, p3, T3F, T4B, T4F, T3B, p3, k2.
12th row: As 6th row.
13th row: T3F, p3, C4F, p4, C4F, p3, T3B.
14th row: As 4th row.
15th row: P1, T3F, [T4B, T4F] twice, T3B, p1.
16th row: As 2nd row.
Rep these 16 rows.

16.14

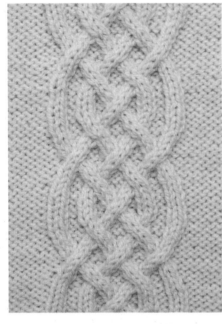

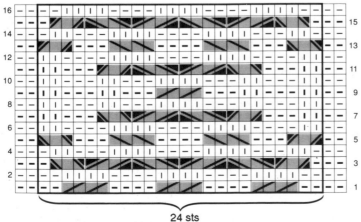

24 sts

16.15

Multiple of 8 sts + 4.
1st row (right side): P5, C2B, *p6, C2B; rep from * to last 5 sts, p5.
2nd row: K5, p2, *k6, p2; rep from * to last 5 sts, k5.
3rd row: P4, *T2B, T2F, p4; rep from * to end.
4th row: K4, *p1, k2, p1, k4; rep from * to end.
5th row: P3, *T2B, p2, T2F, p2; rep from * to last st, p1.
6th row: K3, *p1, k4, p1, k2; rep from * to last st, k1.
7th row: P2, *T2B, p4, T2F; rep from * to last 2 sts, p2.
8th row: K1, p2, *k6, p2; rep from * to last st, k1.
9th row: P1, C2B, *p6, C2B; rep from * to last st, p1.
10th row: As 8th row.
11th row: P2, *T2F, p4, T2B; rep from * to last 2 sts, p2.
12th row: As 6th row.
13th row: P3, *T2F, p2, T2B, p2; rep from * to last st, p1.
14th row: As 4th row.
15th row: P4, *T2F, T2B, p4; rep from * to end.
16th row: As 2nd row.
Rep these 16 rows.

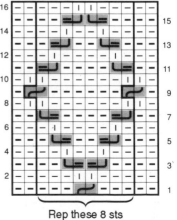

Rep these 8 sts

= C2B. = C2F. = T2B. = T2F. = T3B. = T3F. = C4B.

16.16

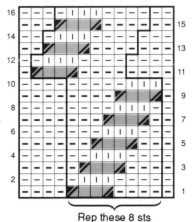

Rep these 8 sts

Multiple of 8 sts + 5.

1st row (right side): P5, *T4R, p4; rep from * to end.

2nd row: K5, *p3, k5; rep from * to end.

3rd row: *P4, T4R; rep from * to last 5 sts, p5.

4th row: K6, p3, *k5, p3; rep from * to last 4 sts, k4.

5th row: P3, *T4R, p4; rep from * to last 2 sts, p2.

6th row: K7, p3, *k5, p3; rep from * to last 3 sts, k3.

7th row: P2, *T4R, p4; rep from * to last 3 sts, p3.

8th row: K8, p3, *k5, p3; rep from * to last 2 sts, k2.

9th row: P1, *T4R, p4; rep from * to last 4 sts, p4.

10th row: K9, p3, *k5, p3; rep from * to last st, k1.

11th row: P8, T4R, *p4, T4R; rep from * to last st, p1.

12th row: K2, *p3, k5; rep from * to last 3 sts, k3.

13th row: P7, T4R, *p4, T4R; rep from * to last 2 sts, p2.

14th row: K3, *p3, k5; rep from * to last 2 sts, k2.

15th row: P6, T4R, *p4, T4R; rep from * to last 3 sts, p3.

16th row: K4, *p3, k5; rep from * to last st, k1.

Rep these 16 rows.

16.17

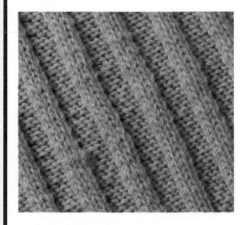

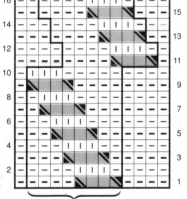

Rep these 8 sts

Multiple of 8 sts + 5.

1st row (right side): *P4, T4L; rep from * to last 5 st5, p5.

2nd row: K5, *p3, k5; rep from * to end.

3rd row: P5, *T4L, p4; rep from * to end.

4th row: K4, *p3, k5; rep from * to last st, k1.

5th row: P6, T4L, *p4, T4L; rep from * to last 3 sts, p3.

6th row: K3, *p3, k5; rep from * to last 2 sts, k2.

7th row: P7, T4L, *p4, T4L; rep from * to last 2 sts, p2.

8th row: K2, *p3, k5; rep from * to last 3 sts, k3.

9th row: P8, T4L, *p4, T4L; rep from * to last st, p1.

10th row: K1, *p3, k5; rep from * to last 4 sts, k4.

11th row: P1, *T4L, p4; rep from * to last 4 sts, p4.

12th row: K8, p3, *k5, p3; rep from * to last 2 sts, k2.

13th row: P2, *T4L, p4; rep from * to last 3 sts, p3.

14th row: K7, p3, *k5, p3; rep from * to last 3 sts, k3.

15th row: P3, *T4L, p4; rep from * to last 2 sts, p2.

16th row: K6, p3, *k5, p3; rep from * to last 4 sts, k4.

Rep these 16 rows.

16.18

Multiple of 6 sts + 2.

1st row (right side): P4, T3B, *p3, T3B; rep from * to last st, p1.

2nd row: K2, *p2, k4; rep from * to end.

3rd row: *P3, T3B; rep from * to last 2 sts, p2.

4th row: K3, p2, *k4, p2; rep from * to last 3 sts, k3.

5th row: P2, *T3B, p3; rep from * to end.

6th row: *K4, p2; rep from * to last 2 sts, k2.

7th row: P1, *T3B, p3; rep from * to last st, p1.

8th row: K5, p2, *k4, p2; rep from * to last st, k1.

9th row: P1, *T3F, p3; rep from * to last st, p1.

10th row: As 6th row.

11th row: P2, *T3F, p3; rep from * to end.

12th row: As 4th row.

13th row: *P3, T3F; rep from * to last 2 sts, p2.

14th row: As 2nd row.

15th row: P4, T3F, *p3, T3F; rep from * to last st, p1.

16th row: K1, *p2, k4; rep from * to last st, k1.

Rep these 16 rows.

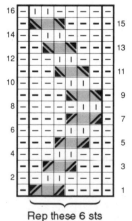

Rep these 6 sts

Note: This stitch is also very effective when worked as a panel of 8 or 14 sts on a background of reverse st st.

◺ = C4F. ◤ = T4B. ◺ = T4F. ◻ = T4R. ◻ = T4L.

Accessories

Child's Hat and Mittens

Measurements
To fit 3 to 7 years
Hat: Width round head 48 cm [19¼ ins].
Mittens: Width round palm 17 cm [6¾ ins].

Materials
Double Knitting (Sports Weight) yarn
Hat: 100 grams [4 ounces]
Mittens: 50 grams [2 ounces]
Pair needles each size 3¼mm (UK 10, USA 3 or 4) and 4mm (UK 8, USA 6).
Cable needle.

The quantities of yarn stated are based on average requirements and are therefore approximate.
For abbreviations see pages 20 and 21.
Figures or instructions given in [ ]s should be repeated as stated after the brackets.

Tension
22 sts and 30 rows = 10 cm [4 ins] square measured over st st using larger needles.

Special Abbreviations
M1 (Make 1 stitch) = pick up strand of yarn lying between last st worked and next st and knit into back of it.

T3B (Twist 3 Back) = slip next st on to cable needle and hold at back of work, knit next 2 sts from left-hand needle, then purl st from cable needle.

T3F (Twist 3 Front) = slip next 2 sts on to cable needle and hold at front of work, purl next st from left-hand needle, then knit sts from cable needle.

C4B (Cable 4 Back) = slip next 2 sts on to cable needle and hold at back of work, knit next 2 sts from left-hand needle, then knit sts from cable needle.

C4F (Cable 4 Front) = slip next 2 sts on to cable needle and hold at front of work, knit next 2 sts from left-hand needle, then knit sts from cable needle.

C5F (Cable 5 Front) = slip next 3 sts on to cable needle and hold at front of work, knit next 2 sts from left-hand needle, now place first st (purl) on cable needle back on to left-hand needle and purl this st, then knit sts from cable needle.

MB (Make Bobble) = [k1, p1, k1, p1, k1] into next st, turn and k4, turn and p4, turn and k2tog, k1, k2tog, turn and p3tog (bobble completed).

Panel A (9 sts)
1st row (right side): K2, p2, C4F, p1.
2nd row: K1, p4, k2, p2.
3rd row: T3F, T3B, T3F.
4th row: P2, k2, p4, k1.
5th row: P1, C4B, p2, k2.
6th row: P2, k2, p4, k1.
7th row: T3B, T3F, T3B.
8th row: K1, p4, k2, p2.
These 8 rows form Panel A.

Panel B (13 sts)
1st row (right side): T3B, p7, T3F.
2nd row: P2, k9, p2.
3rd row: K2, p4, MB, p4, k2.
4th row: P2, k9, p2.
5th row: T3F, p7, T3B.
6th row: K1, p2, k7, p2, k1.
7th row: P1, T3F, p5, T3B, p1.
8th row: K2, p2, k5, p2, k2.
9th row: P2, T3F, p3, T3B, p2.
10th row: K3, [p2, k3] twice.
11th row: P3, T3F, p1, T3B, p3.
12th row: K4, p2, k1, p2, k4.
13th row: P4, C5F, p4.
14th row: K4, p2, k1, p2, k4.
15th row: P3, T3B, p1, T3F, p3.
16th row: K3, [p2, k3] twice.
17th row: P2, T3B, p3, T3F, p2.
18th row: K2, p2, k5, p2, k2.
19th row: P1, T3B, p5, T3F, p1.
20th row: K1, p2, k7, p2, k1.
21st row: P1, k2, p3, MB, p3, k2, p1.
22nd row: K1, p2, k7, p2, k1.
23rd to 34th rows: As 7th to 18th rows.
35th row: P2, k2, p2, MB, p2, k2, p2.
36th row: K2, p2, k5, p2, k2.
37th row: P2, T3F, p3, T3B, p2.
38th row: K3, [p2, k3] twice.
These 38 rows form Panel B.

Panel C (15 sts)
1st row (right side): P2, T3B, p5, T3F, p2.
2nd row: K2, p2, k7, p2, k2.
3rd row: P2, k2, p3, MB, p3, k2, p2.
4th row: K2, p2, k7, p2, k2.
5th row: P2, T3F, p5, T3B, p2.
6th row: K3, p2, k5, p2, k3.
7th row: P3, T3F, p3, T3B, p3.
8th row: K4, p2, k3, p2, k4.
9th row: P4, T3F, p1, T3B, p4.
10th row: K5, p2, k1, p2, k5.
11th row: P5, C5F, p5.
12th row: K5, p2, k1, p2, k5.
13th row: P4, T3B, p1, T3F, p4.
14th row: K4, p2, k3, p2, k4.
15th row: P3, T3B, p3, T3F, p3.
16th row: K3, p2, k5, p2, k3.
These 16 rows form Panel C.

Hat
Using smaller needles cast on 114 sts.
1st row: K2, *p2, k2; rep from * to end.
2nd row: P2, *k2, p2; rep from * to end.
Rep these 2 rows until rib measures 10 cm [4 ins] ending with a 2nd row.
Next row (increase): Rib 6, *inc in next st, rib 5; rep from * to end. 132 sts.
Change to larger needles and commence pattern.
1st row (right side): P2, *work 1st row of Panel A across next 9 sts, p2, work 1st row of Panel B across next 13 sts, p2; rep from * to end.
2nd row: K2, *work 2nd row of Panel B, k2, work 2nd row of Panel A, k2; rep from * to end.
These 2 rows form reverse st st at each side and between cables.
Keeping pattern correct as set and re-peating the 8 rows of Panel A throughout, work 36 rows straight, thus ending with a 6th row of Panel A and the 38th row of Panel B.

Shape Crown
1st row (decrease): P2, *work 7th row of Panel A, p1, p2tog, p2, T3F, p1, T3B, p2, p2tog, p1; rep from * to end. 122 sts remain.
Work 1 row straight.
3rd row (decrease): P2, *work 10 sts p2tog, p2, C5F, p2, p2tog, p1; rep from * to end. 112 sts remain.
Work 1 row straight.
5th row (decrease): P2, *work 10 sts p2tog, p1, k2, p1, k2, p1, p2tog, p1; rep from * to end. 102 sts remain.
Work 1 row straight.
7th row (decrease): P2, *work 10 sts p2tog, C5F, p2tog, p1; rep from * to end. 92 sts remain.
8th row (decrease): *K2, p2tog, k1, p2tog, k2, work 9 sts; rep from * to last 2 sts, k2. 82 sts remain.
9th row (decrease): P2tog, *work 9 sts, p2tog, k3tog, p2tog; rep from * to end. 61 sts remain.
10th row: K1, *p1, k1, work 9 sts, k1; rep from * to end.
11th row (decrease): P1, *k2, p2, C4F, [p2tog] twice; rep from * to end. 51 sts remain.
12th row (decrease): *K2tog, [p2tog] twice, k2tog, p2tog; rep from * to last st, k1. 26 sts remain.
13th row: *K2tog; rep from * to end.
Break yarn, thread through remaining 13 sts, draw up firmly and fasten off.

To Finish
Do not press. Join back seam reversing seam on lower half of rib. Turn back brim. Make a pompon and attach firmly to top of crown.

Accessories

Mittens

Right Hand

Using smaller needles cast on 34 sts and work 18 rows in k2, p2 rib as given for Hat.

Next row (increase): Rib 2, [inc in next st, rib 6] twice, [inc in next st, rib 2] 5 times, inc in next st, rib 2. 42 sts.

Change to larger needles and commence pattern.

1st row (right side): K4, work 1st row of Panel C across next 15 sts, k23.

2nd row: P23, work 2nd row of Panel C, p4.

These 2 rows form the st st at each side of panel.

Keeping the 16 rows of panel correct throughout, continue as follows:

Shape Thumb Gusset

1st row: Work 23 sts in pattern, M1, k3, M1, k16. 44 sts.

Working the increased sts in st st, work 3 rows straight.

5th row: Work 23 sts in pattern, M1, k5, M1, k16. 46 sts.

Work 1 row straight.

7th row: Work 23 sts in pattern, M1, k7, M1, k16. 48 sts.

Continue to inc 2 sts in this way on following 2 alt rows. 52 sts.

Work 1 row straight.

Divide for Thumb

13th row: Work 36 sts, turn.

★ **14th row:** Inc in first st, p11, inc in next st, turn.

Work 10 rows in st st on these 15 sts, thus ending with a purl row.

Next row: *K1, k2tog; rep from * to end.

Next row: *P2tog; rep from * to end.

Break yarn, thread through remaining 4 sts, draw up firmly and fasten off ★.

With right side facing, rejoin yarn and pick up and k3 sts from base of thumb, knit to end. 42 sts.

Keeping pattern and st st correct, work 13 rows straight thus ending with a wrong side row (12th row of panel).

Shape Top

1st row: K1, sl 1, k1, psso, work 17 sts in pattern, k2tog, k3, sl 1, k1, psso, k11, k2tog, k2. 38 sts remain.

Work 3 rows straight.

5th row: K1, sl 1, k1, psso, work 15 sts in pattern, k2tog, k3, sl 1, k1, psso, k9, k2tog, k2. 34 sts remain.

Keeping pattern correct, dec 4 sts in this way on following alt row. 30 sts remain.

Work 1 row straight.

9th row: K1, sl 1, k1, psso, T3F, p3tog, p2tog, T3B, k3tog, k2, sl 1, k1, psso, k5, k2tog, k2.

Cast off remaining 22 sts.

Left Hand

Using smaller needles cast on 34 sts and work 18 rows in k2, p2 rib as given for Hat.

Next row (increase): Rib 2, [inc in next st, rib 2] 5 times, *[inc in next st, rib 6] twice, inc in next st, rib 2. 42 sts.

Change to larger needles and commence pattern.

1st row (right side): K23, work 1st row of Panel C across next 15 sts, k4.

2nd row: P4, work 2nd row of Panel C, p23.

These 2 rows form st st at each side of panel.

Keeping the 16 rows of panel correct throughout, continue as follows:

Shape Thumb Gusset

1st row: K16, M1, k3, M1, work in pattern to end. 44 sts.

Working the increased sts in st st, work 3 rows straight.

5th row: K16, M1, k5, M1, work in pattern to end. 46 sts.

Work 1 row straight

7th row: K16, M1, k7, M1, work in pattern to end. 48 sts.

Continue to inc 2 sts in this way on following 2 alt rows. 52 sts.

Work 1 row straight.

Divide for Thumb

13th row: K29, turn.

Complete Thumb as given for Right Hand from ★ to ★.

With right side facing, rejoin yarn and pick up and k3 sts from base of thumb, work in pattern to end. 42 sts.

Keeping pattern and st st correct, work 13 rows straight thus ending with a wrong side row (12th row of panel).

Shape Top

1st row: K2, sl 1, k1, psso, k11, k2tog, k3, sl 1, k1, psso, work 17 sts in pattern, k2tog, k1. 38 sts remain.

Work 3 rows straight.

5th row: K2, sl 1, k1, psso, k9, k2tog, k3, sl 1, k1, psso, work 15 sts in pattern, k2tog, k1. 34 sts remain.

Dec 4 sts in this way on following alt row. 30 sts remain.

Work 1 row straight.

9th row: K2, sl 1, k1, psso, k5, k2tog, k2, sl 1, k2tog, psso, T3F, p2tog, p3tog, T3B, k2tog, k1.

Cast off remaining 22 sts.

To Finish

Do not press. Join all seams, reversing seam on lower half of cuffs. Turn back cuffs.

Woman's Beret and Gloves

Measurements

Beret: Width round head 56 cm [22½ ins].
Gloves: Width round palm 21 cm [8½ ins].

Materials

Double Knitting (Sports Weight) yarn
Beret: 100 grams [3½ ounces]
Gloves: 100 grams [3½ ounces]
Pair needles each size 3¼mm (UK 10, USA 3 or 4) and 4mm (UK 8, USA 6). Cable needle.

The quantities of yarn stated are based on average requirements and are therefore approximate.

For abbreviations see pages 20 and 21.

Figures or instructions given in [ ]s should be repeated as stated after the brackets.

Tension

22 sts and 30 rows = 10 cm [4 ins] square measured over st st using larger needles.

Panel A

Work as given for Panel A of Child's Hat and Mittens.

Panel B

Work the 38 rows of Panel B as given for the Child's Hat and Mittens, then work 2 more rows as follows:

39th row: P3, T3F, p1, T3B, p3.
40th row: K4, p2, k1, p2, k4.
These 40 rows form Panel B.

Panel C (9 sts)

1st row (right side): T3B, p3, T3F.
2nd row: P2, k5, p2.
3rd row: K2, p2, MB, p2, k2.
4th row: P2, k5, p2.
5th row: T3F, p3, T3B.
6th row: K1, p2, k3, p2, k1.
7th row: P1, T3F, p1, T3B, p1.
8th row: K2, p2, k1, p2, k2.
9th row: P2, C5F, p2.
10th row: K2, p2, k1, p2, k2.
11th row: P1, T3B, p1, T3F, p1.
12th row: K1, p2, k3, p2, k1.
These 12 rows form Panel C.

Beret

Using smaller needles cast on 122 sts.

1st row: K2, *p2, k2; rep from * to end.
2nd row: P2, *k2, p2; rep from * to end.
Rep these 2 rows 3 times more, then 1st row again.

Next row (increase): Rib 2, *inc in each of next 4 sts, rib 1, inc in each of next 5 sts, rib 1, inc in each of next 7 sts, rib 6; rep from * to end. 202 sts.

Change to larger needles and commence pattern.

1st row (right side): P2, *work 1st row of Panel A across next 9 sts, p9, work 1st row of Panel B across next 13 sts, p9; rep from * to end.

2nd row: *K9, work 2nd row of Panel B, k9, work 2nd row of Panel A; rep from * to last 2 sts, k2.

These 2 rows form reverse st st at each side and between cables.

Keeping pattern correct as set and repeating the 8 rows of Panel A through-out, work 18 rows straight, thus ending with a 4th row of Panel A and the 20th row of Panel B.

Shape Crown

21st row (decrease): P2, *work 5th row of Panel A, p1, p2tog, p6, work 21st row of Panel B, p6, p2tog, p1; rep from * to end. 192 sts remain.

Work 3 rows straight.

25th row (decrease): P2, *work 10 sts in pattern, p2tog, work 23 sts in pattern, p2tog, p1; rep from * to end. 182 sts remain.

Work 3 rows straight.

29th row (decrease): P2, *work 10 sts, p2tog, work 21 sts, p2tog, p1; rep from * to end. 172 sts remain.

Continue to dec 10 sts in this way on following 4th row once more, then on following 3 alt rows. 132 sts remain.

Work 1 row straight thus ending with an 8th row of Panel A and the 40th row of Panel B.

41st row (decrease): P2, *work 10 sts, p2tog, p3, C5F, p3, p2tog, p1; rep from * to end. 122 sts remain.

42nd row: K5, p2, k1, p2, k5, *work 9 sts, k5, p2, k1, p2, k5; rep from * to last 11 sts, work to end.

43rd row (decrease): Work 12 sts, p2tog, p2, k2, p1, k2, p2, p2tog, *work 11 sts, p2tog, p2, k2, p1, k2, p2, p2tog; rep from * to last st, p1. 112 sts remain.

44th row: K4, p2, k1, p2, k4, *work 13 sts, p2, k1, p2, k4; rep from * to last 11 sts, work to end.

45th row (decrease): Work 12 sts, p2tog, p1, C5F, p1, p2tog, *work 11 sts, p2tog, p1, C5F, p1, p2tog; rep from * to last st, p1. 102 sts remain.

Work 1 row straight.

47th row (decrease): Work 12 sts, p2tog, k2, p1, k2, p2tog, *work 11 sts, p2tog, k2, p1, k2, p2tog; rep from * to last st, p1. 92 sts remain.

Work 1 row straight.

49th row (decrease): P2, *work 9 sts, p2tog, C5F, p2tog; rep from * to end. 82 sts remain.

50th row (decrease): *K1, p2tog, k1, p2tog, work 10 sts; rep from * to last 2 sts, k2. 72 sts remain.

51st row (decrease): P2, *work 10 sts, p3tog, p1; rep from * to end. 62 sts remain.

52nd row: K3, p2, k2, p4, *k4, p2, k2, p4; rep from * to last 3 sts, k3.

53rd row (decrease): P1, p2tog, C4B, p2, k2, *[p2tog] twice, C4B, p2, k2; rep from * to last 3 sts, p2tog, p1. 52 sts remain.

54th row: K2, *p2, k2, p4, k2; rep from * to end.

55th row (decrease): P2tog, *[k2tog] twice, p2tog, k2tog, p2tog; rep from * to end. 26 sts remain.

56th row: *P2tog; rep from * to end.

Break yarn, thread through remaining 13 sts, draw up firmly and fasten off.

To Finish

Do not press. Join back seam. Make a pompon and attach firmly to top of crown.

Gloves
Right Hand

Using smaller needles cast on 46 sts and work 11 cm [4½ ins] in k2, p2 rib as given for Beret ending with a 2nd row.

Next row (increase): Rib 19, *inc in next st, rib 2; rep from * to end. 55 sts.

Change to larger needles and commence pattern.

Accessories

1st row (right side): P1, work 1st row of Panel A across next 9 sts, p2, work 1st row of Panel C across next 9 sts, p2, work 1st row of Panel A across next 9 sts, p1, k22.

2nd row: P22, k1, work 2nd row of Panel A, k2, work 2nd row of Panel C, k2, work 2nd row of panel A, k1.

These 2 rows form st st and reverse st st at each side and between cables.

Keeping pattern correct and working the 8 rows of each Panel A and the 12 rows of Panel C throughout, work 2 more rows.

Shape Thumb Gusset

1st row: Work 33 sts in pattern, M1, k3, M1, k19. 57 sts.

Working the increased sts in st st, work 3 rows straight.

5th row: Work 33 sts, M1, k5, M1, k19. 59 sts.

Work 3 rows straight.

9th row: Work 33 sts, M1, k7, M1, k19. 61 sts.

Work 1 row straight.

Continue to inc 2 sts in this way on next and following 2 alt rows. 67 sts.

Work 1 row straight thus ending with a wrong side row.

Divide for Thumb

Next row: Work 48 sts, turn.

★ **Next row:** Inc in first st, p13, inc in next st, turn.

Work 14 rows in st st on these 17 sts starting knit.

Next row: K2tog, *k1, k2tog; rep from * to end.

Next row: P1, *p2tog; rep from * to end. Break yarn, thread through remaining sts, draw up firmly and fasten off ★.

With right side facing, rejoin yarn at base of thumb, pick up and k3 sts from base of thumb, k19. 55 sts.

Keeping pattern and st st correct as set, work 10 rows straight thus ending with a right side row.

Next row (decrease): P22, *p2tog, p1; rep from * to end. 44 sts remain.

★★ Divide for Fingers

Next row: K28, turn.

Next row: Inc in first st, p11, inc in next st, turn.

Work 20 rows in st st on these 15 sts for first finger.

Next row: *K1, k2tog; rep from * to end.

Next row: *P2tog; rep from * to end. Break yarn, thread through remaining sts, draw up firmly and fasten off.

With right side facing, rejoin yarn at base of first finger, pick up and k2 sts from base of first finger, k6, turn.

Next row: Inc in first st, p11, inc in next st, turn.

Work 22 rows in st st on these 15 sts for second finger. Complete as given for first finger.

With right side facing, rejoin yarn at base of second finger, pick up and k2 sts from base of second finger, k5, turn.

Next row: Inc in first st, p10, inc in next st, turn.

Work 20 rows in st st on these 14 sts for third finger. Complete as given for thumb.

With right side facing, rejoin yarn at base of third finger, pick up and k2 sts from base of third finger, knit to end.

Work 15 rows in st st on these 12 sts for fourth finger. Complete as given for first finger.

Left Hand

Using smaller needles cast on 46 sts and work 13 cm [5¼ ins] in rib as given for Beret ending with 2nd row.

Next row (increase): *Rib 2, inc in next st; rep from * to last 19 sts, rib to end. 55 sts.

Change to larger needles and commence pattern.

1st row (right side): K22, p1, work 1st row of Panel A across next 9 sts, p2, work 1st row of Panel C across next 9 sts, p2, work 1st row of Panel A across next 9 sts, p1.

2nd row: K1, work 2nd row of Panel A, k2, work 2nd row of Panel C, k2, work 2nd row of Panel A, k1, p22.

These 2 rows form st st and reverse st st at each side and between cables.

Keeping pattern correct and working the 8 rows of each Panel A and the 12 rows of Panel C throughout, work 2 more rows.

Shape Thumb Gusset

1st row: K19, M1, k3, M1, work to end. 57 sts.

Work 3 rows straight.

5th row: K19, M1, k5, M1, work to end. 59 sts.

Work 3 rows straight.

9th row: K19, M1, k7, M1, work to end. 61 sts.

Work 1 row straight.

Continue to inc 2 sts in this way on next and following 2 alt rows. 67 sts.

Work 1 row straight thus ending with a wrong side row.

Divide for Thumb

Next row: K34, turn.

Complete as given for Thumb of Right Hand from ★ to ★.

With right side facing rejoin yarn at base of thumb, pick up and k3 sts from base of thumb, work in pattern to end. 55 sts.

Keeping pattern and st st correct as set, work 10 rows straight thus ending with a right side row.

Next row (decrease): *P1, p2tog; rep from * to last 22 sts, purl to end. 44 sts remain.

Complete as given for Right Hand from ★★ to end.

To Finish

Do not press. Join all seams reversing seam on lower half of cuffs. Turn back cuffs.

16.19

Multiple of 16 sts + 8.

1st row (right side): P2, C4B, *p4, C4B; rep from * to last 2 sts, p2.

2nd row: K2, p4, *k4, p4; rep from * to last 2 sts, k2.

3rd row: P2, k2, *T4F, T4B; rep from * to last 4 sts, k2, p2.

4th row: K2, p2, k2, p4, *k4, p4; rep from * to last 6 sts, k2, p2, k2.

5th row: P2, k2, p2, C4F, *p4, C4F; rep from * to last 6 sts, p2, k2, p2.

6th row: As 4th row.

7th row: P2, k2, *T4B, T4F; rep from * to last 4 sts, k2, p2.

8th row: As 2nd row.

9th and 10th rows: As 1st and 2nd rows.

11th row: P2, k4, *p2, T4B, T4F, p2, k4; rep from * to last 2 sts, p2.

12th row: K2, p4, k2, *p2, k4, p2, k2, p4, k2; rep from * to end.

13th row: P2, C4B, p2, *k2, p4, k2, p2, C4B, p2; rep from * to end.

14th row: As 12th row.

15th row: P2, k4, p2, *T4F, T4B, p2, k4, p2; rep from * to end.

16th row: As 2nd row.

Rep these 16 rows.

16.20

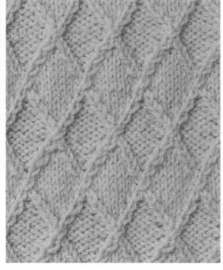

Multiple of 8 sts + 4.

1st row (right side): P5, C2B, *p6, C2B; rep from * to last 5 sts, p5.

2nd row: K5, p2, *k6, p2; rep from * to last 5 sts, k5.

3rd row: P4, *C2B, C2F, p4; rep from * to end.

4th row: K4, *p4, k4; rep from * to end.

5th row: P3, *C2B, k2, C2F, p2; rep from * to last st, p1.

6th row: K3, *p6, k2; rep from * to last st, k1.

7th row: P2, *C2B, k4, C2F; rep from * to last 2 sts, p2.

8th row: Purl.

9th row: K1, C2B, *k6, C2B; rep from * to last st, k1.

10th row: Purl.

11th row: P2, *T2F, k4, T2B; rep from * to last 2 sts, p2.

12th row: As 6th row.

13th row: P3, *T2F, k2, T2B, p2; rep from * to last st, p1.

14th row: As 4th row.

15th row: P4, *T2F, T2B, p4; rep from * to end.

16th row: As 2nd row.

Rep these 16 rows.

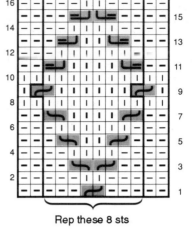

Rep these 8 sts

16.21

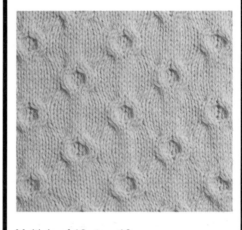

Multiple of 18 sts + 10.

1st row (right side): Knit.

2nd and every alt row: Purl.

3rd row: K1, C4B, C4F, *k10, C4B, C4F; rep from * to last st, k1.

5th row: Knit.

7th row: K1, C4F, C4B, *k10, C4F, C4B; rep from * to last st, k1.

9th row: Knit.

11th row: K10, *C4B, C4F, k10; rep from * to end.

13th row: Knit.

15th row: K10, *C4F, C4B, k10; rep from * to end.

16th row: Purl.

Rep these 16 rows.

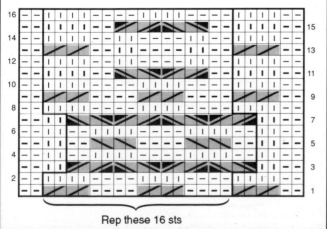

Rep these 16 sts

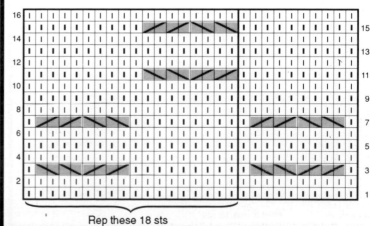

Rep these 18 sts

= C2B. ⌐ = C2F. = T2B. = T2F. = C4B. = C4F. = T4B. = T4F.

16-18 Row Repeats

16.22

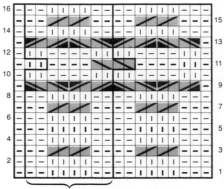

Rep these 8 sts

Multiple of 8 sts + 10.

1st row (right side): P3, k4, *p4, k4; rep from * to last 3 sts, p3.

2nd row: K3, p4, *k4, p4; rep from * to last 3 sts, k3.

3rd row: P3, C4B, *p4, C4B; rep from * to last 3 sts, p3.

4th row: As 2nd row.

5th to 8th rows: Rep the last 4 rows once more.

9th row: P1, *T4B, T4F; rep from * to last st, p1.

10th row: K1, p2, k4, *p4, k4; rep from * to last 3 sts, p2, k1.

11th row: P1, k2, p4, *C4F, p4; rep from * to last 3 sts, k2, p1.

12th row: As 10th row.

13th row: P1, *T4F, T4B; rep from * to last st, p1.

14th and 15th rows: As 2nd and 3rd rows.

16th row: As 2nd row.

Rep these 16 rows.

18.1

Panel of 18 sts on a background of reverse st st.

1st row (right side): P1, T3B, p1, k2, p4, k2, p1, T3F, p1.

2nd row: K1, p2, k2, p2, k4, p2, k2, p2, k1.

3rd row: P1, k2, p2, T3F, p2, T3B, p2, k2, p1.

4th row: K1, p2, k3, p2, k2, p2, k3, p2, k1.

5th row: T2B, T2F, p2, T3F, T3B, p2, T2B, T2F.

6th row: P1, k2, p1, k3, p4, k3, p1, k2, p1.

7th row: K1, p2, k1, p3, C4F, p3, k1, p2, k1.

8th row: As 6th row.

9th row: T2F, p1, k1, p2, T3B, T3F, p2, k1, p1, T2B.

10th row: [K1, p1] twice, k2, [p2, k2] twice, [p1, k1] twice.

11th row: P1, T2F, k1, p1, T3B, p2, T3F, p1, k1, T2B, p1.

12th row: K5, p2, k4, p2, k5.

13th row: P4, T3B, p4, T3F, p4.

14th row: K4, p2, k6, p2, k4.

15th row: P3, T3B, p6, T3F, p3.

16th row: K3, p2, k8, p2, k3.

17th row: P2, T3B, p8, T3F, p2.

18th row: K2, p2, k10, p2, k2.

Rep these 18 rows.

16.23

Multiple of 16 sts + 10.

1st row (right side): K3, C4B, *k4, C4B; rep from * to last 3 sts, k3.

2nd and every alt row: Purl.

3rd row: K1, C4B, C4F, *k8, C4B, C4F; rep from * to last st, k1.

5th row: Knit.

7th row: K1, C4F, C4B, *k8, C4F, C4B; rep from * to last st, k1.

9th row: As 1st row.

11th row: K9, *C4B, C4F, k8; rep from * to last st, k1.

13th row: Knit.

15th row: K9, *C4F, C4B, k8; rep from * to last st, k1.

16th row: Purl.

Rep these 16 rows.

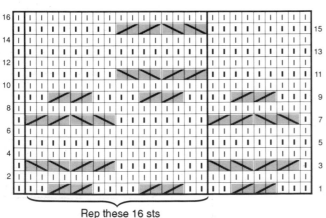

Rep these 16 sts

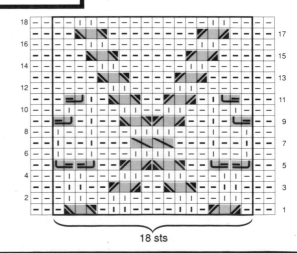

18 sts

⌐⌐ = C2B. ⌐⌐ = T2B. ⌐⌐ = T2F. ◣◣ = C3F. ◢◢ = C3B. ◣◣ = T3B. ◣◣ = T3F. ◣◣ = C4F.

18.2

Panel of 10 sts on a background of reverse st st.

1st row (right side): K10.
2nd row: P10.
3rd row: C10B.
4th row: P10.

5th to 8th rows: Rep 1st and 2nd rows twice.
9th row: K2, C6B, k2.
10th row: P10.
11th to 14th rows: Rep 1st and 2nd rows twice.
15th and 16th rows: As 9th and 10th rows.
17th and 18th rows: As 1st and 2nd rows.
Rep these 18 rows.

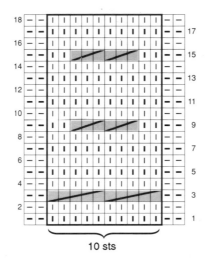

10 sts

18.4

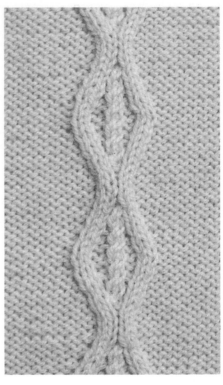

Panel of 12 sts on a background of reverse st st.

1st row (right side): P3, C3B, C3F, p3.
2nd row: K3, p6, k3.
3rd row: P2, T3B, C2B, T3F, p2.
4th row: K2, p2, [k1, p2] twice, k2.
5th row: P1, T3B, p1, C2B, p1, T3F, p1.
6th row: K1, p2, [k2, p2] twice, k1.
7th row: T3B, p2, C2B, p2, T3F.
8th row: P2, [k3, p2] twice.
9th row: T3F, p2, C2B, p2, T3B.
10th row: As 6th row.
11th row: P1, T3F, p1, C2B, p1, T3B, p1.
12th row: As 4th row.
13th row: P2, T3F, C2B, T3B, p2.
14th row: K3, p6, k3.
15th row: P3, T3F, T3B, p3.
16th row: K4, p4, k4.
17th row: P4, k4, p4.
18th row: K4, p4, k4.
Rep these 18 rows.

18.3

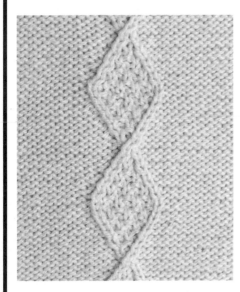

Panel of 11 sts on a background of reverse st st.

Special Abbreviation

T3RP (Twist 3 Right Purl) = slip next 2 sts onto cable needle and hold at back of work, knit next st from left-hand needle, then p1, k1 from cable needle.

1st row (right side): P3, T2B, k1, T2F, p3.
2nd row: K3, p1, [k1, p1] twice, k3.
3rd row: P2, T2B, k1, p1, k1, T2F, p2.
4th row: K2, p1, [k1, p1] 3 times, k2.
5th row: P1, T2B, k1, [p1, k1] twice, T2F, p1.

6th row: K1, [p1, k1] 5 times.
7th row: T2B, k1, [p1, k1] 3 times, T2F.
8th row: P1, [k1, p1] 5 times.
9th row: T2F, p1, [k1, p1] 3 times, T2B.
10th row: As 6th row.
11th row: P1, T2F, p1, [k1, p1] twice, T2B, p1.
12th row: As 4th row.
13th row: P2, T2F, p1, k1, p1, T2B, p2.
14th row: As 2nd row.
15th row: P3, T2F, p1, T2B, p3.
16th row: K4, p1, k1, p1, k4.
17th row: P4, T3RP, p4.
18th row: As 16th row.
Rep these 18 rows.

11 sts

12 sts

18 Row Repeats

18.5

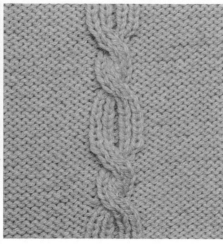

Panel of 12 sts on a background of reverse st st.

1st row (right side): P3, T3B, T3F, p3.
2nd row: K3, p2, k2, p2, k3.
3rd row: P2, T3B, p2, T3F, p2.
4th row: K2, p2, k4, p2, k2.
5th row: P1, T3B, p4, T3F, p1.
6th row: K1, p2, k6, p2, k1.
7th row: T3B, p6, T3F.
8th row: P2, k8, p2.
9th row: T3F, p6, T3B.
10th row: As 6th row.
11th row: P1, T3F, p4, T3B, p1.
12th row: As 4th row.
13th row: P2, T3F, p2, T3B, p2.
14th row: As 2nd row.
15th row: P3, T3F, T3B, p3.
16th row: K4, p4, k4.
17th row: P4, C4B, p4.
18th row: K4, p4, k4.
Rep these 18 rows.

12 sts

18.7

Panel of 8 sts on a background of reverse st st.

Special Abbreviations

T6F rib (Twist 6 Front rib) = slip next 3 sts onto cable needle and hold at front of work, k1, p1, k1 from left-hand needle, then k1, p1, k1 from cable needle.

T4R rib (Twist 4 Right rib) = slip next st onto cable needle and hold at back of work, k1, p1, k1 from left-hand needle, then p1 from cable needle.

T4L rib (Twist 4 Left rib) = slip next 3 sts onto cable needle and hold at front of work, p1 from left-hand needle, then k1, p1, k1 from cable needle.

1st row (right side): P1, k1, p1, k2, p1, k1, p1.
2nd row: K1, p1, k1, p2, k1, p1, k1.
3rd row: P1, T6F rib, p1.
4th row: As 2nd row.
5th row: T4R rib, T4L rib.
6th row: P1, k1, p1, k2, p1, k1, p1.
7th row: K1, p1, k1, p2, k1, p1, k1.
8th to 12th rows: Rep the last 2 rows twice more, then 6th row again.
13th row: T4L rib, T4R rib.
14th to 16th rows: As 2nd to 4th rows.
17th and 18th rows: As 1st and 2nd rows.
Rep these 18 rows.

18.6

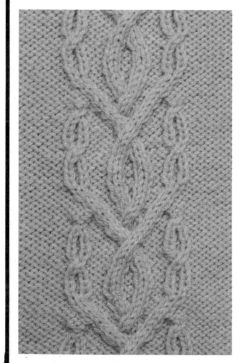

Panel of 22 sts on a background of reverse st st.

1st row (right side): K1, p2, k1, p3, k2, p4, k2, p3, k1, p2, k1.
2nd row: P1, k2, p1, k3, p2, k4, p2, k3, p1, k2, p1.
3rd row: T2F, T2B, p3, T3F, p2, T3B, p3, T2F, T2B.
4th row: K1, C2BW, k5, p2, k2, p2, k5, C2BW, k1.
5th row: T2B, T2F, p4, T3F, T3B, p4, T2B, T2F.
6th row: P1, k2, p1, k5, p4, k5, p1, k2, p1.
7th row: K1, p2, k1, p5, C4B, p5, k1, p2, k1.
8th row: As 6th row.
9th row: T2F, T2B, p3, C4B, C4F, p3, T2F, T2B.
10th row: K1, C2BW, k4, p8, k4, C2BW, k1.
11th row: P5, T4B, k4, T4F, p5.
12th row: K5, p2, k2, p4, k2, p2, k5.
13th row: P3, T4B, p2, C4B, p2, T4F, p3.
14th row: K3, p2, k4, p4, k4, p2, k3.
15th row: P1, T4B, p3, T3B, T3F, p3, T4F, p1.
16th row: K1, p2, k5, p2, k2, p2, k5, p2, k1.
17th row: T2B, T2F, p3, T3B, p2, T3F, p3, T2B, T2F.
18th row: As 2nd row.
Rep these 18 rows.

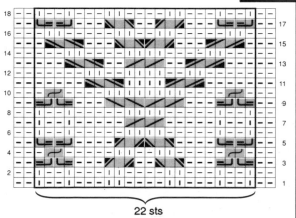

22 sts

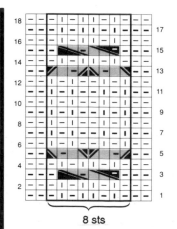

8 sts

$\boxed{V}$ = PB1. = C2BW. = T2B. = T2F. = T3B. = T3F. = C4F. = C4B.

20.1

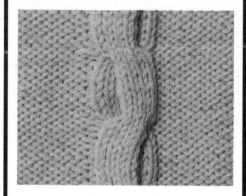

Panel of 10 sts on a background of reverse st st.

1st row (right side): K10.
2nd row: P10.
3rd row: C10F.
4th row: P10.
5th to 12th rows: Rep 1st and 2nd rows 4 times.
13th row: C10B.
14th row: P10.
15th to 20th rows: Rep 1st and 2nd rows 3 times.
Rep these 20 rows.

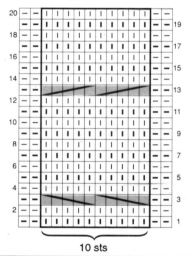

20.3

Panel of 6 sts on a background of reverse st st.

1st row (right side): K6.
2nd row: P6.
3rd row: C6F.
4th row: P6.
5th to 10th rows: Rep 1st and 2nd rows once, then rep 1st to 4th rows once.
11th to 20th rows: Rep 1st and 2nd rows 5 times.
Rep these 20 rows.

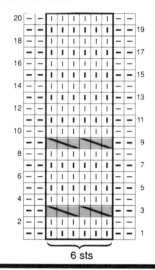

20.4

Panel of 9 sts on a background of reverse st st.

1st row (right side): K9.
2nd row: P9.
3rd row: K3, C6F.
4th row: P9.
5th to 10th rows: Rep 1st and 2nd rows twice, then rep 3rd and 4th rows once.
11th and 12th rows: As 1st and 2nd rows.
13th row: C6B, k3.
14th row: P9.
15th to 18th rows: Rep 1st and 2nd rows twice.
19th and 20th rows: As 13th and 14th rows.
Rep these 20 rows.

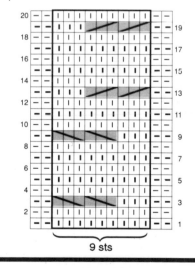

20.2

Panel of 7 sts on a background of reverse st st.

1st row (right side): [T2F] twice, p3.
2nd row: K3, [PB1, k1] twice.
3rd row: P1, [T2F] twice, p2.
4th row: K2, PB1, k1, PB1, k2.
5th row: P2, [T2F] twice, p1.
6th row: [K1, PB1] twice, k3.
7th row: P3, [T2F] twice.
8th row: PB1, k1, PB1, k4.
9th row: P4, k1, p1, k1.
10th row: As 8th row.
11th row: P3, [T2B] twice.
12th row: As 6th row.
13th row: P2, [T2B] twice, p1.
14th row: As 4th row.
15th row: P1, [T2B] twice, p2.
16th row: As 2nd row.
17th row: [T2B] twice, p3.
18th row: K4, PB1, k1, PB1.
19th row: K1, p1, k1, p4.
20th rows: As 18th row.
Rep these 20 rows.

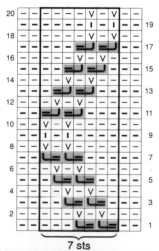

= T4F. = T4B. = C6B. = C6F. = C10B. = C10F.

20 Row Repeats

20.5

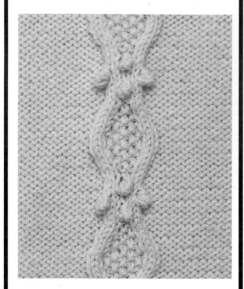

Panel of 11 sts on a background of reverse st st.

Special Abbreviation

● **MB#8 (Make Bobble number 8)** see page 21.

1st row (right side): P3, k2, MB#8, k2, p3.
2nd row: K3, p5, k3.
3rd row: P3, MB#8, k3, MB#8, p3.
4th row: K3, p5, k3.
5th and 6th rows: As 1st and 2nd rows.
7th row: P2, T3B, p1, T3F, p2.
8th row: K2, p2, k1, p1, k1, p2, k2.
9th row: P1, T3B, k1, p1, k1, T3F, p1.
10th row: K1, p3, k1, p1, k1, p3, k1.
11th row: T3B, p1, [k1, p1] twice, T3F.
12th row: P2, k1, [p1, k1] 3 times, p2.
13th row: K3, p1, [k1, p1] twice, k3.
14th row: As 12th row.
15th row: T3F, p1, [k1, p1] twice, T3B.
16th row: As 10th row.
17th row: P1, T3F, k1, p1, k1, T3B, p1.
18th row: As 8th row.
19th row: P2, T3F, p1, T3B, p2.
20th row: K3, p5, k3.
Rep these 20 rows.

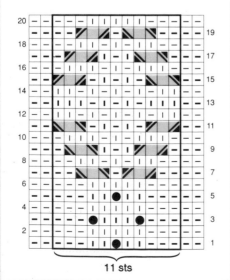

11 sts

20.6

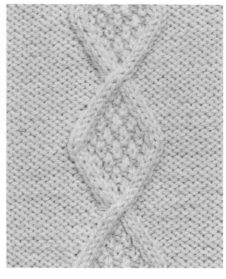

Panel of 13 sts on a background of reverse st st.

1st row (right side): P3, C3B, p1, C3F, p3.
2nd row: K3, p3, k1, p3, k3.
3rd row: P2, C3B, p1, k1, p1, C3F, p2.
4th row: K2, p3, k1, p1, k1, p3, k2.
5th row: P1, C3B, p1, [k1, p1] twice, C3F, p1.
6th row: K1, p3, k1, [p1, k1] twice, p3, k1.
7th row: C3B, p1, [k1, p1] 3 times, C3F.
8th row: P3, k1, [p1, k1] 3 times, p3.
9th row: K2, p1, [k1, p1] 4 times, k2.

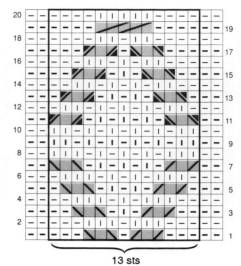

13 sts

10th row: P2, k1, [p1, k1] 4 times, p2.
11th row: T3F, p1, [k1, p1] 3 times, T3B.
12th row: K1, p2, k1, [p1, k1] 3 times, p2, k1.
13th row: P1, T3F, p1, [k1, p1] twice, T3B, p1.
14th row: K2, p2, k1, [p1, k1] twice, p2, k2.
15th row: P2, T3F, p1, k1, p1, T3B, p2.
16th row: K3, p2, k1, p1, k1, p2, k3.
17th row: P3, T3F, p1, T3B, p3.
18th row: K4, p2, k1, p2, k4.
19th row: P4, C5B, p4.
20th row: K4, p5, k4.
Rep these 20 rows.

20.7

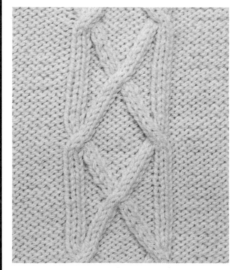

Panel of 16 sts on a background of reverse st st.

1st row (right side): K2, p3, T3B, T3F, p3, k2.
2nd row: P2, k3, p2, k2, p2, k3, p2.
3rd row: K2, p2, T3B, p2, T3F, p2, k2.
4th row: P2, k2, p2, k4, p2, k2, p2.
5th row: K2, p1, T3B, p4, T3F, p1, k2.
6th row: P2, k1, p2, k6, p2, k1, p2.
7th row: K2, T3B, p6, T3F, k2.

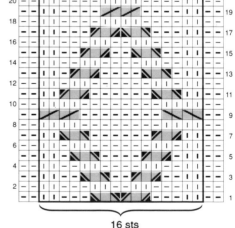

16 sts

8th row: P4, k8, p4.
9th row: C4F, p8, C4B.
10th row: As 8th row.
11th row: K2, T3F, p6, T3B, k2.
12th row: As 6th row.
13th row: K2, p1, T3F, p4, T3B, p1, k2.
14th row: As 4th row.
15th row: K2, p2, T3F, p2, T3B, p2, k2.
16th row: As 2nd row.
17th row: K2, p3, T3F, T3B, p3, k2.
18th row: P2, k4, p4, k4, p2.
19th row: K2, p4, C4B, p4, k2.
20th row: As 18th row.
Rep these 20 rows.

⊐⊏ = C2FW. ⊐⊏ = C2BW. ⊟⌐ = T2B. ⌐⊟ = T2F. ◣◥ = C3F. ◢◤ = C3B. ◢◤ = T3B. ◣◥ = T3F.

20.8

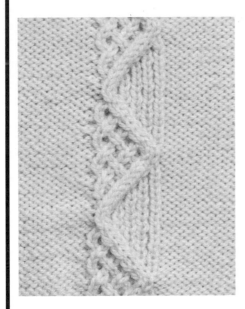

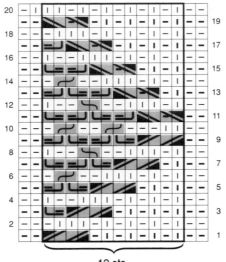

12 sts

Panel of 12 sts on a background of reverse st st.

1st row (right side): [K1, p1] 4 times, T4B.
2nd row: K1, p3, [k1, p1] 4 times.
3rd row: [K1, p1] 3 times, T4B, T2F.
4th row: P1, k2, p3, [k1, p1] 3 times.
5th row: [K1, p1] twice, T4B, T2F, T2B.
6th row: K1, C2BW, k2, p3, [k1, p1] twice.
7th row: K1, p1, T4B, T2F, T2B, T2F.
8th row: P1, k2, C2FW, k2, p3, k1, p1.

9th row: T4B, [T2F, T2B] twice.
10th row: K1, C2BW, k2, C2BW, k3, p2.
11th row: T4FP, [T2B, T2F] twice.
12th row: As 8th row.
13th row: K1, p1, T4FP, T2B, T2F, T2B.
14th row: As 6th row.
15th row: [K1, p1] twice, T4FP, T2B, T2F.
16th row: As 4th row.
17th row: [K1, p1] 3 times, T4FP, T2B.
18th row: As 2nd row.
19th row: [K1, p1] 4 times, T4FP.
20th row: P2, [k1, p1] 5 times.
Rep these 20 rows.

20.9

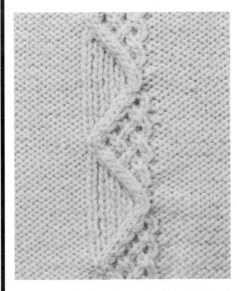

Panel of 12 sts on a background of reverse st st.

1st row (right side): T4F, [p1, k1] 4 times.
2nd row: [P1, k1] 4 times, p3, k1.
3rd row: T2B, T4F, [p1, k1] 3 times.
4th row: [P1, k1] 3 times, p3, k2, p1.
5th row: T2F, T2B, T4F, [p1, k1] twice.
6th row: [P1, k1] twice, p3, k2, C2FW, k1.
7th row: T2B, T2F, T2B, T4F, p1, k1.
8th row: P1, k1, p3, k2, C2BW, k2, p1.

12 sts

9th row: [T2F, T2B] twice, T4F.
10th row: P2, k3, C2FW, k2, C2FW, k1.
11th row: [T2B, T2F] twice, T4BP.
12th row: As 8th row.
13th row: T2F, T2B, T2F, T4BP, p1, k1.
14th row: As 6th row.
15th row: T2B, T2F, T4BP, [p1, k1] twice.
16th row: As 4th row.
17th row: T2F, T4BP, [p1, k1] 3 times.
18th row: As 2nd row.
19th row: T4BP, [p1, k1] 4 times.
20th row: [P1, k1] 5 times, p2.
Rep these 20 rows.

20.10

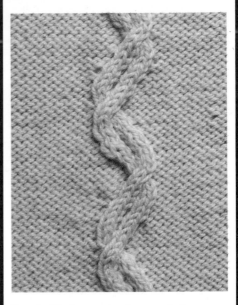

Panel of 9 sts on a background of reverse st st.

1st row (right side): P3, T4B, k2.
2nd row: P2, k2, p2, k3.
3rd row: P1, T4B, p1, T3B.
4th row: K1, p2, k3, p2, k1.
5th row: T3B, p1, T4B, p1.
6th row: K3, p2, k2, p2.
7th row: K2, T4B, p3.
8th row: K5, p4.
9th row: C4B, p5.
10th row: K5, p4.
11th row: K2, T4F, p3.
12th row: As 6th row.
13th row: T3F, p1, T4F, p1.
14th row: As 4th row.
15th row: P1, T4F, p1, T3F.
16th row: As 2nd row.
17th row: P3, T4F, k2.
18th row: P4, k5.
19th row: P5, C4B.
20th row: P4, k5.
Rep these 20 rows.

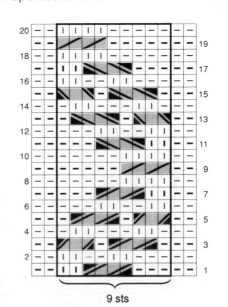

9 sts

| = C4F. | = C4B. | = T4F. | = T4B. | = T4BP | = T4FP. | = C5B.

20 Row Repeats

20.11

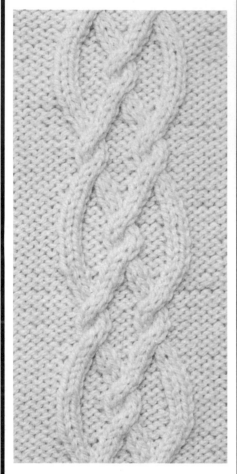

Panel of 16 sts on a background of reverse st st.

1st row (right side): K2, p4, k4, p4, k2.
2nd row: P2, k4, p4, k4, p2.
3rd row: K2, p4, C4B, p4, k2.
4th row: As 2nd row.
5th row: [T3F, p2, T3B] twice.
6th row: K1, p2, [k2, p2] 3 times, k1.
7th row: P1, T3F, T3B, p2, T3F, T3B, p1.
8th row: K2, p4, k4, p4. k2.
9th row: P2, C4B, p4, C4B, p2.
10th row: As 8th row.
11th row: P2, k4, p4, k4, p2.

20.12

12th and 13th rows: As 8th and 9th rows.
14th row: As 8th row.
15th row: P1, T3B, T3F, p2, T3B, T3F, p1.
16th row: As 6th row.
17th row: [T3B, p2, T3F] twice.
18th and 19th rows: As 2nd and 3rd rows.
20th row: As 2nd row.
Rep these 20 rows.

Panel starts with 15 sts and is worked on a background of reverse st st. The number of sts within the panel varies, therefore work between markers.

1st row (right side): P3, T2B, [k1, p1] twice, k1, T2F, p3.
2nd row: K3, p2, [k1, p1] twice, k1, p2, k3.
3rd row: P2, C2B, [p1, k1] 3 times, p1, C2F, p2.
4th row: K2, [p1, k1] 5 times, p1, k2.
5th row: P1, T2B, [k1, p1] twice, M3, [p1, k1] twice, T2F, p1. (17 sts)
6th row: K1, p2, k1, p1, k1, p5, k1, p1, k1, p2, k1.
7th row: C2B, [p1, k1] twice, p1, M1K, k3, M1K, [p1, k1] twice, p1, C2F. (19 sts)
8th row: [P1, k1] 3 times, p7, [k1, p1] 3 times.
9th row: KB1, [k1, p1] 3 times, M1K, k5, M1K, [p1, k1] 3 times, KB1. (21 sts)
10th row: [P1, k1] 3 times, p9, [k1, p1] 3 times.
11th row: KB1, [k1, p1] 3 times, k2, sl 1, k2tog, psso, k2, [p1, k1] 3 times, KB1. (19 sts)
12th row: As 8th row.
13th row: KB1, [k1, p1] 3 times, k1, sl 1, k2tog, psso, k1, [p1, k1] 3 times, KB1. (17 sts)
14th row: [P1, k1] 3 times, p5, [k1, p1] 3 times.
15th row: KB1, [k1, p1] 3 times, yb, sl 1, k2tog, psso, [p1, k1] 3 times, KB1. (15 sts)
16th row: [P1, k1] 3 times, p3, [k1, p1] 3 times.
17th row: T2F, p1, k1, p1, T2B, k1, T2F, p1, k1, p1, T2B.
18th row: K1, p2, [k1, p3] twice, k1, p2, k1.
19th row: P1, T2F, k1, C2B, p1, k1, p1, C2F, k1, T2B, p1.
20th row: K4, [p1, k1] 3 times, p1, k4.
Rep these 20 rows.

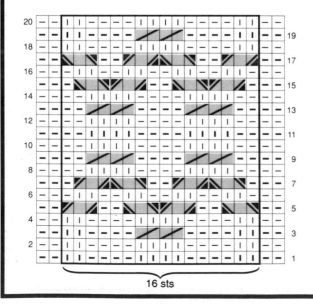

16 sts

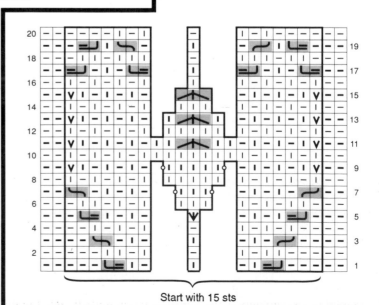

Start with 15 sts

$\boxed{\text{V}}$ = KB1. $\boxed{\circ}$ = M1K. $\boxed{\bullet}$ = M1P. $\boxed{\text{V}}$ = M3. $\boxed{\diagdown}$ = p2tog. $\boxed{\diagup}$ = p3tog. $\boxed{\wedge}$ = sl 1, k2tog, psso. $\boxed{}$ = C2B. $\boxed{}$ = C2F.

20.13

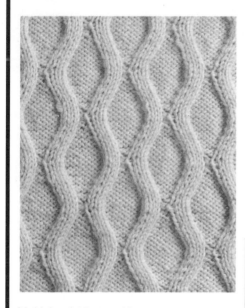

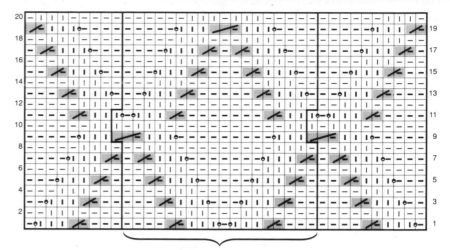

Rep these 18 sts

Multiple of 18 sts + 19.

1st row (right side): P1, *M1P, k3, p2tog, p7, p2tog, k3, M1P, p1; rep from * to end.

2nd row: K2, p3, k9, p3, *k3, p3, k9, p3; rep from * to last 2 sts, k2.

3rd row: P2, M1P, k3, p2tog, p5, p2tog, k3, M1P, *p3, M1P, k3, p2tog, p5, p2tog, k3, M1P; rep from * to last 2 sts, p2.

4th row: K3, p3, k7, p3, *k5, p3, k7, p3; rep from * to last 3 sts, k3.

5th row: P3, M1P, k3, p2tog, p3, p2tog, k3, M1P, *p5, M1P, k3, p2tog, p3, p2tog, k3, M1P; rep from * to last 3 sts, p3.

6th row: K4, p3, k5, p3, *k7, p3, k5, p3; rep from * to last 4 sts, k4.

7th row: P4, M1P, k3, p2tog, p1, p2tog, k3, M1P, *p7, M1P, k3, p2tog, p1, p2tog, k3, M1P; rep from * to last 4 sts, p4.

8th row: K5, p3, k3, p3, *k9, p3, k3, p3; rep from * to last 5 sts, k5.

9th row: P5, M1P, k3, p3tog, k3, M1P, *p9, M1P, k3, p3tog, k3, M1P; rep from * to last 5 sts, p5.

10th row: K6, p3, k1, p3, *k11, p3, k1, p3; rep from * to last 6 sts, k6.

11th row: P4, p2tog, k3, M1P, p1, M1P, k3, p2tog, *p7, p2tog, k3, M1P, p1, M1P, k3, p2tog; rep from * to last 4 sts, p4.

12th row: As 8th row.

13th row: P3, p2tog, k3, M1P, p3, M1P, k3, p2tog, *p5, p2tog, k3, M1P, p3, M1P, k3, p2tog; rep from * to last 3 sts, p3.

14th row: As 6th row.

15th row: P2, p2tog, k3, M1P, p5, M1P, k3, p2tog, *p3, p2tog, k3, M1P, p5, M1P, k3, p2tog; rep from * to last 2 sts, p2.

16th row: As 4th row.

17th row: P1, *p2tog, k3, M1P, p7, M1P, k3, p2tog, p1; rep from * to end.

18th row: As 2nd row.

19th row: P2tog, k3, M1P, p9, M1P, k3, *p3tog, k3, M1P, p9, M1P, k3; rep from * to last 2 sts, p2tog.

20th row: K1, *p3, k11, p3, k1; rep from * to end.

Rep these 20 rows.

20.14

Multiple of 14 sts + 15.

1st row (right side): K4, C3B, p1, C3F, *k7, C3B, p1, C3F; rep from * to last 4 sts, k4.

2nd row: P7, k1, *p13, k1; rep from * to last 7 sts, p7.

3rd row: K3, C3B, p1, k1, p1, C3F, *k5, C3B, p1, k1, p1, C3F; rep from * to last 3 sts, k3.

4th row: P6, k1, p1, k1, *p11, k1, p1, k1; rep from * to last 6 sts, p6.

5th row: K2, C3B, p1, [k1, p1] twice, C3F, *k3, C3B, p1, [k1, p1] twice, C3F; rep from * to last 2 sts, k2.

6th row: P5, k1, [p1, k1] twice, *p9, k1, [p1, k1] twice; rep from * to last 5 sts, p5.

7th row: K1, *C3B, p1, [k1, p1] 3 times, C3F, k1; rep from * to end.

8th row: P4, k1, [p1, k1] 3 times, *p7, k1, [p1, k1] 3 times; rep from * to last 4 sts, p4.

9th row: K3, p1, [k1, p1] 4 times, *C5B, p1, [k1, p1] 4 times, rep from * to last 3 sts, k3.

10th row: P3, k1, [p1, k1] 4 times, *p5, k1, [p1, k1] 4 times; rep from * to last 3 sts, p3.

11th row: K1, *C3F, p1, [k1, p1] 3 times, C3B, k1; rep from * to end.

12th row: As 8th row.

13th row: K2, C3F, p1, [k1, p1] twice, C3B, *k3, C3F, p1, [k1, p1] twice, C3B; rep from * to last 2 sts, k2.

14th row: As 6th row.

15th row: K3, C3F, p1, k1, p1, C3B, *k5, C3F, p1, k1, p1, C3B; rep from * to last 3 sts, k3.

16th row: As 4th row.

17th row: K4, C3F, p1, C3B, *k7, C3F, p1, C3B; rep from * to last 4 sts, k4.

18th row: As 2nd row.

19th row: K5, C5B, *k9, C5B; rep from * to last 5 sts, k5.

20th row: Purl.

Rep these 20 rows.

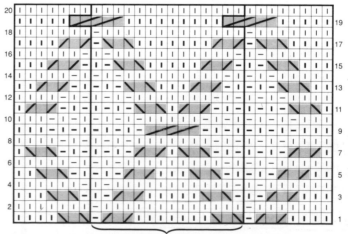

Rep these 14 sts

| =⌐⌐ | = T2B. | ⌐= | = T2F. | ◢◤ | = C3B. | ◣◥ | = C3F. | ◢◤ | = T3B. | ◣◥ | = T3F. | = C4B. | = C5B. |

61

20 Row Repeats

20.15

Multiple of 12 sts + 14.

1st row (right side): K4, C3B, C3F, *k6, C3B, C3F; rep from * to last 4 sts, k4.

2nd and every alt row: Purl.

3rd row: K3, C3B, k2, C3F, *k4, C3B, k2, C3F; rep from * to last 3 sts, k3.

5th row: *K2, C3B, k4, C3F; rep from * to last 2 sts, k2.

7th row: K1, *C3B, k6, C3F; rep from * to last st, k1.

9th row: K11, *C4B, k8; rep from * to last 3 sts, k3.

11th row: K1, *C3F, k6, C3B; rep from * to last st, k1.

13th row: *K2, C3F, k4, C3B; rep from * to last 2 sts, k2.

15th row: K3, C3F, k2, C3B, *k4, C3F, k2, C3B; rep from * to last 3 sts, k3.

17th row: K4, C3F, C3B, *k6, C3F, C3B; rep from * to last 4 sts, k4.

19th row: K5, C4B, *k8, C4B; rep from * to last 5 sts, k5.

20th row: Purl.

Rep these 20 rows.

20.16

Multiple of 16 sts + 5.

Special Abbreviation

● **MB#4 (Make Bobble number 4)** see page 21.

1st row (right side): P6, [T2B] twice, p1, [T2F] twice, *p7, [T2B] twice, p1, [T2F] twice; rep from * to last 6 sts, p6.

2nd row: K6, PB1, k1, PB1, k3, PB1, k1, PB1, *k7, PB1, k1, PB1, k3, PB1, k1, PB1; rep from * to last 6 sts, k6.

3rd row: P5, *[T2B] twice, p3, [T2F] twice, p5; rep from * to end.

4th row: K5, *PB1, k1, PB1, k5; rep from * to end.

5th row: P4, *[T2B] twice, p5, [T2F] twice, p3; rep from * to last st, p1.

6th row: K4, *PB1, k1, PB1, k7, PB1, k1, PB1, k3; rep from * to last st, k1.

7th row: P3, *[T2B] twice, p7, [T2F] twice, p1; rep from * to last 2 sts, p2.

8th row: K3, PB1, k1, PB1, k9, *[PB1, k1] 3 times, PB1, k9; rep from * to last 6 sts, PB1, k1, PB1, k3.

9th row: P2, MB#4, *k1, p1, k1, p9, k1, p1, k1, MB#4; rep from * to last 2 sts, p2.

10th row: As 8th row.

20.17

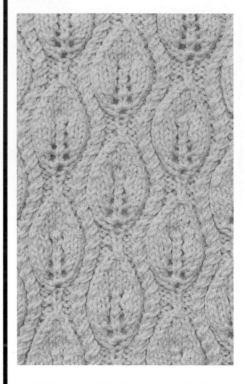

11th row: P3, *[T2F] twice, p7, [T2B] twice, p1; rep from * to last 2 sts, p2.

12th row: As 6th row.

13th row: P4, *[T2F] twice, p5, [T2B] twice, p3; rep from * to last st, p1.

14th row: As 4th row.

15th row: P5, *[T2F] twice, p3, [T2B] twice, p5; rep from * to end.

16th row: As 2nd row.

17th row: P6, [T2F] twice, p1, [T2B] twice, *p7, [T2F] twice, p1, [T2B] twice; rep from * to last 6 sts, p6.

18th row: K7, PB1, [k1, PB1] 3 times, *k9, PB1, [k1, PB1] 3 times; rep from * to last 7 sts, k7.

19th row: P7, k1, p1, k1, MB#4, k1, p1, k1, *p9, k1, p1, k1, MB#4, k1, p1, k1; rep from * to last 7 sts, p7.

20th row: As 18th row.

Rep these 20 rows.

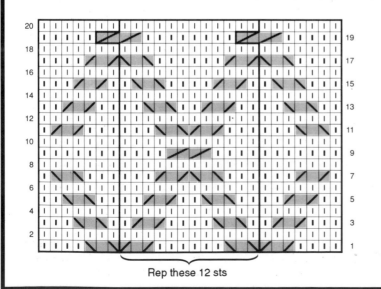

Rep these 12 sts

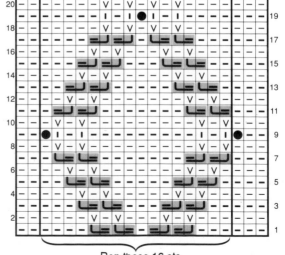

Rep these 16 sts

Ⅴ = KB1.   Ⅴ = PB1.   Ⅴ = M3.   ◆ = yf.   ◩ = sl 1, k1, psso.   ◪ = k2tog.   ◪ = sl 1, k2tog, psso.   ⟋ = C2B.

Cast on a multiple of 22 sts + 21.

Note: Only count sts after 1st, 2nd, 19th and 20th rows.

1st row (right side): P2, C2B, p2, k2, sl 1, k1, psso, yf, k1, yf, k2tog, k2, p2, C2B, p2, *KB1, p2, C2B, p2, k2, sl 1, k1, psso, yf, k1, yf, k2tog, k2, p2, C2B, p2; rep from * to end.

2nd row: K2, p2, k2, p9, k2, p2, k2, *p1, k2, p2, k2, p9, k2, p2, k2; rep from * to end.

3rd row: P2, C2B, p2, yb, sl 1, k1, psso, k5, k2tog, p2, C2B, p2, *M3, p2, C2B, p2, yb, sl 1, k1, psso, k5, k2tog, p2, C2B, p2; rep from * to end.

4th row: K2, p2, k2, p7, k2, p2, k2, *p3, k2, p2, k2, p7, k2, p2, k2; rep from * to end.

5th row: P2, C2B, p2, yb, sl 1, k1, psso, k3, k2tog, p2, C2B, p2, *k1, [yf, k1] twice, p2, C2B, p2, yb, sl 1, k1, psso, k3, k2tog, p2, C2B, p2; rep from * to end.

6th row: K2, p2, k2, *p5, k2, p2, k2; rep from * to end.

7th row: P2, C2B, p2, yb, sl 1, k1, psso, k1, k2tog, p2, C2B, p2, *k2, yf, k1, yf, k2, p2, C2B, p2, yb, sl 1, k1, psso, k1, k2tog, p2, C2B, p2; rep from * to end.

8th row: K2, p2, k2, p3, k2, p2, k2, *p7, k2, p2, k2, p3, k2, p2, k2; rep from * to end.

9th row: P2, C2B, p2, yb, sl 1, k2tog, psso, p2, C2B, p2, *k3, yf, k1, yf, k3, p2, C2B, p2, yb, sl 1, k2tog, psso, p2, C2B, p2; rep from * to end.

10th row: K2, p2, k2, p1, k2, p2, k2, *p9, k2, p2, k2, p1, k2, p2, k2; rep from * to end.

11th row: P2, C2B, p2, KB1, p2, C2B, p2, *k2, sl 1, k1, psso, yf, k1, yf, k2tog, k2, p2, C2B, p2, KB1, p2, C2B, p2; rep from * to end.

12th row: As 10th row.

13th row: P2, C2B, p2, M3, p2, C2B, p2, *yb, sl 1, k1, psso, k5, k2tog, p2, C2B, p2, M3, p2, C2B, p2; rep from * to end.

14th row: As 8th row.

15th row: P2, C2B, p2, k1, [yf, k1] twice, p2, C2B, p2, *yb, sl 1, k1, psso, k3, k2tog, p2, C2B, p2, k1, [yf, k1] twice, p2, C2B, p2; rep from * to end.

16th row: As 6th row.

17th row: P2, C2B, p2, k2, yf, k1, yf, k2, p2, C2B, p2, *yb, sl 1, k1, psso, k1, k2tog, p2, C2B, p2, k2, yf, k1, yf, k2, p2, C2B, p2; rep from * to end.

18th row: As 4th row.

19th row: P2, C2B, p2, k3, yf, k1, yf, k3, p2, C2B, p2, *yb, sl 1, k2tog, psso, p2, C2B, p2, k3, yf, k1, yf, k3, p2, C2B, p2; rep from * to end.

20th row: As 2nd row.

Rep these 20 rows.

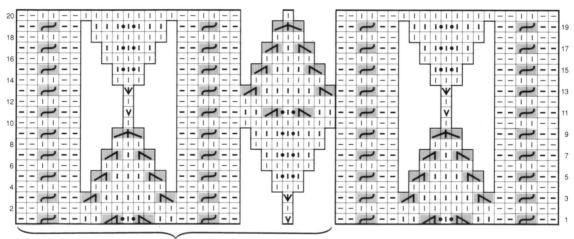

Rep these sts

20.18

Multiple of 8 sts + 2.

1st row (right side): P5, T4R, *p4, T4R; rep from * to last st, p1.

2nd row: K2, *p3, k5; rep from * to end.

3rd row: *P4, T4R; rep from * to last 2 sts, p2.

4th row: K3, p3, *k5, p3; rep from * to last 4 sts, k4.

5th row: P3, T4R, *p4, T4R; rep from * to last 3 sts, p3.

6th row: K4, p3, *k5, p3; rep from * to last 3 sts, k3.

7th row: P2, *T4R, p4; rep from * to end.

8th row: *K5, p3; rep from * to last 2 sts, k2.

9th row: P1, *T4R, p4; rep from * to last st, p1.

10th row: K6, p3, *k5, p3; rep from * to last st, k1.

11th row: P1, *T4L, p4; rep from * to last st, p1.

12th row: As 8th row.

13th row: P2, *T4L, p4; rep from * to end.

14th row: As 6th row.

15th row: P3, T4L, *p4, T4L; rep from * to last 3 sts, p3.

16th row: As 4th row.

17th row: *P4, T4L; rep from * to last 2 sts, p2.

18th row: As 2nd row.

19th row: P5, T4L, *p4, T4L; rep from * to last st, p1.

20th row: K1, *p3, k5; rep from * to last st, k1.

Rep these 20 rows.

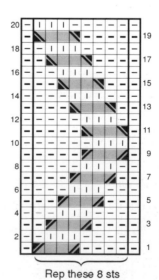

Rep these 8 sts

Note: This stitch is also very effective when worked as a panel of 10 or 18 sts on a background of reverse st st.

◻◻ = T2B. ◻◻ = T2F. ◻◻ = C3B. ◻◻ = C3F. ◻◻ = C4B. ◻◻ = T4R. ◻◻ = T4L.

20-22 Row Repeats

20.19

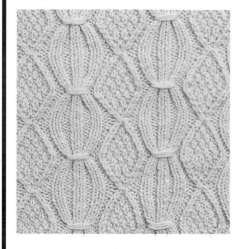

Rep these sts

Cast on a multiple of 17 sts + 14.

Note: Only count sts after 1st, 2nd, 19th and 20th rows.

Special Abbreviation

Cluster 10 rib = [k2, p2] twice, k2, slip these 10 sts onto cable needle. Wrap yarn 3 times anticlockwise round 10 sts. Slip sts back onto right-hand needle.

1st row (right side): [P2, k2] 3 times, p2, *C3L, [p2, k2] 3 times, p2; rep from * to end.

2nd row: [K2, p2] 3 times, k2, *p3, [k2, p2] 3 times, k2; rep from * to end.

3rd row: [P2, k2] 3 times, p2, *M1P, k1, p1, k1, M1P, [p2, k2] 3 times, p2; rep from * to end.

4th row: [K2, p2] 3 times, k2, *C2FW, k1, C2BW, [k2, p2] 3 times, k2; rep from * to end.

5th row: [P2, k2] 3 times, p2, *M1P, [k1, p1] twice, k1, M1P, [p2, k2] 3 times, p2; rep from * to end.

6th row: [K2, p2] 3 times, k2, *C2FW, k1, p1, k1, C2BW, [k2, p2] 3 times, k2; rep from * to end.

7th row: [P2, k2] 3 times, p2, *M1P, [k1, p1] 3 times, k1, M1P, [p2, k2] 3 times, p2; rep from * to end.

8th row: [K2, p2] 3 times, k2, *C2FW, [k1, p1] twice, k1, C2BW, [k2, p2] 3 times, k2; rep from * to end.

9th row: [P2, k2] 3 times, p2, *M1P, [k1, p1] 4 times, k1, M1P, [p2, k2] 3 times, p2; rep from * to end.

10th row: [K2, p2] 3 times, k2, *C2FW, [k1, p1] 3 times, k1, C2BW, [k2, p2] 3 times, k2; rep from * to end.

11th row: P2, cluster 10 rib, p2, *[k1, p1] 5 times, k1, p2, cluster 10 rib, p2; rep from * to end.

12th row: [K2, p2] 3 times, k2, *[k1, k1] 5 times, p1, [k2, p2] 3 times, k2; rep from * to end.

13th row: [P2, k2] 3 times, p2, *yb, sl 1, k1, psso, [p1, k1] 3 times, p1, k2tog, [p2, k2] 3 times, p2; rep from * to end.

14th row: [K2, p2] 3 times, k2, *[p1, k1] 4 times, p1, [k2, p2] 3 times, k2; rep from * to end.

15th row: [P2, k2] 3 times, p2, *yb, sl 1, k1, psso, [p1, k1] twice, p1, k2tog, [p2, k2] 3 times, p2; rep from * to end.

16th row: [K2, p2] 3 times, k2, *[p1, k1] 3 times, p1, [k2, p2] 3 times, k2; rep from * to end.

17th row: [P2, k2] 3 times, p2, *yb, sl 1, k1, psso, p1, k1, p1, k2tog, [p2, k2] 3 times, p2; rep from * to end.

18th row: [K2, p2] 3 times, k2, *[p1, k1] twice, p1, [k2, p2] 3 times, k2; rep from * to end.

19th row: [P2, k2] 3 times, p2, *yb, sl 1, k1, psso, p1, k2tog, [p2, k2] 3 times, p2; rep from * to end.

20th row: [K2, p2] 3 times, k2, *p1, k1, p1, [k2, p2] 3 times, k2; rep from * to end.

Rep these 20 rows.

22.1

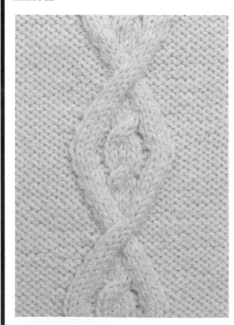

Panel of 16 sts on a background of reverse st st.

1st row (right side): P4, C4R, C4L, p4.

2nd row: K4, p8, k4.

3rd row: P3, C4R, k2, C4L, p3.

4th row: K3, p10, k3.

5th row: P2, T4R, k4, T4L, p2.

6th row: K2, p3, k1, p4, k1, p3, k2.

7th row: P1, T4R, p1, C4B, p1, T4L, p1.

8th row: K1, p3, k2, p4, k2, p3, k1.

9th row: T4R, p2, k4, p2, T4L.

10th row: P3, k3, p4, k3, p3.

11th row: T4L, p2, k4, p2, T4R.

12th row: As 8th row.

13th row: P1, T4L, p1, C4B, p1, T4R, p1.

14th row: As 6th row.

15th row: P2, T4L, k4, T4R, p2.

16th row: K3, p10, k3.

17th row: P3, T4L, k2, T4R, p3.

18th row: K4, p8, k4.

19th row: P4, T4L, T4R, p4.

20th row: K5, p6, k5.

21st row: P5, C6B, p5.

22nd row: K5, p6, k5.

Rep these 22 rows.

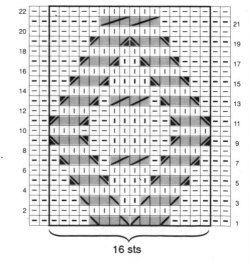

16 sts

⊤ = M1P. ◣ = k2tog. ◥ = sl 1, k1, psso. = C2BW. = C2FW. = C3B. = C3F. = C3L. = T3B. = T3F. = C4B.

22.2

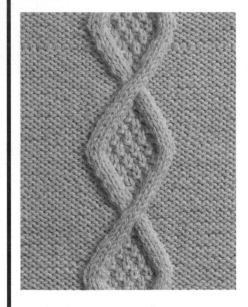

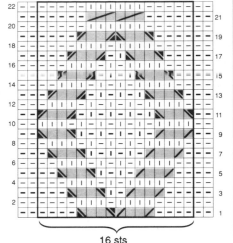

16 sts

Panel of 16 sts on a background of reverse st st.

1st row (right side): P4, C4R, T4L, p4.
2nd row: K4, p3, k1, p4, k4.
3rd row: P3, C4R, p1, k1, T4L, p3.
4th row: K3, p3, k1, p1, k1, p4, k3.
5th row: P2, C4R, [p1, k1] twice, T4L, p2.
6th row: K2, p3, k1, [p1, k1] twice, p4, k2.
7th row: P1, C4R, [p1, k1] 3 times, T4L, p1.
8th row: K1, p3, k1, [p1, k1] 3 times, p4, k1.

9th row: C4R, [p1, k1] 4 times, T4L.
10th row: P3, k1, [p1, k1] 4 times, p4.
11th row: T4L, [k1, p1] 4 times, T4R.
12th row: As 8th row.
13th row: P1, T4L, [k1, p1] 3 times, T4R, p1.
14th row: As 6th row.
15th row: P2, T4L, [k1, p1] twice, T4R, p2.
16th row: As 4th row.
17th row: P3, T4L, k1, p1, T4R, p3.
18th row: As 2nd row.
19th row: P4, T4L, T4R, p4.
20th row: K5, p6, k5.
21st row: P5, C6B, p5.
22nd row: K5, p6, k5.
Rep these 22 rows.

22.3

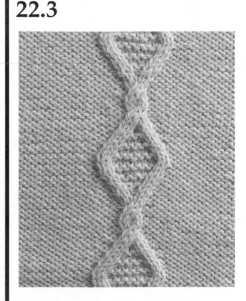

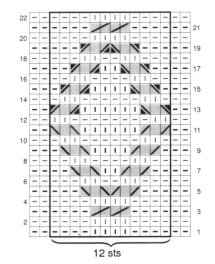

12 sts

Panel of 12 sts on a background of reverse st st.

1st row (right side): P4, k4, p4.
2nd row: K4, p4, k4.
3rd row: P4, C4B, p4.
4th row: K4, p4, k4.
5th row: P3, C3B, C3F, p3.
6th row: K3, p2, k2, p2, k3.
7th row: P2, C3B, k2, C3F, p2.
8th row: K2, p2, k4, p2, k2.

9th row: P1, C3B, k4, C3F, p1.
10th row: K1, p2, k6, p2, k1.
11th row: C3B, k6, C3F.
12th row: P2, k8, p2.
13th row: T3F, k6, T3B.
14th row: As 10th row.
15th row: P1, T3F, k4, T3B, p1.
16th row: As 8th row.
17th row: P2, T3F, k2, T3B, p2.
18th row: As 6th row.
19th row: P3, T3F, T3B, p3.
20th to 22nd rows: As 2nd to 4th rows.
Rep these 22 rows.

24.1

Panel of 12 sts on a background of reverse st st.

1st row (right side): K12.
2nd row: P12.
3rd row: C12B.
4th row: P12.
5th to 10th rows: Rep 1st and 2nd rows 3 times.
11th row: K2, C8B, k2.
12th row: P12.
13th to 18th rows: Rep 1st and 2nd rows 3 times.
19th and 20th rows: As 11th and 12th rows.
21st to 24th rows: Rep 1st and 2nd rows twice.
Rep these 24 rows.

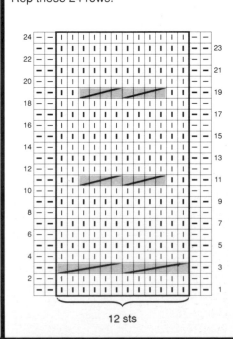

12 sts

= C4R. = C4L. = T4R. = T4L. = C6B. = C8B. = C12B.

24 Row Repeats

24.2

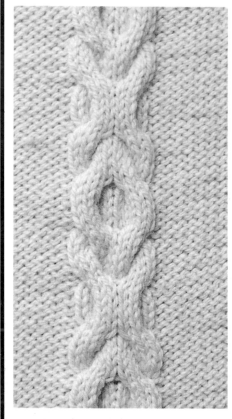

Panel of 12 sts on a background of reverse st st.

1st row (right side): K12.
2nd row: P12.
3rd row: C6B, C6F.
4th row: P12.
5th to 8th rows: Rep 1st and 2nd rows twice.
9th and 10th rows: As 3rd and 4th rows.
11th to 14th rows: Rep 1st and 2nd rows twice.
15th row: C6F, C6B.
16th row: P12.
17th and 20th rows: Rep 1st and 2nd rows twice.
21st and 22nd rows: As 15th and 16th rows.
23rd and 24th rows: As 1st and 2nd rows.
Rep these 24 rows.

24.4

Panel of 14 sts on a background of reverse st st.

1st row (right side): P4, C3B, C3F, p4.
2nd row: K4, [PB1] 6 times, k4.
3rd row: P3, T3B, C2B, T3F, p3.
4th row: K3, *[PB1] twice, k1; rep from * twice more, k2.
5th row: P2, T3B, p1, C2B, p1, T3F, p2.
6th row: *K2, [PB1] twice; rep from * twice more, k2.

24.3

Panel of 12 sts on a background of reverse st st.

1st row (right side): P2, k8, p2.
2nd row: K2, p8, k2.
3rd row: P3, C3B, T3F, p3.
4th row: K3, p3, k1, p2, k3.
5th row: P2, T3B, k1, p1, C3F, p2.
6th row: K2, p2, k1, p1, k1, p3, k2.
7th row: P1, C3B, [p1, k1] twice, T3F, p1.
8th row: K1, p3, k1, [p1, k1] twice, p2, k1.
9th row: T3B, [k1, p1] 3 times, C3F.
10th row: P2, k1, [p1, k1] 3 times, p3.
11th row: T3F, [k1, p1] 3 times, T3B.
12th row: As 8th row.
13th row: P1, T3F, [p1, k1] twice, T3B, p1.
14th row: As 6th row.
15th row: P2, T3F, k1, p1, T3B, p2.
16th row: As 4th row.
17th row: P3, T3F, T3B, p3.
18th row: K4, p4, k4.
19th row: P2, C4B, C4F, p2.
20th row: K2, p8, k2.
21st and 22nd rows: As 1st and 2nd rows.
23rd and 24th rows: As 19th and 20th rows.
Rep these 24 rows.

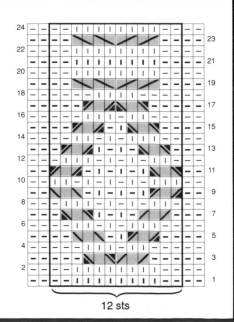

V = PB1. ⤵ = C2B. ⤴ = T2B. ⬕ = T2F. ⟋ ⟋ = C3B. ⟍ ⟍ = C3F. ⟋ = T3B. ⟍ = T3F. ⟋⟋ = C4B. ⟍⟍ = C4F.

7th row: P1, T3B, p1, T2B, T2F, p1, T3F, p1.

8th row: K1, [PB1] twice, k2, [PB1, k2] twice, [PB1] twice, k1.

9th row: T3B, p1, T2B, p2, T2F, p1, T3F.

10th row: [PB1] twice, k2, PB1, k4, PB1, k2, [PB1] twice.

11th row: K2, p2, k1, p4, k1, p2, k2.

12th row: As 10th row.

13th row: T3F, p1, T2F, p2, T2B, p1, T3B.

14th row: As 8th row.

15th row: P1, T3F, p1, T2F, T2B, p1, T3B, p1.

16th row: As 6th row.

17th row: P2, T3F, p1, C2B, p1, T3B, p2.

18th row: As 4th row.

19th row: P3, T3F, C2B, T3B, p3.

20th row: As 2nd row.

21st row: P4, T3F, T3B, p4.

22nd row: K5, [PB1] 4 times, k5.

23rd row: P5, C4B, p5.

24th row: As 22nd row.

Rep these 24 rows.

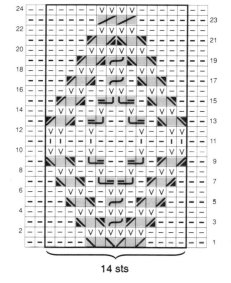

14 sts

24.5

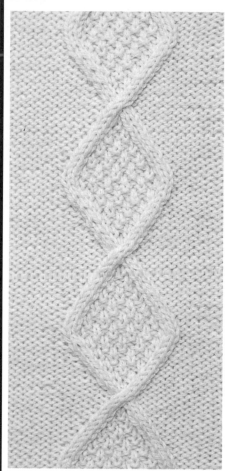

Panel of 15 sts on a background of reverse st st.

1st row (right side): P4, C3B, p1, C3F, p4.

2nd row: K4, p3, k1, p3, k4.

3rd row: P3, C3B, p1, k1, p1, C3F, p3.

4th row: K3, p3, k1, p1, k1, p3, k3.

5th row: P2, C3B, p1, [k1, p1] twice, C3F, p2.

6th row: K2, p3, k1, [p1, k1] twice, p3, k2.

7th row: P1, C3B, p1, [k1, p1] 3 times, C3F, p1.

8th row: K1, p3, k1, [p1, k1] 3 times, p3, k1.

9th row: C3B, p1, [k1, p1] 4 times, C3F.

10th row: P3, k1, [p1, k1] 4 times, p3.

11th row: K2, p1, [k1, p1] 5 times, k2.

12th row: P2, k1, [p1, k1] 5 times, p2.

13th row: T3F, p1, [k1, p1] 4 times, T3B.

14th row: K1, p2, k1, [p1, k1] 4 times, p2, k1.

15th row: P1, T3F, p1, [k1, p1] 3 times, T3B, p1.

16th row: K2, p2, k1, [p1, k1] 3 times, p2, k2.

17th row: P2, T3F, p1, [k1, p1] twice, T3B, p2.

18th row: K3, p2, k1, [p1, k1] twice, p2, k3.

19th row: P3, T3F, p1, k1, p1, T3B, p3.

20th row: K4, p2, k1, p1, k1, p2, k4.

21st row: P4, T3F, p1, T3B, p4.

22nd row: K5, p2, k1, p2, k5.

23rd row: P5, C5B, p5.

24th row: K5, p5, k5.

Rep these 24 rows.

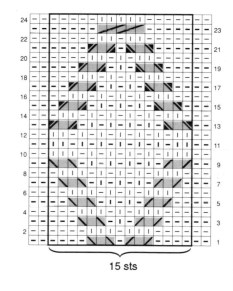

15 sts

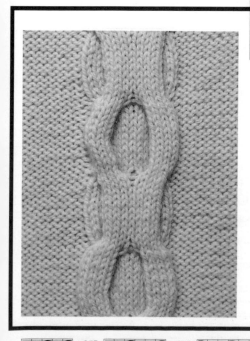

24.6

Panel of 20 sts on a background of reverse st st.

1st row (right side): K20.

2nd row: P20.

3rd row: C10B, C10F.

4th row: P20.

5th to 14th rows: Rep 1st and 2nd rows 5 times.

15th row: C10F, C10B.

16th row: P20.

17th to 24th rows: Rep 1st and 2nd rows 4 times.

Rep these 24 rows.

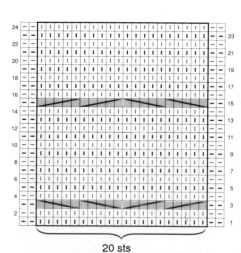

20 sts

= C5B.   = C6B.   = C6F.   = C10B.   = C10F.

24 Row Repeats

24.7

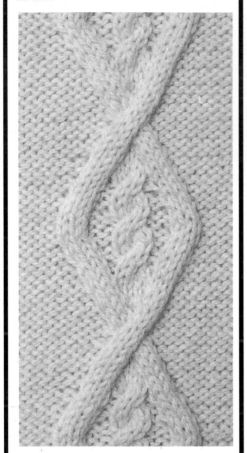

Panel of 16 sts on a background of reverse st st.

1st row (right side): P4, C4R, C4L, p4.
2nd row: K4, p8, k4.
3rd row: P3, C4R, k2, C4L, p3.
4th row: K3, p10, k3.
5th row: P2, T4R, k4, T4L, p2.
6th row: K2, p3, k1, p4, k1, p3, k2.
7th row: P1, T4R, p1, C4B, p1, T4L, p1.
8th row: K1, p3, k2, p4, k2, p3, k1.
9th row: T4R, p2, k4, p2, T4L.
10th row: P3, k3, p4, k3, p3.
11th row: K3, p3, C4B, p3, k3.
12th row: As 10th row.

13th row: T4L, p2, k4, p2, T4R.
14th row: As 8th row.
15th row: P1, T4L, p1, C4B, p1, T4R, p1.
16th row: As 6th row.
17th row: P2, T4L, k4, T4R, p2.
18th row: K3, p10, k3.
19th row: P3, T4L, k2, T4R, p3.
20th row: K4, p8, k4.
21st row: P4, T4L, T4R, p4.
22nd row: K5, p6, k5.
23rd row: P5, C6B, p5.
24th row: K5, p6, k5.
Rep these 24 rows.

24.8

Panel of 18 sts on a background of reverse st st.

1st row (right side): P5, k1, p2, C2F, p2, k1, p5.
2nd row: K5, PB1, k2, [PB1] twice, k2, PB1, k5.
3rd row: P4, T2B, p1, T2B, T2F, p1, T2F, p4.
4th row: K4, PB1, [k2, PB1] 3 times, k4.
5th row: P3, T2B, p1, T2B, p2, T2F, p1, T2F, p3.
6th row: K3, PB1, k2, PB1, k4, PB1, k2, PB1, k3.
7th row: P2, T2B, p1, C2B, p4, C2F, p1, T2F, p2.
8th row: K2, PB1, k2, [PB1] twice, k4, [PB1] twice, k2, PB1, k2.
9th row: [P1, T2B] twice, T2F, p2, T2B, [T2F, p1] twice.
10th row: K1, PB1, [k2, PB1] 5 times, k1.
11th row: T2B, p1, T2B, p2, T2F, T2B, p2, T2F, p1, T2F.
12th row: PB1, k2, PB1, k4, [PB1] twice, k4, PB1, k2, PB1.
13th row: K1, p2, k1, p4, C2F, p4, k1, p2, k1.
14th row: As 12th row.
15th row: T2F, p1, T2F, p2, T2B, T2F, p2, T2B, p1, T2B.
16th row: As 10th row.
17th row: [P1, T2F] twice, T2B, p2, T2F, [T2B, p1] twice.
18th row: As 8th row.
19th row: P2, T2F, p1, T2F, p4, T2B, p1, T2B, p2.
20th row: As 6th row.
21st row: P3, T2F, p1, T2F, p2, T2B, p1, T2B, p3.
22nd row: As 4th row.
23rd row: P4, T2F, p1, T2F, T2B, p1, T2B, p4.
24th row: As 2nd row.
Rep these 24 rows.

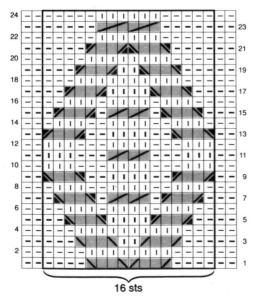

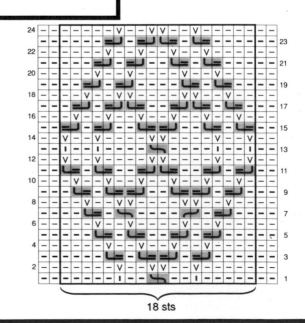

V = PB1.   ⌐ = C2B.   ⌐ = C2F.   ⌐ = T2B.   ⌐ = T2F.   ⟋⟋ = C4B.   ⟋⟋ = C4R.   ⟍⟍ = C4L.

24.9

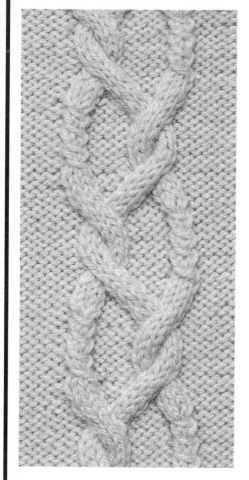

Panel of 17 sts on a background of reverse st st.

Special Abbreviation

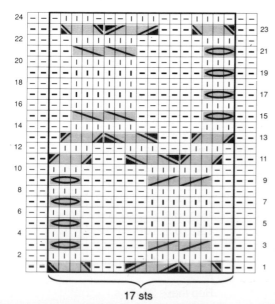 **Bind 3** = slip 1 st with yarn at back of work, k1, yf, k1, pass slipped st over the k1, yf, k1.

1st row (right side): P1, T4L, T5R, p3, T4L.
2nd row: P3, k6, p6, k2.
3rd row: P2, C6B, p6, bind 3.
4th row: As 2nd row.
5th row: P2, k6, p6, bind 3.

24.10

6th row: As 2nd row.
7th and 8th rows: Rep the last 2 rows once more.
9th row: As 3rd row.
10th row: As 2nd row.
11th row: P1, T4R, T5L, p3, T4R.
12th row: K1, p3, [k3, p3] twice, k1.
13th row: T4R, p3, T5L, T4R, p1.
14th row: K2, p6, k6, p3.
15th row: Bind 3, p6, C6F, p2.
16th row: As 14th row.
17th row: Bind 3, p6, k6, p2.
18th row: As 14th row.
19th and 20th rows: Rep the last 2 rows once more.
21st row: As 15th row.
22nd row: As 14th row.
23rd row: T4L, p3, T5R, T4L, p1.
24th row: As 12th row.
Rep these 24 rows.

Panel of 24 sts on a background of reverse st st.

1st row (right side): P5, [T2B] 3 times, k2, [T2F] 3 times, p5.
2nd row: K5, [p1, k1] twice, p2, k2, p2, [k1, p1] twice, k5.
3rd row: P4, [T2B] 3 times, k1, p2, k1, [T2F] 3 times, p4.
4th row: K4, p1, [k1, p1] twice, k2, p2, k2, p1, [k1, p1] twice, k4.
5th row: P3, [T2B] 3 times, p2, k2, p2, [T2F] 3 times, p3.
6th row: K3, [p1, k1] 3 times, p2, k2, p2, [k1, p1] 3 times, k3.
7th row: P2, [T2B] 3 times, p1, k2, p2, k2, p1, [T2F] 3 times, p2.
8th row: K2, [p1, k1] twice, p3, k2, p2, k2, p3, [k1, p1] twice, k2.
9th row: P1, [T2B] 3 times, k2, [p2, k2] twice, [T2F] 3 times, p1.
10th row: K1, [p1, k1] twice, p2, [k2, p2] 3 times, k1, [p1, k1] twice.
11th row: [T2B] 3 times, k1, p2, [k2, p2] twice, k1, [T2F] 3 times.
12th row: P1, [k1, p1] twice, k2, [p2, k2] 3 times, p1, [k1, p1] twice.
13th row: [T2F] 3 times, p1, k2, [p2, k2] twice, p1, [T2B] 3 times.
14th row: As 10th row.
15th row: P1, [T2F] 3 times, p2, [k2, p2] twice, [T2B] 3 times, p1.
16th row: As 8th row.
17th row: P2, [T2F] 3 times, k1, p2, k2, p2, k1, [T2B] 3 times, p2.
18th row: As 6th row.
19th row: P3, [T2F] 3 times, k2, p2, k2, [T2B] 3 times, p3.
20th row: As 4th row.
21st row: P4, [T2F] 3 times, p1, k2, p1, [T2B] 3 times, p4.
22nd row: As 2nd row.
23rd row: P5, [T2F] 3 times, p2, [T2B] 3 times, p5.
24th row: K6, [p1, k1] twice, p4, [k1, p1] twice, k6.
Rep these 24 rows.

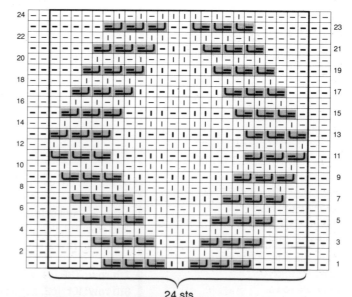

17 sts   24 sts

 = T4R.   = T4L.   = T5R.   = T5L.   = C6B.   = C6F.

24 Row Repeats

24.11

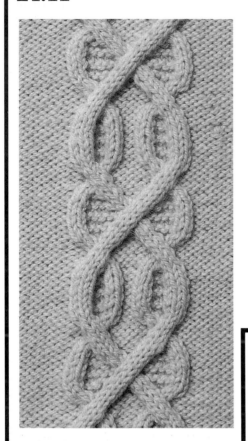

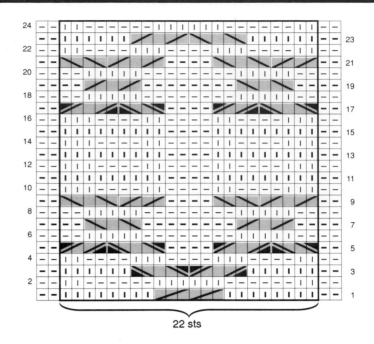

22 sts

Panel of 22 sts on a background of reverse st st.

Special Abbreviations

C5R (Cable 5 Right) = slip next 2 sts onto cable needle and hold at back of work, knit next 3 sts from left-hand needle, then knit sts from cable needle.

C5L (Cable 5 Left) = slip next 3 sts onto cable needle and hold at front of work, knit next 2 sts from left-hand needle, then knit sts from cable needle.

1st row (right side): K8, C6B, k8.
2nd row: P2, k6, p6, k6, p2.
3rd row: K6, T5R, T5L, k6.
4th row: P2, k4, [p3, k4] twice, p2.
5th row: T4F, T5R, p4, T5L, T4B.
6th row: K2, p5, k8, p5, k2.
7th row: P2, C5R, p8, C5L, p2.
8th row: As 6th row.
9th row: C5R, C4F, p4, C4B, C5L.
10th row: P3, k4, [p2, k4] twice, p3.
11th row: K9, p4, k9.
12th to 16th rows: Rep the last 2 rows twice more, then 10th row again.
17th row: T5L, T4B, p4, T4F, T5R.
18th row: As 6th row.
19th row: P2, C5L, p8, C5R, p2.
20th row: As 6th row.
21st row: C4B, C5L, p4, C5R, C4F.
22nd row: As 4th row.
23rd row: K6, C5L, C5R, k6.
24th row: As 2nd row.
Rep these 24 rows.

24.12

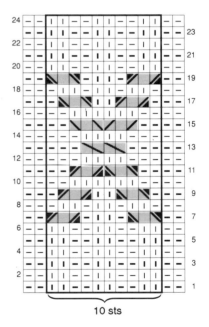

10 sts

Panel of 10 sts on a background of reverse st st.
1st row (right side): K2, [p2, k2] twice.
2nd row: P2, [k2, p2] twice.
3rd to 6th rows: Rep the last 2 rows twice more.
7th row: T3F, p1, k2, p1, T3B.
8th row: K1, [p2, k1] 3 times.

9th row: P1, T3F, k2, T3B, p1.
10th row: K2, p6, k2.
11th row: P2, T3F, T3B, p2.
12th row: K3, p4, k3.
13th row: P3, C4F, p3.
14th row: K3, p4, k3.
15th row: P2, C3B, C3F, p2.
16th row: K2, p6, k2.
17th row: P1, T3B, k2, T3F, p1.
18th row: K1, [p2, k1] 3 times.
19th row: T3B, p1, k2, p1, T3F.
20th row: P2, [k2, p2] twice.
21st to 24th rows: Rep 1st and 2nd rows twice.
Rep these 24 rows.

= C3B. = C3F. = T3B. = T3F. = C4B. = C4F.

24.13

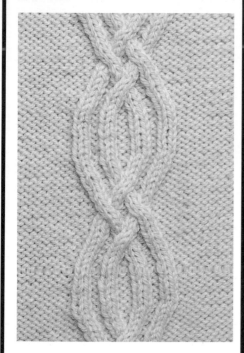

Panel of 18 sts on a background of reverse st st.

1st row (right side): K2, p3, k2, p4, k2, p3, k2.

2nd row: P2, k3, p2, k4, p2, k3, p2.

3rd row: T3F, p2, T3F, [p2, T3B] twice.

4th row: K1, p2, k3, p2, k2, p2, k3, p2, k1.

5th row: P1, T3F, p2, T3F, T3B, p2, T3B, p1.

6th row: K2, p2, k3, p4, k3, p2, k2.

7th row: P2, T3F, p2, C4B, p2, T3B, p2.

8th row: K3, p2, k2, p4, k2, p2, k3.

9th row: P3, [T3F, T3B] twice, p3.

10th row: K4, p4, k2, p4, k4.

11th row: P4, C4F, p2, C4F, p4.

12th row: As 10th row.

13th row: P3, [T3B, T3F] twice, p3.

14th row: As 8th row.

15th row: P2, T3B, p2, C4B, p2, T3F, p2.

24.14

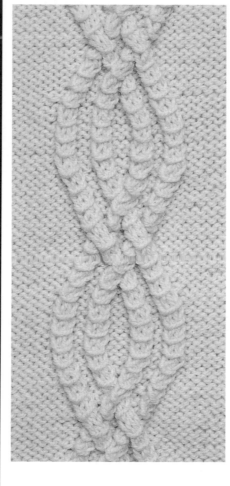

16th row: As 6th row.

17th row: P1, T3B, p2, T3B, T3F, p2, T3F, p1.

18th row: As 4th row.

19th row: T3B, p2, T3B, [p2, T3F] twice.

20th row: As 2nd row.

21st to 24th rows: Rep 1st and 2nd rows twice.

Rep these 24 rows.

Panel of 18 sts on a background of reverse st st.

Special Abbreviation

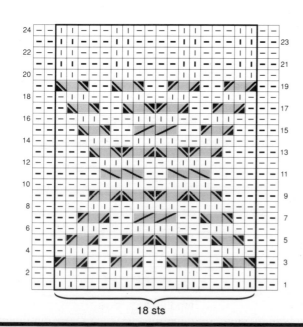 **Bind 2** = yarn over needle to make a st, p2, pass new st over the 2 purl sts.

1st row (right side): K2, p3, k2, p4, k2, p3, k2.

2nd row: Bind 2, k3, bind 2, k4, bind 2, k3, bind 2.

3rd row: T3F, p2, T3F, [p2, T3B] twice.

4th row: K1, bind 2, k3, bind 2, k2, bind 2, k3, bind 2, k1.

5th row: P1, T3F, p2, T3F, T3B, p2, T3B, p1.

6th row: K2, bind 2, k3, bind 2, p2, k3, bind 2, k2.

7th row: P2, T3F, p2, C4B, p2, T3B, p2.

8th row: K3, bind 2, k2, [bind 2] twice, k2, bind 2, k3.

9th row: P3, [T3F, T3B] twice, p3.

10th row: K4, p2, bind 2, k2, p2, bind 2, k4.

11th row: P4, C4F, p2, C4F, p4.

12th row: K4, [bind 2] twice, k2, [bind 2] twice, k4.

13th row: P3, [T3B, T3F] twice, p3.

14th row: K3, bind 2, k2, bind 2, p2, k2, bind 2, k3.

15th row: P2, T3B, p2, C4B, p2, T3F, p2.

16th row: K2, bind 2, k3, [bind 2] twice, k3, bind 2, k2.

17th row: P1, T3B, p2, T3B, T3F, p2, T3F, p1.

18th row: As 4th row.

19th row: T3B, p2, T3B, [p2, T3F] twice.

20th row: As 2nd row.

21st to 24th rows: Rep 1st and 2nd rows twice.

Rep these 24 rows.

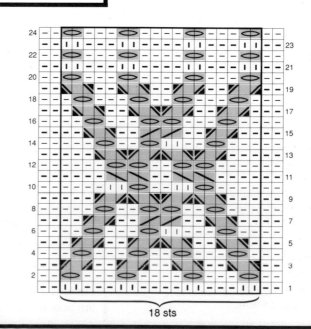

18 sts

18 sts

▨ = T4B.	◳ = T4F.	▨ = T5R.	◳ = T5L.	▨ = C6B.

24 Row Repeats

24.15

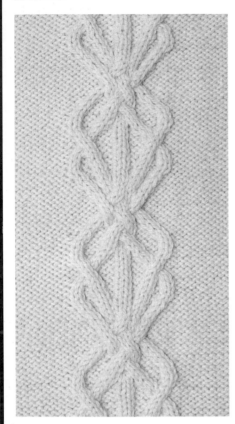

Panel of 22 sts on a background of reverse st st.

1st row (right side): P6, C4B, k2, C4F, p6.
2nd row: K6, p10, k6.
3rd row: P4, T4B, k2, C4B, T4F, p4.
4th row: K4, p2, k2, p6, k2, p2, k4.
5th row: P2, T4B, p1, T3B, k2, T3F, p1, T4F, p2.
6th row: K2, p2, k3, p2, [k1, p2] twice, k3, p2, k2.
7th row: T4B, p2, T3B, p1, k2, p1, T3F, p2, T4F.
8th row: P2, k4, p2, [k2, p2] twice, k4, p2.
9th row: K2, p3, T3B, p2, k2, p2, T3F, p3, k2.

10th row: P2, [k3, p2] 4 times.
11th row: T4F, T3B, p3, k2, p3, T3F, T4B.
12th row: K2, p4, k4, p2, k4, p4, k2.
13th row: P2, C4B, p4, k2, p4, C4F, p2.
14th row: As 12th row.
15th row: T4B, T4F, p2, k2, p2, T4B, T4F.
16th row: As 8th row.
17th row: K2, p4, T4F, k2, T4B, p4, k2.
18th row: P2, k6, p6, k6, p2.
19th row: T4F, p4, C4F, k2, p4, T4B.
20th row: K2, p2, k4, p6, k4, p2, k2.
21st row: P2, T4F, p2, k2, C4B, p2, T4B, p2.
22nd row: As 4th row.
23rd row: P4, T4F, C4F, k2, T4B, p4.
24th row: K6, p10, k6.
Rep these 24 rows.

24.16

Panel of 20 sts on a background of reverse st st.

1st row (right side): P6, T4BP, T4FP, p6.
2nd row: K6, [p2, k1] twice, p2, k6.
3rd row: P4, T4B, p1, k2, p1, T4F, p4.
4th row: K4, [p2, k3] twice, p2, k4.
5th row: P2, T4B, p2, C2B, C2F, p2, T4F, p2.
6th row: K2, p2, k4, p4, k4, p2, k2.
7th row: T4B, p2, C4B, C4F, p2, T4F.
8th row: P2, k4, p8, k4, p2.
9th row: T4F, C4B, k4, C4F, T4B.
10th row: K2, p16, k2.
11th row: P2, C4B, k8, C4F, p2.
12th row: K2, p16, k2.
13th row: T4B, T4F, k4, T4B, T4F.
14th row: As 8th row.

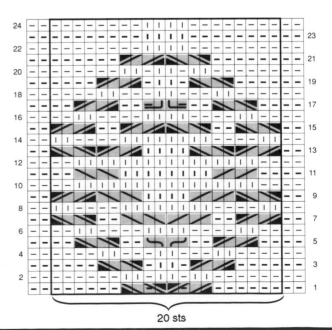

15th row: T4F, p2, T4F, T4B, p2, T4B.
16th row: As 6th row.
17th row: P2, T4F, p2, T2F, T2B, p2, T4B, p2.
18th row: As 4th row.
19th row: P4, T4F, p1, k2, p1, T4B, p4.
20th row: As 2nd row.
21st row: P6, T4F, T4B, p6.
22nd row: K8, p4, k8.
23rd row: P8, k4, p8.
24th row: K8, p4, k8.
Rep these 24 rows.

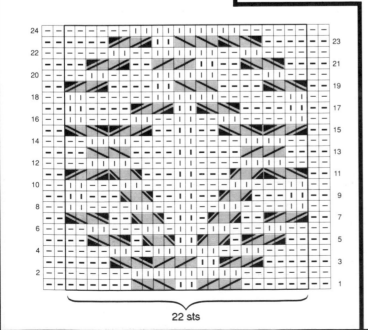

= C2B. = C2F. = T2B. = T2F. = T3B. = T3F. = C4B. = C4F. = T4B.

24.17

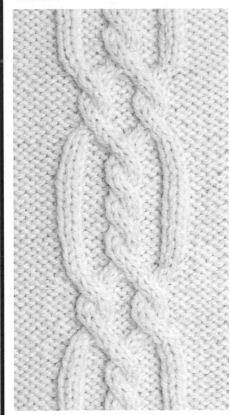

Panel of 16 sts on a background of reverse st st.

1st row (right side): P2, C4F, p4, C4F, p2.
2nd row: K2, p4, k4, p4, k2.
3rd row: P2, k4, p4, k4, p2.
4th row: As 2nd row.
5th and 6th rows: As 1st and 2nd rows.
7th row: [T4B, T4F] twice.
8th row: P2, k4, p4, k4, p2.
9th row: K2, p4, C4F, p4, k2.
10th row: As 8th row.
11th row: K2, p4, k4, p4, k2.
12th row: As 8th row.
13th to 22nd rows: Rep the last 4 rows twice more, then 9th and 10th rows again.
23rd row: [T4F, T4B] twice.
24th row: As 2nd row.
Rep these 24 rows

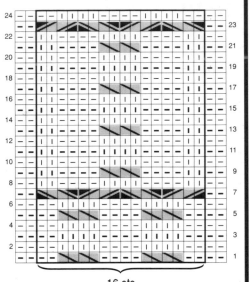

16 sts

24.18

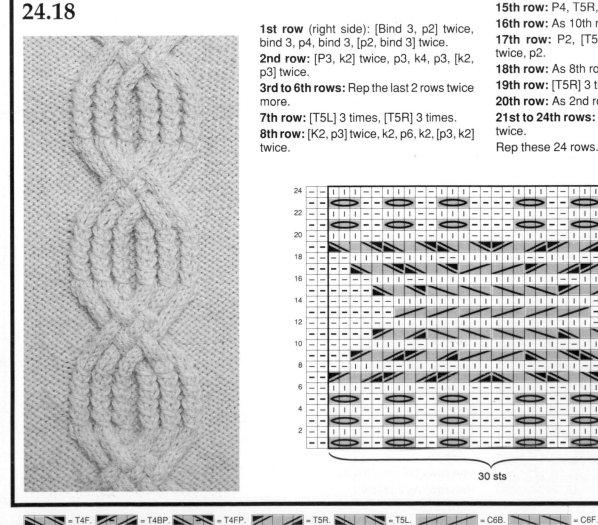

Panel of 30 sts on a background of reverse st st.

Special Abbreviation

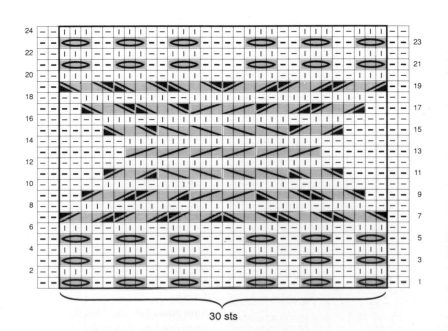

Bind 3 = slip 1 st with yarn at back of work, k1, yf, k1, pass slipped st over the k1, yf, k1.

1st row (right side): [Bind 3, p2] twice, bind 3, p4, bind 3, [p2, bind 3] twice.
2nd row: [P3, k2] twice, p3, k4, p3, [k2, p3] twice.
3rd to 6th rows: Rep the last 2 rows twice more.
7th row: [T5L] 3 times, [T5R] 3 times.
8th row: [K2, p3] twice, k2, p6, k2, [p3, k2] twice.

9th row: P2, [T5L] twice, C6B, [T5R] twice, p2.
10th row: K4, p3, k2, p12, k2, p3, k4.
11th row: P4, T5L, [C6F] twice, T5R, p4.
12th row: K6, p18, k6.
13th row: P6, [C6B] 3 times, p6.
14th row: K6, p18, k6.
15th row: P4, T5R, [C6F] twice, T5L, p4.
16th row: As 10th row.
17th row: P2, [T5R] twice, C6B, [T5L] twice, p2.
18th row: As 8th row.
19th row: [T5R] 3 times, [T5L] 3 times.
20th row: As 2nd row.
21st to 24th rows: Rep 1st and 2nd rows twice.
Rep these 24 rows.

30 sts

= T4F. = T4BP. = T4FP. = T5R. = T5L. = C6B. = C6F.

73

24 Row Repeats

24.19

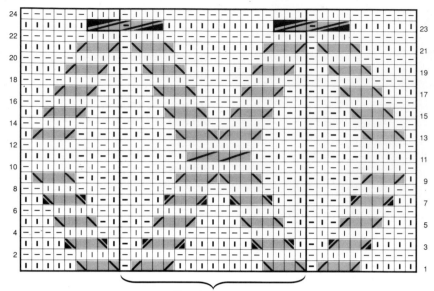

Rep these 17 sts

Multiple of 17 sts + 19.

Special Abbreviation

T7BP (Twist 7 Back Purl) = slip next 4 sts onto cable needle and hold at back of work, knit next 3 sts from left-hand needle, then p1, k3 from cable needle.

1st row (right side): K5, C4R, p1, C4L, *k8, C4R, p1, C4L; rep from * to last 5 sts, k5.

2nd row: K5, p4, k1, p4, *k8, p4, k1, p4; rep from * to last 5 sts, k5.

3rd row: K4, T4R, k1, p1, k1, T4L, *k6, T4R, k1, p1, k1, T4L; rep from * to last 4 sts, k4.

4th row: K4, p3, k1, [p1, k1] twice, p3, *k6, p3, k1, [p1, k1] twice, p3; rep from * to last 4 sts, k4.

5th row: K3, C4R, p1, [k1, p1] twice, C4L, *k4, C4R, p1, [k1, p1] twice, C4L; rep from * to last 3 sts, k3.

6th row: K3, p4, k1, [p1, k1] twice, p4, *k4, p4, k1, [p1, k1] twice, p4; rep from * to last 3 sts, k3.

7th row: K2, *T4R, k1, [p1, k1] 3 times, T4L, k2; rep from * to end.

8th row: K2, *p3, k1, [p1, k1] 4 times, p3, k2; rep from * to end.

9th row: K1, *C4R, p1, [k1, p1] 4 times, C4L; rep from * to last st, k1.

10th row: K1, p4, k1, [p1, k1] 4 times, *p8, k1, [p1, k1] 4 times; rep from * to last 5 sts, p4, k1.

11th row: K5, [p1, k1] 5 times, *C6B, k1, [p1, k1] 5 times; rep from * to last 4 sts, k4.

12th row: As 10th row.

13th row: K1, *C4L, p1, [k1, p1] 4 times, C4R; rep from * to last st, k1.

14th row: As 8th row.

15th row: K2, *C4L, k1, [p1, k1] 3 times, C4R, k2; rep from * to end.

16th row: As 6th row.

17th row: K3, C4L, p1, [k1, p1] twice, C4R, *k4, C4L, p1, [k1, p1] twice, C4R; rep from * to last 3 sts, k3.

18th row: As 4th row.

19th row: K4, C4L, k1, p1, k1, C4R, *k6, C4L, k1, p1, k1, C4R; rep from * to last 4 sts, k4.

20th row: As 2nd row.

21st row: K5, C4L, p1, C4R, *k8, C4L, p1, C4R; rep from * to last 5 sts, k5.

22nd row: K6, p3, k1, p3, *k10, p3, k1, p3; rep from * to last 6 sts, k6.

23rd row: K6, T7BP, *k10, T7BP; rep from * to last 6 sts, k6.

24th row: As 22nd row.

Rep these 24 rows.

24.20

Panel of 16 sts on a background of reverse st st.

Special Abbreviations

T8B rib (Twist 8 Back rib) = slip next 4 sts onto cable needle and hold at back of work, k1, p2, k1 from left-hand needle, then k1, p2, k1 from cable needle.

T8F rib (Twist 8 Front rib) = slip next 4 sts onto cable needle and hold at front of work, k1, p2, k1 from left-hand needle, then k1, p2, k1 from cable needle.

1st row (right side): K1, p2, [k2, p2] 3 times, k1.

2nd row: P1, k2, [p2, k2] 3 times, p1.

3rd row: T8B rib, T8F rib.

4th row: As 2nd row.

5th to 14th rows: Rep 1st and 2nd rows 5 times.

15th row: T8F rib, T8B rib.

16th row: As 2nd row.

17th to 24th rows: Rep 1st and 2nd rows 4 times.

Rep these 24 rows.

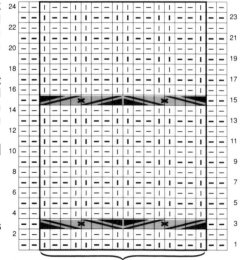

16 sts

V = KB1.   **V** = PB1.   = C2B.   = C2F.   = T2B.   = T2F.   = C4R.   = C4L.

24.21

Multiple of 16 sts + 18.

1st row (right side): P5, T4R, T4L, *p8, T4R, T4L; rep from * to last 5 sts, p5.

2nd row: K5, p3, k2, p3, *k8, p3, k2, p3; rep from * to last 5 sts, k5.

3rd row: P4, T4R, p2, T4L, *p6, T4R, p2, T4L; rep from * to last 4 sts, p4.

4th row: [K4, p3] twice, *k6, p3, k4, p3; rep from * to last 4 sts, k4.

5th row: P3, T4R, p4, T4L, *p4, T4R, p4, T4L; rep from * to last 3 sts, p3.

6th row: K3, p3, k6, p3, *k4, p3, k6, p3; rep from * to last 3 sts, k3.

7th row: *P2, T4R, p6, T4L; rep from * to last 2 sts, p2.

8th row: *K2, p3, k8, p3; rep from * to last 2 sts, k2.

9th row: P1, *T4R, p8, T4L; rep from * to last st, p1.

10th row: K1, p3, k10, *p6, k10; rep from * to last 4 sts, p3, k1.

11th row: P1, k3, p10, *C6B, p10; rep from * to last 4 sts, k3, p1.

12th row: As 10th row.

13th row: P1, *T4L, p8, T4R; rep from * to last st, p1.

14th row: As 8th row.

15th row: *P2, T4L, p6, T4R; rep from * to last 2 sts, p2.

24.22

Panel of 18 sts on a background of reverse st st.

1st row (right side): KB1, p1, T2B, p3, C2B, C2F, p3, T2F, p1, KB1.

16th row: As 6th row.

17th row: P3, T4L, p4, T4R, *p4, T4L, p4, T4R; rep from * to last 3 sts, p3.

18th row: As 4th row.

19th row: P4, T4L, p2, T4R, *p6, T4L, p2, T4R; rep from * to last 4 sts, p4.

20th row: As 2nd row.

21st row: P5, T4L, T4R, *p8, T4L, T4R; rep from * to last 5 sts, p5.

22nd row: K6, p6, *k10, p6; rep from * to last 6 sts, k6.

23rd row: P6, C6B, *p10, C6B; rep from * to last 6 sts, p6.

24th row: As 22nd row.

Rep these 24 rows.

2nd row: PB1, k1, p1, k4, p1, [PB1] twice, p1, k4, p1, k1, PB1.

3rd row: KB1, T2B, p3, T2B, [KB1] twice, T2F, p3, T2F, KB1.

4th row: P2, k4, p1, k1, [PB1] twice, k1, p1, k4, p2.

5th row: T2B, p3, C2B, p1, [KB1] twice, p1, C2F, p3, T2F.

6th row: K5, p1, PB1, k1, [PB1] twice, k1, PB1, p1, k5.

7th row: P4, T2B, KB1, p1, [KB1] twice, p1, KB1, T2F, p4.

8th row: K4, p1, k1, PB1, k1, [PB1] twice, k1, PB1, k1, p1, k4.

9th row: P3, C2B, p1, KB1, p1, [KB1] twice, p1, KB1, p1, C2F, p3.

10th row: K3, p1, [PB1, k1] twice, [PB1] twice, [k1, PB1] twice, p1, k3.

11th row: P2, T2B, [KB1, p1] twice, [KB1] twice, [p1, KB1] twice, T2F, p2.

12th row: K2, p1, k1, [PB1, k1] twice, [PB1] twice, k1, [PB1, k1] twice, p1, k2.

13th row: P1, C2B, p1, [KB1, p1] twice, [KB1] twice, [p1, KB1] twice, p1, C2F, p1.

14th row: K1, p1, [PB1, k1] 3 times, [PB1] twice, [k1, PB1] 3 times, p1, k1.

15th row: T2B, [KB1, p1] twice, KB1, C2B, C2F, KB1, [p1, KB1] twice, T2F.

16th row: [PB1, k1] 3 times, p6, [k1, PB1] 3 times.

17th row: [KB1, p1] 3 times, T2B, k2, T2F, [p1, KB1] 3 times.

18th row: [PB1, k1] 3 times, p1, k1, p2, k1, p1, [k1, PB1] 3 times.

19th row: KB1, [p1, KB1] twice, T2B, p1, C2B, p1, T2F, KB1, [p1, KB1] twice.

20th row: [PB1, k1] twice, p2, [k2, p2] twice, [k1, PB1] twice.

21st row: [KB1, p1] twice, T2B, p2, k2, p2, T2F, [p1, KB1] twice.

22nd row: [PB1, k1] twice, p1, k3, p2, k3, p1, [k1, PB1] twice.

23rd row: KB1, p1, KB1, T2B, p3, C2B, p3, T2F, KB1, p1, KB1.

24th row: PB1, k1, p2, [k4, p2] twice, k1, PB1.

Rep these 24 rows.

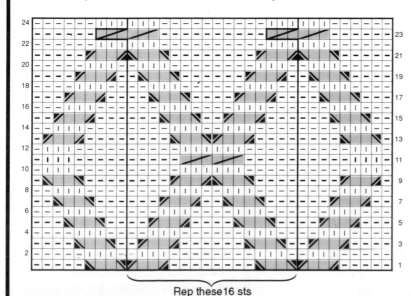

Rep these 16 sts

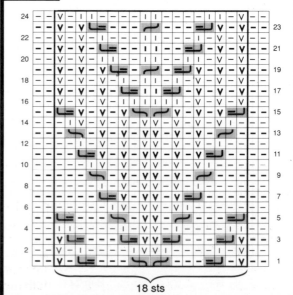

18 sts

◨ = T4R. ◨ = T4L. ◨ = C6B.

24 Row Repeats

24.23

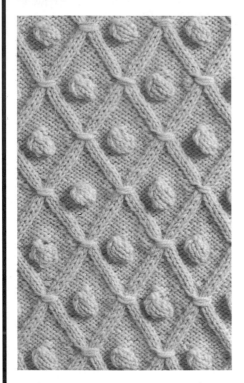

Multiple of 16 sts + 17.

Special Abbreviations

Cluster 5 = knit next 5 sts and slip them onto cable needle. Wrap yarn 4 times anti-clockwise round these 5 sts, then slip sts back onto right-hand needle.

● **MB#4 (Make Bobble number 4)** see page 21.

1st row (right side): P1, *M1P, k2, p2tog, p7, p2tog, k2, M1P, p1; rep from * to end.
2nd row: K2, p2, k9, p2, *k3, p2, k9, p2; rep from * to last 2 sts, k2.
3rd row: P2, M1P, k2, p2tog, p5, p2tog, k2, M1P, *p3, M1P, k2, p2tog, p5, p2tog, k2, M1P; rep from * to last 2 sts, p2.

4th row: K3, p2, k7, p2, *k5, p2, k7, p2; rep from * to last 3 sts, k3.
5th row: P3, M1P, k2, p2tog, p3, p2tog, k2, M1P, *p5, M1P, k2, p2tog, p3, p2tog, k2, M1P; rep from * to last 3 sts, p3.
6th row: K4, p2, k5, p2, *k7, p2, k5, p2; rep from * to last 4 sts, k4.
7th row: P4, M1P, k2, p2tog, p1, p2tog, k2, M1P, *p7, M1P, k2, p2tog, p1, p2tog, k2, M1P; rep from * to last 4 sts, p4.
8th row: K5, p2, k3, p2, *k9, p2, k3, p2; rep from * to last 5 sts, k5.
9th row: P5, M1P, k2, p3tog, k2, M1P, *p9, M1P, k2, p3tog, k2, M1P; rep from * to last 5 sts, p5.
10th row: K6, p2, k1, p2, *k11, p2, k1, p2; rep from * to last 6 sts, k6.
11th row: P6, cluster 5, *p5, MB#4, p5, cluster 5; rep from * to last 6 sts, p6.
12th row: As 10th row.
13th row: P4, p2tog, k2, M1P, p1, M1P, k2, p2tog, *p7, p2tog, k2, M1P, p1, M1P, k2, p2tog; rep from * to last 4 sts, p4.
14th row: As 8th row.
15th row: P3, p2tog, k2, M1P, p3, M1P, k2, p2tog, *p5, p2tog, k2, M1P, p3, M1P, k2, p2tog; rep from * to last 3 sts, p3.
16th row: As 6th row.
17th row: P2, p2tog, k2, M1P, p5, M1P, k2, p2tog, *p3, p2tog, k2, M1P, p5, M1P, k2, p2tog; rep from * to last 2 sts, p2.
18th row: As 4th row.
19th row: P1, *p2tog, k2, M1P, p7, M1P, k2, p2tog, p1; rep from * to end.
20th row: As 2nd row.
21st row: P2tog, k2, M1P, p9, *M1P, k2, p3tog, k2, M1P, p9; rep from * to last 4 sts, M1P, k2, p2tog.
22nd row: K1, *p2, k11, p2, k1; rep from * to end.
23rd row: P1, k2, p5, MB#4, p5, *cluster 5, p5, MB#4, p5; rep from * to last 3 sts, k2, p1.
24th row: As 22nd row.
Rep these 24 rows.

24.24

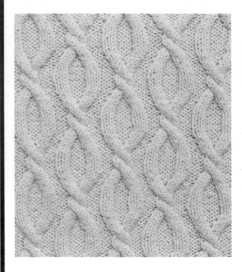

Multiple of 26 sts + 16.

1st row (right side): P2, k3, p6, k3, *p4, k6, p4, k3, p6, k3; rep from * to last 2 sts, p2.
2nd row: K2, p3, k6, p3, *k4, p6, k4, p3, k6, p3; rep from * to last 2 sts, k2.
3rd row: P2, k3, p6, k3, *p4, C6F, p4, k3, p6, k3; rep from * to last 2 sts, p2.
4th row: As 2nd row.
5th row: P2, T4L, p4, T4R, *p3, T4R, T4L, p3, T4L, p4, T4R; rep from * to last 2 sts, p2.

24.25

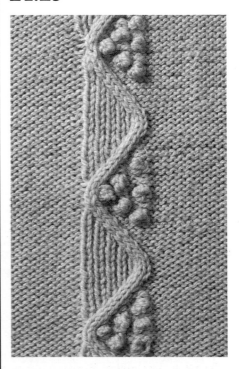

Panel of 12 sts on a background of reverse st st.

Special Abbreviation

● **MB#8 (Make Bobble number 8)** see page 21.

1st row (right side): K2, [p1, k1] 5 times.

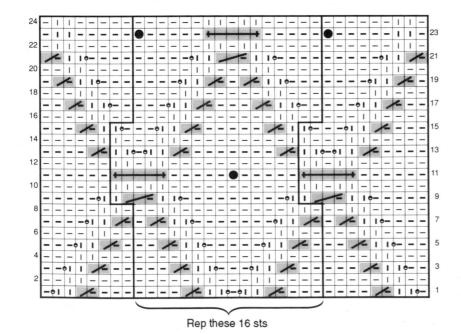

Rep these 16 sts

= M1P. = p2tog. = p3tog. = T4B. = T4F. = T4BP. = T4FP.

6th row: K3, p3, [k4, p3] twice, *k2, p3, [k4, p3] 3 times; rep from * to last 22 sts, k2, p3, [k4, p3] twice, k3.

7th row: P3, T4L, p2, T4R, p3, *T4R, p2, T4L, p3, T4L, p2, T4R, p3; rep from * to end.

8th row: K4, p3, k2, *[p3, k4] 3 times, p3, k2; rep from * to last 7 sts, p3, k4.

9th row: P4, T4L, T4R, p3, *T4R, p4, T4L, p3, T4L, T4R, p3; rep from * to last st, p1.

10th row: K5, p6, k4, *p3, k6, p3, k4, p6, k4; rep from * to last st, k1.

11th row: P5, C6F, p4, *k3, p6, k3, p4, C6F, p4; rep from * to last st, p1.

12th row: As 10th row.

13th row: P5, k6, p4, *k3, p6, k3, p4, k6, p4; rep from * to last st, p1.

14th to 16th rows: As 10th to 12th rows

17th row: P4, T4R, T4L, p3, *T4L, p4, T4R, p3, T4R, T4L, p3; rep from * to last st, p1.

18th row: As 8th row.

19th row: P3, T4R, p2, T4L, p3, *T4L, p2, T4R, p3, T4R, p2, T4L, p3; rep from * to end.

20th row: As 6th row.

21st row: P2, T4R, p4, T4L, *p3, T4L, T4R, p3, T4R, p4, T4L; rep from * to last 2 sts, p2.

22nd to 24th rows: As 2nd to 4th rows. Rep these 24 rows.

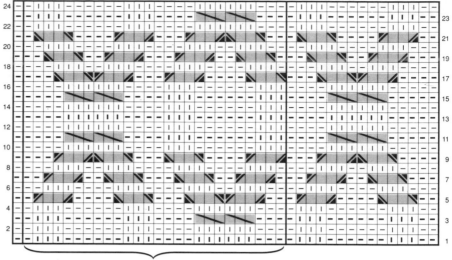

Rep these 26 sts

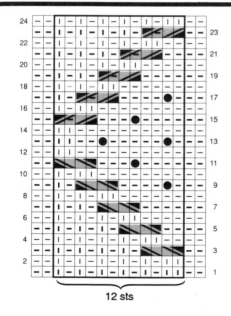

12 sts

2nd row: [P1, k1] 5 times, p2.
3rd row: T4F, [p1, k1] 4 times.
4th row: [P1, k1] 4 times, p2, k2.
5th row: P2, T4F, [p1, k1] 3 times.
6th row: [P1, k1] 3 times, p2, k4.
7th row: P4, T4F, [p1, k1] twice.
8th row: [P1, k1] twice, p2, k6.
9th row: P1, MB#8, p4, T4F, p1, k1.
10th row: P1, k1, p2, k8.
11th row: P4, MB#8, p3, T4F.
12th row: P2, k10.
13th row: P1, MB#8, p5, MB#8, p2, k2.
14th row: P2, k10.

24.26

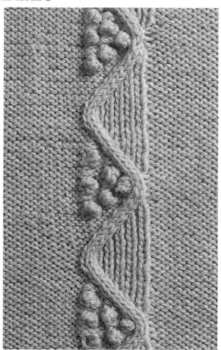

Panel of 12 sts on a background of reverse st st.

Special Abbreviation

⬤ **MB#8 (Make Bobble number 8)** see page 21.

1st row (right side): [K1, p1] 5 times, k2.

15th row: P4, MB#8, p3, T4BP.
16th row: As 10th row.
17th row: P1, MB#8, p4, T4BP, p1, k1.
18th row: As 8th row.
19th row: P4, T4BP, [p1, k1] twice.
20th row: As 6th row.
21st row: P2, T4BP, [p1, k1] 3 times.
22nd row: As 4th row.
23rd row: T4BP, [p1, k1] 4 times.
24th row: As 2nd row.
Rep these 24 rows.

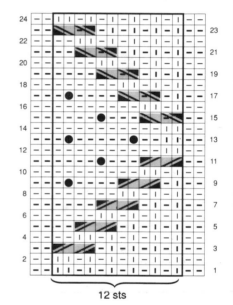

12 sts

2nd row: P2, [k1, p1] 5 times.
3rd row: [K1, p1] 4 times, T4B.
4th row: K2, p2, [k1, p1] 4 times.
5th row: [K1, p1] 3 times, T4B, p2.
6th row: K4, p2, [k1, p1] 3 times.
7th row: [K1, p1] twice, T4B, p4.
8th row: K6, p2, [k1, p1] twice.
9th row: K1, p1, T4B, p4, MB#8, p1.
10th row: K8, p2, k1, p1.
11th row: T4B, p3, MB#8, p4.
12th row: K10, p2.
13th row: K2, p2, MB#8, p5, MB#8, p1.
14th row: K10, p2.
15th row: T4FP, p3, MB#8, p4.
16th row: As 10th row.
17th row: K1, p1, T4FP, p4, MB#8, p1.
18th row: As 8th row.
19th row: [K1, p1] twice, T4FP, p4.
20th row: As 6th row.
21st row: [K1, p1] 3 times, T4FP, p2.
22nd row: As 4th row.
23rd row: [K1, p1] 4 times, T4FP.
24th row: P2, [k1, p1] 5 times.
Rep these 24 rows.

◪▨ = T4R. ◣◥ = T4L. ◩◪ = C6F.

24 - 28 Row Repeats

24.27

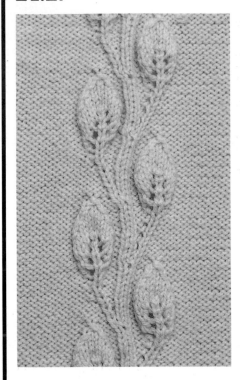

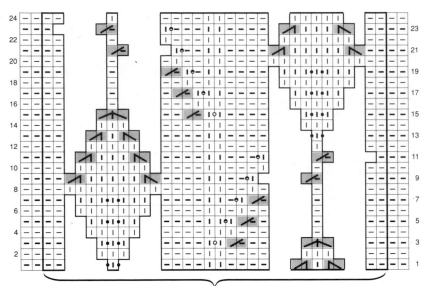

Start with 20 sts

Panel starts with 20 sts and is worked on a background of reverse st st. The number of sts within the panel varies, therefore work between markers.

1st row (right side): P2, yb, sl 1, k1, psso, k1, k2tog, p4, k2, p4, yon, k1, yfrn, p2.

2nd row: K2, p3, k4, p2, k4, p3, k2.

3rd row: P2, yb, sl 1, k2tog, psso, p2, p2tog, k1, M1K, k1, p4, k1, [yf, k1] twice, p2.

4th row: K2, p5, k4, p3, k6.

5th row: P4, p2tog, k1, M1P, k2, p4, k2, yf, k1, yf, k2, p2. (22 sts)

6th row: K2, p7, k4, p2, k1, p1, k5.

7th row: P3, p2tog, k1, M1P, p1, k2, p4, k3, yf, k1, yf, k3, p2. (24 sts)

8th row: K2, p9, k4, p2, k2, p1, k4.

9th row: P2, p2tog, k1, M1P, p2, k2, p4, yb, sl 1, k1, psso, k5, k2tog, p2. (22 sts)

10th row: K2, p7, k4, p2, k3, p1, k3.

11th row: P1, p2tog, k1, M1P, p3, k2, p4, yb, sl 1, k1, psso, k3, k2tog, p2. (20 sts)

12th row: K2, p5, k4, p2, k4, p1, k2.

13th row: P2, yon, k1, yfrn, p4, k2, p4, yb, sl 1, k1, psso, k1, k2tog, p2.

14th row: K2, p3, k4, p2, k4, p3, k2.

15th row: P2, k1, [yf, k1] twice, p4, k1, M1K, k1, p2tog, p2, yb, sl 1, k2tog, psso, p2.

16th row: K6, p3, k4, p5, k2.

17th row: P2, k2, yf, k1, yf, k2, p4, k2, M1P, k1, p2tog, p4. (22 sts)

18th row: K5, p1, k1, p2, k4, p7, k2.

19th row: P2, k3, yf, k1, yf, k3, p4, k2, p1, M1P, k1, p2tog, p3. (24 sts)

20th row: K4, p1, k2, p2, k4, p9, k2.

21st row: P2, yb, sl 1, k1, psso, k5, k2tog, p4, k2, p2, M1P, k1, p2tog, p2. (22 sts)

22nd row: K3, p1, k3, p2, k4, p7, k2.

23rd row: P2, yb, sl 1, k1, psso, k3, k2tog, p4, k2, p3, M1P, k1, p2tog, p1. (20 sts)

24th row: K2, p1, k4, p2, k4, p5, k2.
Rep these 24 rows.

28.1

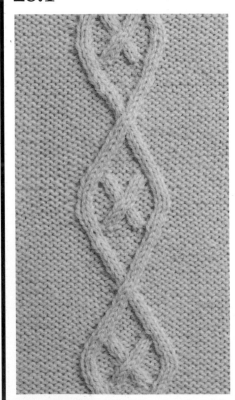

Panel of 16 sts on a background of reverse st st.

1st row (right side): P5, T3B, T3F, p5.

2nd row: K5, p2, k2, p2, k5.

3rd row: P4, T3B, p2, T3F, p4.

4th row: [K4, p2] twice, k4.

5th row: P3, T3B, p4, T3F, p3.

6th row: K3, p2, k6, p2, k3.

7th row: P2, T3B, p6, T3F, p2.

8th row: K2, p2, k8, p2, k2.

9th row: P1, T3B, T3F, p2, T3B, T3F, p1.

10th row: K1, p2, [k2, p2] 3 times, k1.

11th row: [T3B, p2, T3F] twice.

12th row: P2, k4, p4, k4, p2.

13th row: K2, p4, C4B, p4, k2.

14th row: As 12th row.

15th row: [T3F, p2, T3B] twice.

16th row: As 10th row.

17th row: P1, T3F, T3B, p2, T3F, T3B, p1.

18th row: As 8th row.

19th row: P2, T3F, p6, T3B, p2.

20th row: As 6th row.

21st row: P3, T3F, p4, T3B, p3.

22nd row: As 4th row.

23rd row: P4, T3F, p2, T3B, p4.

24th row: As 2nd row.

25th row: P5, T3F, T3B, p5.

26th row: K6, p4, k6.

27th row: P6, C4B, p6.

28th row: K6, p4, k6.
Rep these 28 rows.

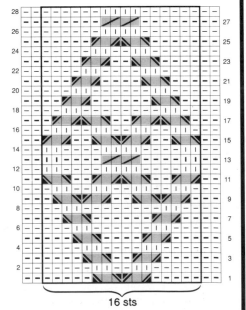

16 sts

○̣ = M1P. ○̇ = M1K. ● = yf. = sl 1, k1, psso. = sl 1, k2tog, psso. = k2tog. = p2tog. = C3B.

28.2

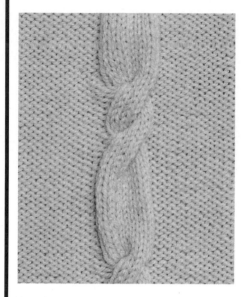

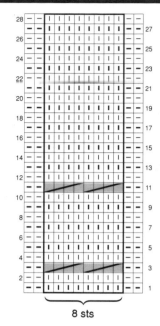

8 sts

Panel of 8 sts on a background of reverse st st.

1st row (right side): K8.
2nd row: P8.
3rd row: C8B.
4th row: P8.
5th to 12th rows: Rep 1st and 2nd rows twice, then rep 1st to 4th rows once.
13th to 28th rows: Rep 1st and 2nd rows 8 times.

Rep these 28 rows.

28.3

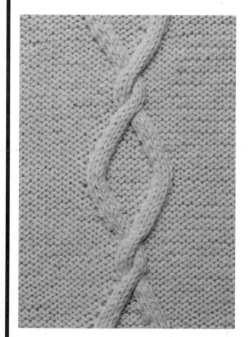

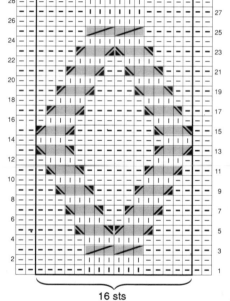

16 sts

Panel of 16 sts on a background of reverse st st.

1st row (right side): P5, k6, p5.
2nd row: K5, p6, k5.
3rd row: P5, C6B, p5.
4th row: K5, p6, k5.
5th row: P4, T4R, T4L, p4.
6th row: K4, p3, k2, p3, k4.
7th row: P3, T4R, p2, T4L, p3.
8th row: K3, p3, k4, p3, k3.
9th row: P2, T4R, p4, T4L, p2.
10th row: K2, p3, k6, p3, k2.
11th row: P1, T4R, p6, T4L, p1.
12th row: K1, p3, k8, p3, k1.
13th row: T4R, p8, T4L.
14th row: P3, k10, p3.
15th row: T4L, p8, T4R.
16th row: As 12th row.
17th row: P1, T4L, p6, T4R, p1.
18th row: As 10th row.
19th row: P2, T4L, p4, T4R, p2.
20th row: As 8th row.
21st row: P3, T4L, p2, T4R, p3.
22nd row: As 6th row.
23rd row: P4, T4L, T4R, p4.
24th to 26th rows: As 2nd to 4th rows.
27th and 28th rows: As 1st and 2nd rows.

Rep these 28 rows.

28.4

Panel of 12 sts on a background of reverse st st.

1st row (right side): P3, C3B, C3F, p3.
2nd row: K3, p6, k3.
3rd row: P2, C3B, k2, C3F, p2.
4th row: K2, p8, k2.
5th row: P1, C3B, k4, C3F, p1.
6th row: K1, p10, k1.
7th row: C3B, k6, C3F.
8th row: P12.
9th row: T3F, k6, T3B.
10th row: K1, p10, k1.
11th row: P1, T3F, k4, T3B, p1.
12th row: K2, p8, k2.
13th row: P2, T3F, k2, T3B, p2.
14th row: K3, p6, k3.
15th row: P3, T3F, T3B, p3.
16th row: K4, p4, k4.
17th row: P4, C4B, p4.
18th row: K4, p4, k4.
19th to 22nd rows: As 1st to 4th rows.
23rd to 28th rows: As 13th to 18th rows.

Rep these 28 rows.

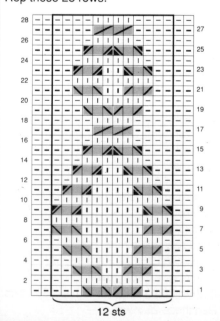

12 sts

NN = C3F. NN = T3B. NN = T3F. / = C4B. / = T4R. NN = T4L. / = C6B.

28.5

Panel of 13 sts on a background of reverse st st.

1st row (right side): P3, C3B, p1, C3F, p3.
2nd row: K3, p3, k1, p3, k3.
3rd row: P2, T3B, KB1, p1, KB1, T3F, p2.
4th row: K2, p2, k1, [p1, k1] twice, p2, k2.
5th row: P1, C3B, p1, [KB1, p1] twice, C3F, p1.
6th row: K1, p3, k1, [p1, k1] twice, p3, k1.
7th row: T3B, KB1, [p1, KB1] 3 times, T3F.
8th row: P2, k1, [p1, k1] 4 times, p2.
9th row: T3F, KB1, [p1, KB1] 3 times, T3B.
10th row: As 6th row.
11th row: P1, T3F, p1, [KB1, p1] twice, T3B, p1.
12th row: As 4th row.
13th row: P2, T3F, KB1, p1, KB1, T3B, p2.
14th row: As 2nd row.
15th row: P3, T3F, p1, T3B, p3.
16th row: K4, p2, k1, p2, k4.
17th row: P4, T5BP, p4.
18th row: As 16th row.
19th row: P3, T3B, p1, T3F, p3.
20th row: K3, [p2, k3] twice.
21st row: P2, T3B, p3, T3F, p2.
22nd row: K2, p2, k5, p2, k2.
23rd row: P2, T3F, p3, T3B, p2.
24th row: As 20th row.
25th to 28th rows: As 15th to 18th rows.
Rep these 28 rows.

Panel of 15 sts on a background of reverse st st.

Special Abbreviation

● **MB#6 (Make Bobble number 6)** see page 21.

1st row (right side): P5, k2, MB#6, k2, p5.
2nd row: K5, p5, k5.
3rd row: P5, MB#6, k3, MB#6, p5.
4th row: K5, p5, k5.
5th and 6th rows: As 1st and 2nd rows.
7th row: P4, C3B, p1, C3F, p4.
8th row: K4, p3, k1, p3, k4.
9th row: P3, C3B, p1, k1, p1, C3F, p3.
10th row: K3, p3, k1, p1, k1, p3, k3.
11th row: P2, C3B, p1, [k1, p1] twice, C3F, p2.
12th row: K2, p3, k1, [p1, k1] twice, p3, k2.
13th row: P1, C3B, p1, [k1, p1] 3 times, C3F, p1.
14th row: K1, p3, k1, [p1, k1] 3 times, p3, k1.
15th row: C3B, p1, [k1, p1] 4 times, C3F.
16th row: P3, k1, [p1, k1] 4 times, p3.
17th row: K2, p1, [k1, p1] 5 times, k2.
18th row: P2, p1, [k1, p1] 5 times, p2.
19th row: T3F, p1, [k1, p1] 4 times, T3B.
20th row: K1, p2, k1, [p1, k1] 4 times, p2, k1.
21st row: P1, T3F, p1, [k1, p1] 3 times, T3B, p1.
22nd row: K2, p2, k1, [p1, k1] 3 times, p2, k2.
23rd row: P2, T3F, p1, [k1, p1] twice, T3B, p2.
24th row: K3, p2, k1, [p1, k1] twice, p2, k3.
25th row: P3, T3F, p1, k1, p1, T3B, p3.
26th row: K4, p2, k1, p1, k1, p2, k4.
27th row: P4, T3F, p1, T3B, p4.
28th row: K5, p5, k5.
Rep these 28 rows.

28.6

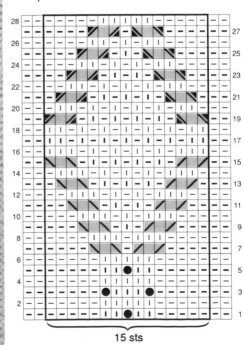

15 sts

V = KB1.   = C3B.   = C3F.   = T3B.   = T3F.   = C4B.   = T4R.

28.7

Panel of 16 sts on a background of reverse st st.

1st row (right side): K2, p4, k4, p4, k2.
2nd row: P2, k4, p4, k4, p2.
3rd row: K2, p4, C4B, p4, k2.
4th row: As 2nd row.
5th row: [T3F, p2, T3B] twice.
6th row: K1, p2, [k2, p2] 3 times, k1.
7th row: P1, T3F, T3B, p2, T3F, T3B, p1.

28.8

Panel of 22 sts on a background of reverse st st.

Special Abbreviation

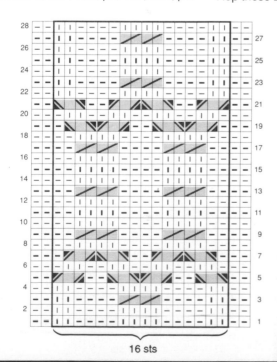 **Bind 3** = slip 1 st with yarn at back of work, k1, yf, k1, pass slipped st over the k1, yf, k1.

1st row (right side): K3, p3, k3, p4, k3, p3, k3.
2nd row: P3, k3, p3, k4, p3, k3, p3.
3rd row: Bind 3, p3, bind 3, p4, bind 3, p3, bind 3.
4th row: As 2nd row.
5th row: T4L, p2, T4L, [p2, T4R] twice.
6th row: K1, p3, k3, p3, k2, p3, k3, p3, k1.
7th row: P1, T4L, p2, T4L, T4R, p2, T4R, p1.
8th row: K2, p3, k3, p6, k3, p3, k2.
9th row: P2, T4L, p2, C6B, p2, T4R, p2.
10th row: K3, p3, k2, p6, k2, p3, k3.
11th row: P3, [T4L, T4R] twice, p3.
12th row: K4, p6, k2, p6, k4.
13th row: P4, C6F, p2, C6F, p4.
14th row: As 12th row.

8th row: K2, p4, k4, p4, k2.
9th row: P2, C4B, p4, C4B, p2.
10th row: As 8th row.
11th row: P2, k4, p4, k4, p2.
12th to 18th rows: Rep the last 4 rows once more, then 8th to 10th rows again.
19th row: P1, T3B, T3F, p2, T3B, T3F, p1.
20th row: As 6th row.
21st row: [T3B, p2, T3F] twice.
22nd to 24th rows: As 2nd to 4th rows.
25th to 28th rows: As 1st to 4th rows.
Rep these 28 rows.

15th row: P3, [T4R, T4L] twice, p3.
16th row: As 10th row.
17th row: P2, T4R, p2, C6B, p2, T4L, p2.
18th row: As 8th row.
19th row: P1, T4R, p2, T4R, T4L, p2, T4L, p1.
20th row: As 6th row.
21st row: T4R, p2, T4R, [p2, T4L] twice.
22nd to 24th rows: As 2nd to 4th rows.
25th row to 28th rows: As 1st to 4th rows.
Rep these 28 rows.

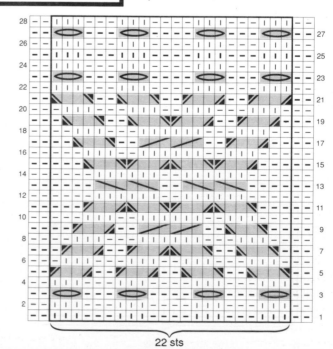

16 sts

22 sts

= T4L. = T5BP. = C6B. = C6F.

28 Row Repeats

28.9

Panel of 26 sts on a background of reverse st st.

1st row (right side): K6, [p4, k6] twice.
2nd row: P6, [k4, p6] twice.
3rd row: C6B, [p4, C6B] twice.
4th row: As 2nd row.
5th to 8th rows: As 1st to 4th rows.
9th row: K3, T5L, p2, k6, p2, T5R, k3.
10th row: [P3, k2] twice, p6, [k2, p3] twice.

28.10

11th row: [T5L] twice, k6, [T5R] twice.
12th row: K2, p3, k2, p12, k2, p3, k2.
13th row: P2, T5L, [C6F] twice, T5R, p2.
14th row: K4, p18, k4.
15th row: P4, [C6B] 3 times, p4.
16th row: K4, p18, k4.
17th row: P2, T5R, [C6F] twice, T5L, p2.
18th row: As 12th row.
19th row: [T5R] twice, k6, [T5L] twice.
20th row: As 10th row.
21st row: K3, T5R, p2, k6, p2, T5L, k3.
22nd to 28th rows: As 2nd to 8th rows.
Rep these 28 rows.

Panel of 17 sts on a background of st st.

Special Abbreviation

● **MB#7 (Make Bobble number 7)** see page 21.

1st row (right side): K5, T3B, p1, T3F, k5.
2nd row: P7, k3, p7.
3rd row: K4, T3B, p3, T3F, k4.
4th row: P6, k5, p6.
5th row: K3, T3B, p5, T3F, k3.
6th row: P5, k7, p5.
7th row: K2, T3B, p2, k3, p2, T3F, k2.
8th row: P4, k3, [PB1] 3 times, k3, p4.
9th row: K1, T3B, p2, T2B, k1, T2F, p2, T3F, k1.
10th row: P3, k3, PB1, [k1, PB1] twice, k3, p3.
11th row: T3B, p3, k1, [p1, k1] twice, p3, T3F.
12th row: P2, k4, PB1, [k1, PB1] twice, k4, p2.
13th row: K2, p3, T2B, p1, k1, p1, T2F, p3, k2.
14th row: P2, k3, PB1, [k2, PB1] twice, k3, p2.
15th row: C3F, p2, MB#7, p2, k1, p2, MB#7, p2, C3B.
16th row: P3, k5, PB1, k5, p3.
17th row: K1, C3F, p4, k1, p4, C3B, k1.
18th row: P4, k4, PB1, k4, p4.
19th row: K2, C3F, p3, MB#7, p3, C3B, k2.
20th row: P5, k7, p5.
21st row: K3, C3F, p5, C3B, k3.
22nd row: P6, k5, p6.
23rd row: K4, C3F, p3, C3B, k4.
24th row: P7, k3, p7.
25th row: K5, C3F, p1, C3B, k5.
26th row: P17.
27th row: K6, C5B, k6.
28th row: P17.
Rep these 28 rows.

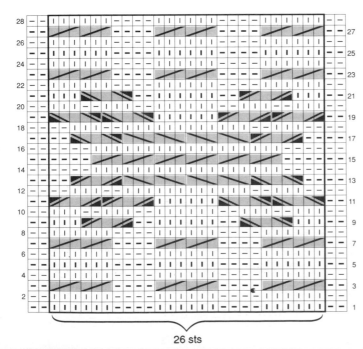

26 sts

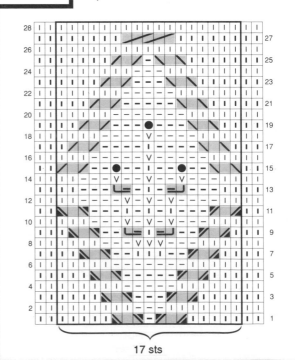

17 sts

V = PB1. ⌐ = C2B. ⌐ = C2F. ⌐ = T2B. ⌐ = T2F. ╱ = C3B. ╲ = C3F. ╱ = T3B. ╲ = T3F. ╱ = T4R.

28.11

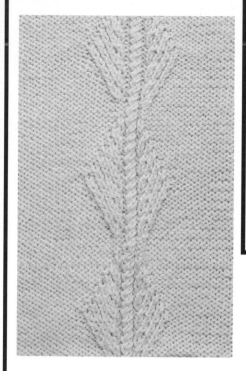

Panel of 18 sts on a background of reverse st st.

1st row (right side): P5, [C2B, p1] twice, C2F, p5.

2nd row: K5, *[PB1] twice, k1; rep from * twice more, k4.

3rd row: P4, T2B, k1, p1, C2B, p1, k1, T2F, p4.

4th row: K4, [PB1, k1] twice, [PB1] twice, [k1, PB1] twice, k4.

5th row: P3, T2B, [C2B, p1] twice, C2F, T2F, p3.

6th row: K3, PB1, k1, *[PB1] twice, k1; rep from * twice more, PB1, k3.

7th row: P2, [T2B] twice, k1, p1, C2B, p1, k1, [T2F] twice, p2.

8th row: K2, [PB1, k1] 3 times, [PB1] twice, [k1, PB1] 3 times, k2.

28.12

Panel of 20 sts on a background of reverse st st.

Special Abbreviations

Cluster 6 = knit next 6 sts and slip them onto cable needle. Wrap yarn 4 times anticlockwise round these 6 sts. Slip sts back onto right-hand needle.

Bind 3 = slip 1 st with yarn at back of work, k1, yf, k1, pass slipped st over the k1, yf, k1.

1st row (right side): Bind 3, p4, k6, p4, bind 3.

2nd row: P3, k4, p6, k4, p3.

3rd row: Bind 3, p4, C6B, p4, bind 3.

9th row: P1, [T2B] twice, [C2B, p1] twice, C2F, [T2F] twice, p1.

10th row: K1, [PB1, k1] twice, *[PB1] twice, k1; rep from * twice more, [PB1, k1] twice.

11th row: [T2B] 3 times, k1, p1, C2B, p1, k1, [T2F] 3 times.

12th row: [PB1, k1] 4 times, [PB1] twice, [k1, PB1] 4 times.

13th and 14th rows: As 9th and 10th rows.

15th and 16th rows: As 7th and 8th rows.

17th and 18th rows: As 5th and 6th rows.

19th and 20th rows: As 3rd and 4th rows.

21st and 22nd rows: As 1st and 2nd rows.

23rd row: P6, k1, p1, C2B, p1, k1, p6.

24th row: K6, PB1, k1, [PB1] twice, k1, PB1, k6.

25th row: P8, C2B, p8.

26th row: K8, [PB1] twice, k8.

27th row: P8, C2B, p8.

28th row: K8, [PB1] twice, k8.

Rep these 28 rows.

4th row: As 2nd row.

5th row: Bind 3, p3, T4R, T4L, p3, bind 3.

6th row: P3, k3, p3, k2, p3, k3, p3.

7th row: T5L, T4R, p2, T4L, T5R.

8th row: K2, p6, k4, p6, k2.

9th row: P2, C6B, p4, C6F, p2.

10th row: As 8th row.

11th row: [T5R, T5L] twice.

12th row: As 2nd row.

13th row: K3, p4, cluster 6, p4, k3.

14th row: As 2nd row.

15th row: [T5L, T5R] twice.

16th to 18th rows: As 8th to 10th rows.

19th row: T5R, T4L, p2, T4R, T5L.

20th row: As 6th row.

21st row: Bind 3, p3, T4L, T4R, p3, bind 3.

22nd to 24th rows: As 2nd to 4th rows.

25th to 28th rows: Rep 1st and 2nd rows twice.

Rep these 28 rows.

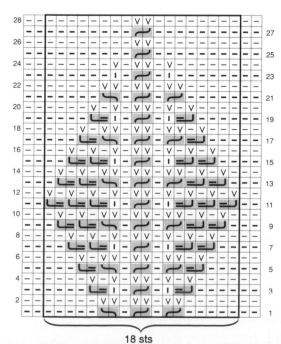

18 sts

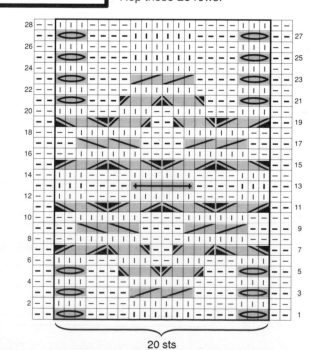

20 sts

= T4L.   = C5B.   = T5R.   = T5L.   = C6B.   = C6F.

28 Row Repeats

28.13

Panel starts with 37 sts and is worked on a background of reverse st st. The number of stitches in panel varies therefore work between markers.

Special Abbreviations

T9FP (Twist 9 Front Purl) = slip next 4 sts onto cable needle and hold at front of work, k4, p1 from left-hand needle, then knit sts from cable needle.

C12XR (Cable 12X Right) = slip next 8 sts onto cable needle and hold at back of work, knit next 4 sts from left-hand needle, slip last 4 sts from cable needle back onto left-hand needle and knit these 4 sts, then knit sts from cable needle.

C12XL (Cable 12X Left) = slip next 8 sts onto cable needle and hold at front of work, knit next 4 sts from left-hand needle, slip last 4 sts from cable needle back onto left-hand needle and knit these 4 sts, then knit sts from cable needle.

1st row (right side): [P2, k4] 3 times, p1, [k4, p2] 3 times.

2nd row: [K2, p4] 3 times, k1, [p4, k2] 3 times.

3rd row: P2, k4, p2, C4F, p2, k4, p1, k4, p2, C4B, p2, k4, p2.

4th row: As 2nd row.

5th and 6th rows: As 1st and 2nd rows.

7th row: P2, k4, p2, C4F, p2, T9FP, p2, C4B, p2, k4, p2.

8th row: As 2nd row.

9th row: P2, M1P, [k4, p2] twice, k4, M1P, p1, M1P, [k4, p2] twice, k4, M1P, p2. (41 sts)

10th row: K3, [p4, k2] twice, p4, k3, [p4, k2] twice, p4, k3.

11th row: P3, M1P, k4, p2tog, C4F, p2tog, k4, M1P, p3, M1P, k4, p2tog, C4B, p2tog, k4, M1P, p3.

12th row: K4, [p4, k1] twice, p4, k5, [p4, k1] twice, p4, k4.

13th row: P4, M1P, k3, sl 1, k1, psso, k4, k2tog, k3, M1P, p5, M1P, k3, sl 1, k1, psso, k4, k2tog, k3, M1P, p4.

14th row: K5, p12, k7, p12, k5.

15th row: P5, M1P, k4, C4F, k4, M1P, p7, M1P, k4, C4B, k4, M1P, p5. (45 sts)

16th row: K6, p12, k9, p12, k6.

17th row: P6, C12XR, p9, C12XL, p6.

18th row: As 16th row.

19th row: P4, p2tog, k4, C4F, k4, p2tog, p5, p2tog, k4, C4B, k4, p2tog, p4. (41 sts)

20th row: As 14th row.

21st row: P3, p2tog, [k4, M1P] twice, k4, p2tog, p3, p2tog, [k4, M1P] twice, k4, p2tog, p3.

22nd row: As 12th row.

23rd row: P2, p2tog, k4, M1P, p1, C4F, p1, M1P, k4, p2tog, p1, p2tog, k4, M1P, p1, C4B, p1, M1P, k4, p2tog, p2.

24th row: As 10th row.

25th row: P1, p2tog, [k4, p2] twice, k4, p3tog, [k4, p2] twice, k4, p2tog, p1. (37 sts)

26th row: As 2nd row.

27th row: As 7th row.

28th row: As 2nd row.

Rep these 28 rows.

28.14

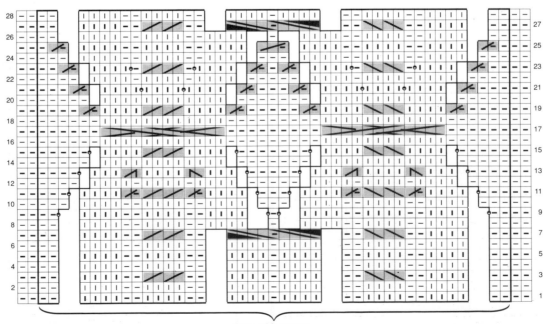

Start with 37 sts

⊥ = M1P.   ∖ = sl 1, k1, psso.   ∕ = k2tog.   ∕ = p2tog.   ∕ = p3tog.   = C2FW.   = T2B.   = T2F.

Multiple of 12 sts + 14.

1st row (right side): P5, k4, *p8, k4; rep from * to last 5 sts, p5.

2nd row: K5, p4, *k8, p4; rep from * to last 5 sts, k5.

3rd row: P5, C4B, *p8, C4B; rep from * to last 5 sts, p5.

4th row: As 2nd row.

5th row: P4, T3B, C3F, *p6, T3B, C3F; rep from * to last 4 sts, p4.

6th row: K4, p2, k1, p3, *k6, p2, k1, p3; rep from * to last 4 sts, k4.

7th row: P3, T3B, k1, p1, C3F, *p4, T3B, k1, p1, C3F; rep from * to last 3 sts, p3.

8th row: K3, p2, k1, p1, k1, p3, *k4, p2, k1, p1, k1, p3; rep from * to last 3 sts, k3.

9th row: P2, *T3B, [k1, p1] twice, C3F, p2; rep from * to end.

10th row: K2, *p2, k1, [p1, k1] twice, p3, k2; rep from * to end.

11th row: P1, *T3B, [k1, p1] 3 times, C3F; rep from * to last st, p1.

12th row: K1, p2, k1, [p1, k1] 3 times, *p5, k1, [p1, k1] 3 times; rep from * to last 4 sts, p3, k1.

13th row: P1, k3, [p1, k1] 3 times, p1, *C4B, [k1, p1] 4 times; rep from * to last 3 sts, k2, p1.

14th row: K1, p3, k1, [p1, k1] 3 times, *p5, k1, [p1, k1] 3 times; rep from * to last 3 sts, p2, k1.

15th row: P1, k2, p1, [k1, p1] 3 times, *k5, p1, [k1, p1] 3 times; rep from * to last 4 sts, k3, p1.

16th to 18th rows: As 12th to 14th rows.

19th row: P1, *T3F, [k1, p1] 3 times, T3B; rep from * to last st, p1.

20th row: K2, *p3, k1, [p1, k1] twice, p2, k2; rep from * to end.

21st row: P2, *T3F, [k1, p1] twice, T3B, p2; rep from * to end.

22nd row: K3, p3, k1, p1, k1, p2, *k4, p3, k1, p1, k1, p2; rep from * to last 3 sts, k3.

23rd row: P3, T3F, k1, p1, T3B, *p4, T3F, k1, p1, T3B; rep from * to last 3 sts, p3.

24th row: K4, p3, k1, p2, *k6, p3, k1, p2; rep from * to last 4 sts, k4.

25th row: P4, T3F, T3B, *p6, T3F, T3B; rep from * to last 4 sts, p4.

26th to 28th rows: Rep 2nd and 3rd rows once, then 2nd row again.

Rep these 28 rows.

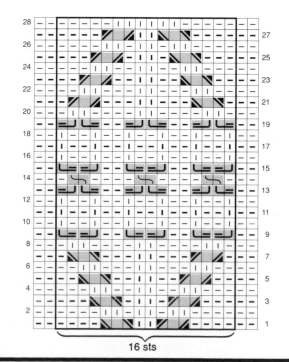

28.15

Panel of 16 sts on a background of reverse st st.

1st row (right side): P4, T3B, k2, T3F, p4.

2nd row: K4, p2, [k1, p2] twice, k4.

3rd row: P3, T3B, p1, k2, p1, T3F, p3.

4th row: K3, p2, [k2, p2] twice, k3.

5th row: P2, T3B, p2, k2, p2, T3F, p2.

6th row: K2, p2, [k3, p2] twice, k2.

7th row: P1, T3B, p3, k2, p3, T3F, p1.

8th row: K1, p2, [k4, p2] twice, k1.

9th row: T2B, T2F, [p2, T2B, T2F] twice.

10th row: P1, [k2, p1] 5 times.

11th row: K1, [p2, k1] 5 times.

12th row: As 10th row.

13th row: T2F, T2B, [p2, T2F, T2B] twice.

14th row: K1, C2FW, [k4, C2FW] twice, k1.

15th to 19th rows: As 9th to 13th rows.

20th row: As 8th row.

21st row: P1, T3F, p3, k2, p3, T3B, p1.

22nd row: As 6th row.

23rd row: P2, T3F, p2, k2, p2, T3B, p2.

24th row: As 4th row.

25th row: P3, T3F, p1, k2, p1, T3B, p3.

26th row: As 2nd row.

27th row: P4, T3F, k2, T3B, p4.

28th row: K5, p6, k5.

Rep these 28 rows.

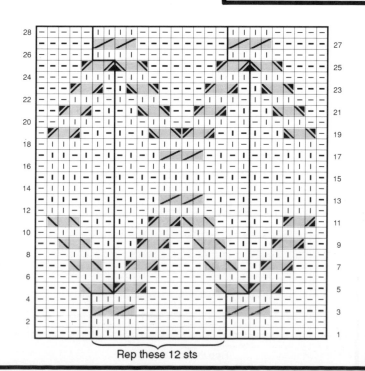

Rep these 12 sts

16 sts

/ / = C3B.　\ \ = C3F.　/ / = T3B.　\ \ = T3F.　/ / = C4B.　\ \ = C4F.

28 Row Repeats

28.16

Multiple of 12 sts + 14.

1st row (right side): P5, k4, *p8, k4; rep from * to last 5 sts, p5.

2nd row: K5, p4, *k8, p4; rep from * to last 5 sts, k5.

3rd row: P5, C4B, *p8, C4B; rep from * to last 5 sts, p5.

4th row: As 2nd row.

5th row: P4, T3B, T3F, *p6, T3B, T3F; rep from * to last 4 sts, p4.

6th row: K4, p2, k2, p2, *k6, p2, k2, p2; rep from * to last 4 sts, k4.

7th row: P3, T3B, p2, T3F, *p4, T3B, p2, T3F; rep from * to last 3 sts, p3.

8th row: K3, p2, *k4, p2; rep from * to last 3 sts, k3.

9th row: *P2, T3B, p4, T3F; rep from * to last 2 sts, p2.

10th row: *K2, p2, k6, p2; rep from * to last 2 sts, k2.

11th row: P1, *T3B, p6, T3F; rep from * to last st, p1.

12th row: K1, p2, k8, *p4, k8; rep from * to last 3 sts, p2, k1.

13th row: P1, k2, p8, *C4B, p8; rep from * to last 3 sts, k2, p1.

14th row: As 12th row.

28.17

Multiple of 12 sts + 16.

1st row (right side): P6, k4, *p3, C2F, p3, k4; rep from * to last 6 sts, p6.

2nd row: K6, p4, *k3, p2, k3, p4; rep from * to last 6 sts, k6.

3rd row: P6, C4B, *p2, T2B, T2F, p2, C4B; rep from * to last 6 sts, p6.

15th row: P1, k2, p8, *k4, p8; rep from * to last 3 sts, k2, p1.

16th to 18th rows: Rep 12th and 13th rows once, then 12th row again.

19th row: P1, *T3F, p6, T3B; rep from * to last st, p1.

20th row: As 10th row.

21st row: *P2, T3F, p4, T3B; rep from * to last 2sts, p2.

22nd row: As 8th row.

23rd row: P3, T3F, p2, T3B, *p4, T3F, p2, T3B; rep from * to last 3 sts, p3.

24th row: As 6th row.

25th row: P4, T3F, T3B, *p6, T3F, T3B; rep from * to last 4 sts, p4.

26th to 28th rows: Rep 2nd and 3rd rows once, then 2nd row again.

Rep these 28 rows.

4th row: K6, p4, *k2, [p1, k2] twice, p4; rep from * to last 6 sts, k6.

5th row: P5, T3B, T3F, *T2B, p2, T2F, T3B, T3F; rep from * to last 5 sts, p5.

6th row: K5, p2, k2, *p3, k4, p3, k2; rep from * to last 7 sts, p2, k5.

7th row: P4, *T3B, p2, T3F, p4; rep from * to end.

8th row: K4, *p2, k4; rep from * to end.

9th row: P3, *C3B, p4, C3F, p2; rep from * to last st, p1.

10th row: K3, p3, k4, p3, *k2, p3, k4, p3; rep from * to last 3 sts, k3.

11th row: P2, *T3B, T2F, p2, T2B, T3F; rep from * to last 2 sts, p2.

12th row: K2, p2, k2, [p1, k2] twice, *p4, k2, [p1, k2] twice; rep from * to last 4 sts, p2, k2.

13th row: P2, k2, p2, T2F, T2B, p2, *C4B, p2, T2F, T2B, p2; rep from * to last 4 sts, k2, p2.

14th row: K2, [p2, k3] twice, *p4, k3, p2, k3; rep from * to last 4 sts, p2, k2.

15th row: P2, k2, p3, C2F, p3, *k4, p3, C2F, p3; rep from * to last 4 sts, k2, p2.

16th row: As 14th row.

17th row: P2, k2, p2, T2B, T2F, p2, *C4B, p2, T2B, T2F, p2; rep from * to last 4 sts, k2, p2.

18th row: As 12th row.

19th row: P2, *T3F, T2B, p2, T2F, T3B; rep from * to last 2 sts, p2.

20th row: As 10th row.

21st row: P3, *T3F, p4, T3B, p2; rep from * to last st, p1.

22nd row: As 8th row.

23rd row: P4, T3F, p2, *C3B, p4, C3F, p2; rep from * to last 7 sts, T3B, p4.

24th row: As 6th row.

25th row: P5, T3F, T3B, *T2F, p2, T2B, T3F, T3B; rep from * to last 5 sts, p5.

26th row: As 4th row.

27th row: P6, C4B, *p2, T2F, T2B, p2, C4B; rep from * to last 6 sts, p6.

28th row: As 2nd row.

Rep these 28 rows.

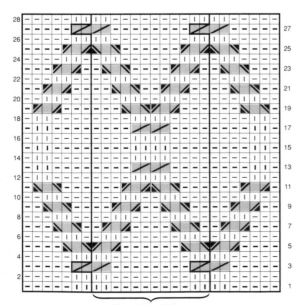

Rep these 12 sts

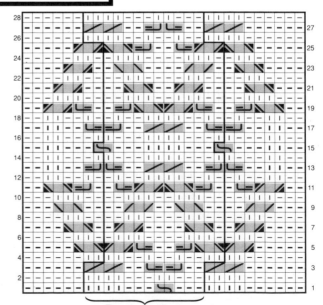

Rep these 12 sts

⌐ = C2B. ⌐ = C2F. ⌐ = T2B. ⌐ = T2F. ⌐ = C3B. ⌐ = C3F. ⌐ = T3B. ⌐ = T3F. ⌐ = C4B. ⌐ = C4F.

28.18

Multiple of 12 sts + 8.

1st row (right side): P3, k2, *T3F, p1, C2B, p1, T3B, k2; rep from * to last 3 sts, p3.

2nd row: K3, p2, *k1, p2; rep from * to last 3 sts, k3.

3rd row: P3, C2B, *p1, T3F, k2, T3B, p1, C2B; rep from * to last 3 sts, p3.

4th row: K3, p2, *k2, p6, k2, p2; rep from * to last 3 sts, k3.

5th row: P3, k2, p2, *C4B, [k2, p2] twice; rep from * to last st, p1.

6th row: As 4th row.

7th row: P3, C2B, *p2, k2, C4F, p2, C2B; rep from * to last 3 sts, p3.

8th row: As 4th row.

9th row: P3, k2, *p2, k6, p2, k2; rep from * to last 3 sts, p3.

10th row: As 4th row.

11th row: P3, C2B, *p2, C4B, k2, p2, C2B; rep from * to last 3 sts, p3.

12th row: As 4th row.

13th row: P3, k2, *p2, k2, C4F, p2, k2; rep from * to last 3 sts, p3.

14th row: As 4th row.

15th row: P3, C2B, *p1, T3B, k2, T3F, p1, C2B; rep from * to last 3 sts, p3.

16th row: As 2nd row.

17th row: P3, k2, *T3B, p1, C2B, p1, T3F, k2; rep from * to last 3 sts, p3.

18th row: K1, p6, *k2, p2, k2, p6; rep from * to last st, k1.

19th row: P1, C4B, *[k2, p2] twice, C4B; rep from * to last 3 sts, k2, p1.

20th row: As 18th row.

21st row: P1, k2, C4F, *p2, C2B, p2, k2, C4F; rep from * to last st, p1.

22nd row: As 18th row.

23rd row: P1, k6, *p2, k2, p2, k6; rep from * to last st, p1.

24th row: As 18th row.

25th row: P1, C4B, k2, *p2, C2B, p2, C4B, k2; rep from * to last st, p1.

26th row: As 18th row.

27th row: P1, k2, C4F, *[p2, k2] twice, C4F; rep from * to last st, p1.

28th row: As 18th row.

Rep these 28 rows.

30.1

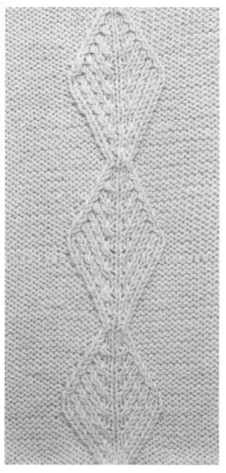

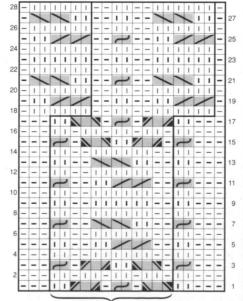

Rep these 12 sts

---

17 sts

Panel of 17 sts on a background of reverse st st.

1st row (right side): P6, T2B, k1, T2F, p6.

2nd row: K6, p5, k6.

3rd row: P5, T2B, k3, T2F, p5.

4th row: K5, p7, k5.

5th row: P4, [T2B] twice, k1, [T2F] twice, p4.

6th row: K4, p9, k4.

7th row: P3, [T2B] twice, k3, [T2F] twice, p3.

8th row: K3, p11, k3.

9th row: P2, [T2B] 3 times, k1, [T2F] 3 times, p2.

10th row: K2, p13, k2.

11th row: P1, [T2B] 3 times, k3, [T2F] 3 times, p1.

12th row: K1, p15, k1.

13th row: [T2B] 4 times, k1, [T2F] 4 times.

14th row: P17.

15th row: K1, [T2B] 3 times, k3, [T2F] 3 times, k1.

16th row: P17.

17th row: T2F, [T2B] 3 times, k1, [T2F] 3 times, T2B.

18th row: K1, p15, k1.

19th row: P1, T2F, [T2B] twice, k3, [T2F] twice, T2B, p1.

20th row: K2, p13, k2.

21st row: P2, T2F, [T2B] twice, k1, [T2F] twice, T2B, p2.

22nd row: K3, p11, k3.

23rd row: P3, T2F, T2B, k3, T2F, T2B, p3.

24th row: K4, p9, k4.

25th row: P4, T2F, T2B, k1, T2F, T2B, p4.

26th row: K5, p7, k5.

27th row: P5, T2F, k3, T2B, p5.

28th row: K6, p5, k6.

29th row: P6, T2F, k1, T2B, p6.

30th row: K7, p3, k7.

Rep these 30 rows.

30-32 Row Repeats

30.2

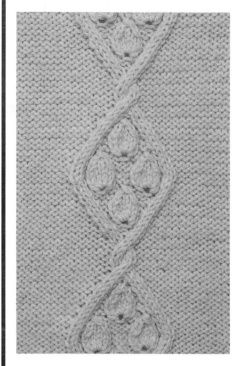

Panel starts with 17 sts and is worked on a background of reverse st st. The number of sts within the panel varies, therefore work between markers.

Special Abbreviation

Inc 4 (increase 4 sts) = [k1, yf, k1, yf, k1] all into next st.

1st row (right side): P5, T3B, p1, T3F, p5.
2nd row: K5, p2, k3, p2, k5.
3rd row: P4, T3B, p1, inc 4, p1, T3F, p4. (21 sts)
4th row: K4, p2, k2, p5, k2, p2, k4.
5th row: P3, T3B, p2, k5, p2, T3F, p3.
6th row: K3, p2, k3, p5, k3, p2, k3.

7th row: P2, T3B, p3, yb, sl 1, k1, psso, k1, k2tog, p3, T3F, p2. (19 sts).
8th row: K2, p2, k4, p2, p3, k4, p2, k2.
9th row: P1, T3B, p1, inc 4, p2, yb, sl 1, k2tog, psso, p2, inc 4, p1, T3F, p1. (25 sts)
10th row: K1, p2, k2, p5, k5, p5, k2, p2, k1.
11th row: T3B, p2, k5, p5, k5, p2, T3F.
12th row: P2, k3, p5, k5, p5, k3, p2.
13th row: T3F, p2, yb, sl 1, k1, psso, k1, k2tog, p5, yb, sl 1, k1, psso, k1, k2tog, p2, T3B. (21 sts)
14th row: K1, p2, k2, p3, k5, p3, k2, p2, k1.
15th row: P1, T3F, p1, yb, sl 1, k2tog, psso, p2, inc 4, p2, yb, sl 1, k2tog, psso, p1, T3B, p1.

16th row: K2, p2, k4, p5, k4, p2, k2.
17th row: P2, T3F, p3, k5, p3, T3B, p2.
18th row: As 6th row.
19th row: P3, T3F, p2, yb, sl 1, k1, psso, k1, k2tog, p2, T3B, p3. (19 sts)
20th row: K4, p2, k2, p3, k2, p2, k4.
21st row: P4, T3F, p1, yb, sl 1, k2tog, psso, p1, T3B, p4. (17 sts)
22nd row: K5, p2, k3, p2, k5.
23rd row: P5, T3F, p1, T3B, p5.
24th row: K6, p2, k1, p2, k6.
25th row: P6, C5B, p6.
26th row: K6, p2, k1, p2, k6.
27th row: P6, k2, p1, k2, p6.
28th to 30th rows: As 24th to 26th rows.
Rep these 30 rows.

Start with 17 sts

32.1

Panel of 16 sts on a background of reverse st st.

1st row (right side): K16.
2nd row: P16.
3rd row: C8B, C8F.
4th row: P16.
5th to 10th rows: Rep 1st and 2nd rows 3 times.
11th and 12th rows: As 3rd and 4th rows.
13th to 18th rows: Rep 1st and 2nd rows 3 times.
19th row: C8F, C8B.
20th row: P16.
21st to 26th rows: Rep 1st and 2nd rows 3 times.
27th and 28th rows: AS 19th and 20th rows.
29th to 32nd rows: Rep 1st and 2nd rows 3 times.
Rep these 32 rows.

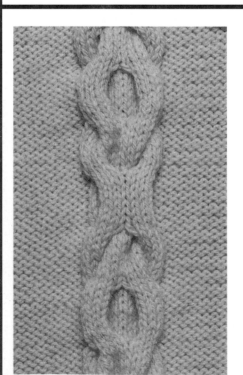

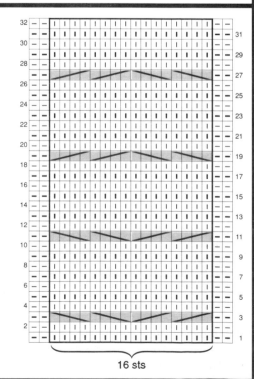

16 sts

= sl 1, k1, psso. = k2tog. = sl 1, k2tog, psso. = T2B. = T2F. = T3B. = T3F.

32.2

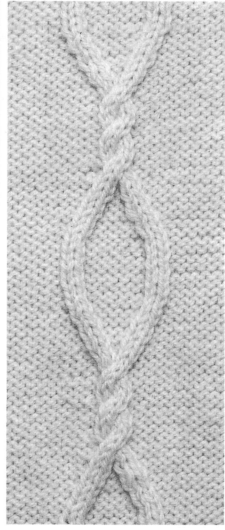

12 sts

Panel of 12 sts on a background of reverse st st.

1st row (right side): P4, k4, p4.
2nd row: K4, p4, k4.
3rd row: P4, C4B, p4.
4th row: K4, p4, k4.
5th row: P3, T3B, T3F, p3.
6th row: K3, p2, k2, p2, k3.
7th row: P2, T3B, p2, T3F, p2.
8th row: K2, p2, k4, p2, k2.
9th row: P1, T3B, p4, T3F, p1.
10th row: K1, p2, k6, p2, k1.
11th row: T3B, p6, T3F.
12th row: P2, k8, p2.
13th row: K2, p8, k2.
14th to 18th rows: Rep the last 2 rows twice more, then 12th row again.
19th row: T3F, p6, T3B.
20th row: As 10th row.
21st row: P1, T3F, p4, T3B, p1.
22nd row: As 8th row.
23rd row: P2, T3F, p2, T3B, p2.
24th row: As 6th row.
25th row: P3, T3F, T3B, p3.
26th to 28th rows: As 2nd to 4th rows.
29th to 32nd rows: As 1st to 4th rows.
Rep these 32 rows.

32.3

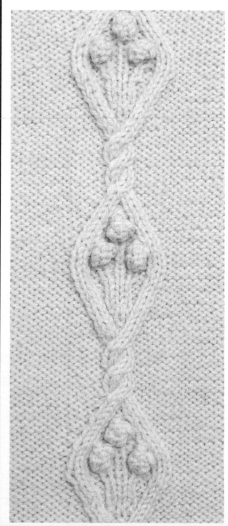

Panel of 15 sts on a background of reverse st st.

Special Abbreviation

● **MD#6 (Make Dobble number 6)** see page 21.

1st row (right side): P5, k2, p1, k2, p5.
2nd row: K5, p2, k1, p2, k5.
3rd row: P5, T5BP, p5.
4th row: As 2nd row.
5th row: P4, T3B, p1, T3F, p4.
6th row: K4, p2, k1, p1, k1, p2, k4.
7th row: P3, T3B, p1, k1, p1, T3F, p3.
8th row: K3, p2, k1, p3, k1, p2, k3.
9th row: P2, T3B, p1, k3, p1, T3F, p2.
10th row: K2, p2, k2, p3, k2, p2, k2.
11th row: P1, T3B, p2, k3, p2, T3F, p1.
12th row: K1, p2, k3, p3, k3, p2, k1.
13th row: T3B, p2, T2B, k1, T2F, p2, T3F.
14th row: P2, k3, p1, [k1, p1] twice k3, p2.
15th row: K2, p2, T2B, p1, k1, p1, T2F, p2, k2.
16th row: P2, k2, [p1, k2] 3 times, p2.
17th row: T3F, p1, MB#6, p2, k1, p2, MB#6, p1, T3B.
18th row: K1, p2, k4, p1, k4, p2, k1.
19th row: P1, T3F, p3, k1, p3, T3B, p1.
20th row: K2, p2, k3, p1, k3, p2, k2.
21st row: P2, T3F, p2, MB#6, p2, T3B, p2.
22nd row: K3, p2, k5, p2, k3.
23rd row: P3, T3F, p3, T3B, p3.
24th row: K4, p2, k3, p2, k4.
25th row: P4, T3F, p1, T3B, p4.
26th, 27th and 28th rows: As 2nd, 3rd and 4th rows.
29th to 32nd rows: As 1st to 4th rows.
Rep these 32 rows.

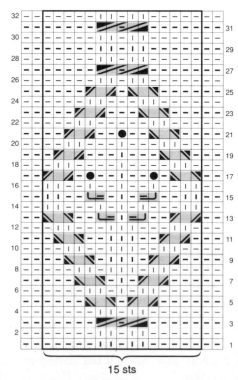

15 sts

= C4B.   = C5B.   = T5BP.   = C8B.   = C8F.

32 Row Repeats

32.4 - 32.5

32.4 (starting with slope to left)
Panel of 9 sts on a background of reverse st st.

1st row (right side): C2F, p7.
2nd row: K6, T2FW, p1.
3rd row: KB1, p1, C2F, p5.
4th row: K4, T2FW, p1, k1, p1.
5th row: [KB1, p1] twice, C2F, p3.
6th row: K2, T2FW, [p1, k1] twice, p1.
7th row: [KB1, p1] 3 times, C2F, p1.
8th row: T2FW, [p1, k1] 3 times, p1.
9th row: [KB1, p1] 4 times, KB1.
10th row: [P1, k1] 3 times, p1, T2FW.
11th row: P1, T2F, [p1, KB1] 3 times.
12th row: [P1, k1] twice, p1, T2FW, k2.
13th row: P3, T2F, [p1, KB1] twice.
14th row: P1, k1, p1, T2FW, k4.
15th row: P5, T2F, p1, KB1.
16th row: P1, T2FW, k6.
17th row: P7, C2B.
18th row: P1, T2BW, k6.
19th row: P5, C2B, p1, KB1.
20th row: P1, k1, p1, T2BW, k4.
21st row: P3, C2B, [p1, KB1] twice.
22nd row: [P1, k1] twice, p1, T2BW, k2.
23rd row: P1, C2B, [p1, KB1] 3 times.
24th row: [P1, k1] 3 times, p1, T2BW.
25th row: [KB1, p1] 4 times, KB1.
26th row: T2BW, [p1, k1] 3 times, p1.
27th row: [KB1, p1] 3 times, T2B, p1.
28th row: K2, T2BW, [p1, k1] twice, p1.
29th row: [KB1, p1] twice, T2B, p3.
30th row: K4, T2BW, p1, k1, p1.
31st row: KB1, p1, T2B, p5.
32nd row: K6, T2BW, p1.
Rep these 32 rows.

32.5 (starting with slope to right)
Work as given for 32.4 **but** starting with 17th row.

32.6

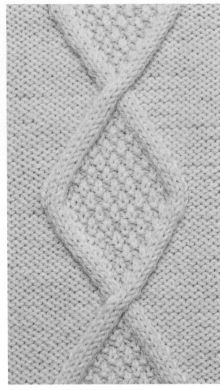

Panel of 21 sts on a background of reverse st st.

1st row (right side): P6, C4R, p1, C4L, p6.
2nd row: K6, p4, k1, p4, k6.
3rd row: P5, C4R, p1, k1, p1, C4L, p5.
4th row: K5, p4, k1, p1, k1, p4, k5.
5th row: P4, C4R, p1, [k1, p1] twice, C4L, p4.
6th row: K4, p4, k1, [p1, k1] twice, p4, k4.
7th row: P3, C4R, p1, [k1, p1] 3 times, C4L, p3.
8th row: K3, p4, k1, [p1, k1] 3 times, p4, k3.
9th row: P2, C4R, p1, [k1, p1] 4 times, C4L, p2.
10th row: K2, p4, k1, [p1, k1] 4 times, p4, k2.
11th row: P1, C4R, p1, [k1, p1] 5 times, C4L, p1.
12th row: K1, p4, k1, [p1, k1] 5 times, p4, k1.
13th row: C4R, p1, [k1, p1] 6 times, C4L.
14th row: P4, k1, [p1, k1] 6 times, p4.
15th row: K3, p1, [k1, p1] 7 times, k3.
16th row: P3, k1, [p1, k1] 7 times, p3.
17th row: T4L, p1, [k1, p1] 6 times, T4R.
18th row: K1, p3, k1, [p1, k1] 6 times, p3, k1.
19th row: P1, T4L, p1, [k1, p1] 5 times, T4R, p1.
20th row: K2, p3, k1, [p1, k1] 5 times, p3, k2.
21st row: P2, T4L, p1, [k1, p1] 4 times, T4R, p2.
22nd row: K3, p3, k1, [p1, k1] 4 times, p3, k3.
23rd row: P3, T4L, p1, [k1, p1] 3 times, T4R, p3.
24th row: K4, p3, k1, [p1, k1] 3 times, p3, k4.
25th row: P4, T4L, p1, [k1, p1] twice, T4R, p4.
26th row: K5, p3, k1, [p1, k1] twice, p3, k5.
27th row: P5, T4L, p1, k1, p1, T4R, p5.
28th row: K6, p3, k1, p1, k1, p3, k6.
29th row: P6, T4L, p1, T4R, p6.
30th row: K7, p3, k1, p3, k7.
31st row: P7, C7B, p7.
32nd row: K7, p7, k7.
Rep these 32 rows.

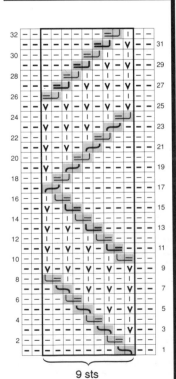

9 sts

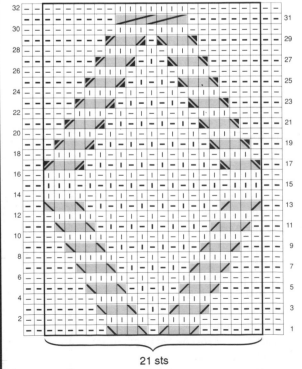

21 sts

V = KB1. ⌐ = C2B. ⌐ = C2F. ⊐ = T2B. ⌐ = T2F. ⊐ = T2BW. ⌐ = T2FW. ╱╱ = C4R. ╲╲ = C4L.

32.7

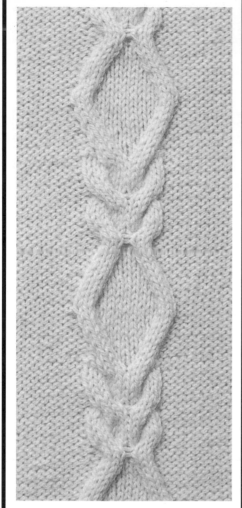

Panel of 16 sts on a background of reverse st st.

1st row (right side): P4, C4R, C4L, p4.
2nd row: K4, p8, k4.
3rd row: P3, C4R, k2, C4L, p3.
4th row: K3, p10, k3.
5th row: P2, C4R, k4, C4L, p2.
6th row: K2, p12, k2.
7th row: P1, C4R, k6, C4L, p1.
8th row: K1, p14, k1.
9th row: C4R, k8, C4L.
10th row: P16.
11th row: T4L, k8, T4R.
12th row: K1, p14, k1.
13th row: P1, T4L, k6, T4R, p1.
14th row: K2, p12, k2.
15th row: P2, T4L, k4, T4R, p2.
16th row: K3, p10, k3.
17th row: P3, T4L, k2, T4R, p3.
18th row: K4, p8, k4.
19th row: P4, T4L, T4R, p4.
20th row: K5, p6, k5.
21st row: P2, C6B, C6F, p2.
22nd row: K2, p12, k2.
23rd row: P2, k12, p2.
24th to 26th rows: Rep the last 2 rows once more, then 22nd row again.
27th to 32nd rows: As 21st to 26th rows.
Rep these 32 rows.

32.8

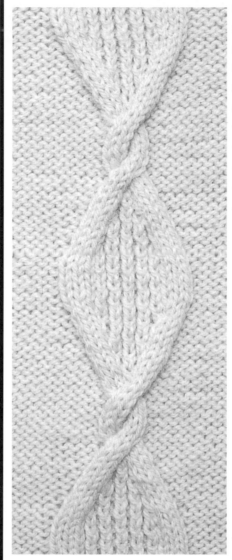

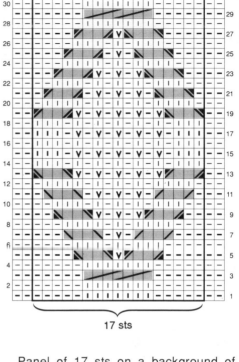

17 sts

Panel of 17 sts on a background of reverse st st.

1st row (right side): P5, k7, p5.
2nd row: K5, p7, k5.
3rd row: P5, C7B, p5.
4th row: K5, p7, k5.
5th row: P4, T4R, KB1, T4L, p4.
6th row: K4, p3, k1, p1, k1, p3, k4.
7th row: P3, C4R, p1, KB1, p1, C4L, p3.
8th row: K3, p4, k1, p1, k1, p4, k3.
9th row: P2, T4R, KB1, [p1, KB1] twice, T4L, p2.
10th row: K2, p3, k1, [p1, k1] 3 times, p3, k2.
11th row: P1, C4R, p1, [KB1, p1] 3 times, C4L, p1.
12th row: K1, p4, k1, [p1, k1] 3 times, p4, k1.
13th row: T4R, KB1, [p1, KB1] 4 times, T4L.
14th row: P3, k1, [p1, k1] 5 times, p3.
15th row: K3, p1, [KB1, p1] 5 times, k3.
16th to 18th rows: Rep the last 2 rows once more, then 14th row again.
19th row: T4L, KB1, [p1, KB1] 4 times, T4R.
20th row: As 12th row.
21st row: P1, T4L, p1, [KB1, p1] 3 times, T4R, p1.
22nd row: As 10th row.
23rd row: P2, T4L, KB1, [p1, KB1] twice, T4R, p2.
24th row: As 8th row.
25th row: P3, T4L, p1, KB1, p1, T4R, p3.
26th row: As 6th row.
27th row: P4, T4L, KB1, T4R, p4.
28th to 30th rows: As 2nd to 4th rows.
31st and 32nd rows: As 1st and 2nd rows.
Rep these 32 rows.

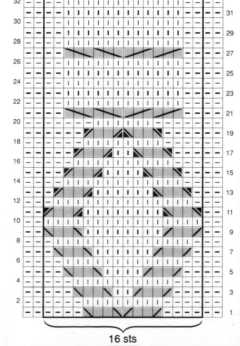

16 sts

= T4R.   = T4L.   = C6B.   = C6F.   = C7B.

32 Row Repeats

32.9

Multiple of 24 sts + 20.

1st row (right side): P2, k4, *p8, k4; rep from * to last 2 sts, p2.

2nd row: K2, p4, *k8, p4; rep from * to last 2 sts, k2.

3rd row: P2, C4B, p8, C4F, *p8, C4B, p8, C4F; rep from * to last 2 sts, p2.

4th row: As 2nd row.

5th row: P2, k2, T4F, p4, T4B, k2, *p8, k2, T4F, p4, T4B, k2; rep from * to last 2 sts, p2.

6th row: [K2, p2] twice, k4, p2, k2, p2, *k8, p2, k2, p2, k4, p2, k2, p2; rep from * to last 2 sts, k2.

7th row: P2, k2, p2, T4F, T4B, p2, k2, *p8, k2, p2, T4F, T4B, p2, k2; rep from * to last 2 sts, p2.

8th row: K2, p2, k4, p4, k4, p2, *k8, p2, k4, p4, k4, p2; rep from * to last 2 sts, k2.

9th row: P2, k2, p4, C4F, p4, k2, *p8, k2, p4, C4F, p4, k2; rep from * to last 2 sts, p2.

10th row: As 8th row.

11th row: P2, k2, p2, T4B, T4F, p2, k2, *p8, k2, p2, T4B, T4F, p2, k2; rep from * to last 2 sts, p2.

12th row: As 6th row.

13th row: P2, k2, T4B, p4, T4F, k2, *p8, k2, T4B, p4, T4F, k2; rep from * to last 2 sts, p2.

14th row: As 2nd row.

15th row: P2, C4F, p8, C4B, *p8, C4F, p8, C4B; rep from * to last 2 sts, p2.

16th row: As 2nd row.

17th and 18th rows: As 1st and 2nd rows.

19th row: P2, T4F, p8, *C4B, p8, C4F, p8; rep from * to last 6 sts, T4B, p2.

20th row: K4, p2, k8, *p4, k8; rep from * to last 6 sts, p2, k4.

21st row: P4, k2, p8, *k2, T4F, p4, T4B, k2, p8; rep from * to last 6 sts, k2, p4.

22nd row: K4, p2, k8, *p2, k2, p2, k4, p2, k2, p2, k8; rep from * to last 6 sts, p2, k4.

23rd row: P4, k2, p8, *k2, p2, T4F, T4B, p2, k2, p8; rep from * to last 6 sts, k2, p4.

24th row: K4, p2, k8, *p2, k4, p4, k4, p2, k8; rep from * to last 6 sts, p2, k4.

25th row: P4, k2, p8, *k2, p4, C4B, p4, k2, p8; rep from * to last 6 sts, k2, p4.

26th row: As 24th row.

27th row: P4, k2, p8, *k2, p2, T4B, T4F, p2, k2, p8; rep from * to last 6 sts, k2, p4.

28th row: As 22nd row.

29th row: P4, k2, p8, *k2, T4B, p4, T4F, k2, p8; rep from * to last 6 sts, k2, p4.

30th row: As 20th row.

31st row: As 3rd row.

32nd row: As 2nd row.

Rep these 32 rows.

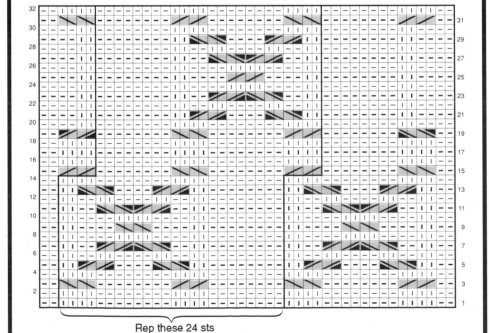

Rep these 24 sts

32.10

Panel of 26 sts on a background of reverse st st.

Special Abbreviations

T4B rib (Twist 4 Back rib) = slip next 2 sts onto cable needle and hold at back of work, knit next 2 sts from left-hand needle, then k1, p1 from cable needle.

T4F rib (Twist 4 Front rib) = slip next 2 sts onto cable needle and hold at front of work, p1, k1 from left-hand needle, then knit sts from cable needle.

1st row (right side): K2, [p2, k2] 6 times.

2nd row: P2, [k2, p2] 6 times.

3rd row: [K2, p2] twice, k2, p1, C2B, C2F, p1, k2, [p2, k2] twice.

4th row: [P2, k2] twice, p2, k1, p4, k1, p2, [k2, p2] twice.

5th row: [K2, p2] twice, k1, T4B, T4F, k1, [p2, k2] twice.

6th row: [P2, k2] twice, p3, k4, p3, [k2, p2] twice.

7th row: K2, p2, k2, p1, T4B, p4, T4F, p1, k2, p2, k2.

8th row: P2, k2, p2, k1, p2, k8, p2, k1, p2, k2, p2.

9th row: K2, p2, k1, T4B, p8, T4F, k1, p2, k2.

10th row: P2, k2, p3, k12, p3, k2, p2.

= C2B.   = C2F.   = C2BW.   = C2FW.   = T2B.   = T2F.   = C4B.

11th row: K2, p1, T4B, p4, C2B, C2F, p4, T4F, p1, k2.

12th row: P2, k1, p2, k6, p4, k6, p2, k1, p2.

13th row: K1, T4B, p4, T4B, T4F, p4, T4F, k1.

14th row: P3, k6, p2, k4, p2, k6, p3.

15th row: K3, p4, T4B, T2F, T2B, T4F, p4, k3.

16th row: P3, k4, p2, k3, C2BW, k3, p2, k4, p3.

17th row: K1, T4FP, T4B, [T2F, T2B] twice, T4F, T4BP, k1.

18th row: P2, k1, p4, k3, C2FW, k2, C2FW, k3, p4, k1, p2.

19th row: K2, p1, T4B, [T2F, T2B] 3 times, T4F, p1, k2.

20th row: P2, k1, p2, k3, C2BW, [k2, C2BW] twice, k3, p2, k1, p2.

21st row: K2, p1, T4F rib, [T2B, T2F] 3 times, T4B rib, p1, k2.

22nd row: P2, k2, p4, k2, C2FW, k2, C2FW, k2, p4, k2, p2.

23rd row: K2, p2, k1, T4FP, [T2B, T2F] twice, T4BP, k1, p2, k2.

24th row: P2, k2, p2, k1, p3, k2, C2BW, k2, p3, k1, p2, k2, p2.

25th row: K2, p2, k2. p1, T4F rib, T2B, T2F, T4B rib, p1, k2, p2, k2.

26th row: [P2, k2] twice, p4, k2, p4, [k2, p2] twice.

27th row: [K2, p2] twice, k1, T4FP, T4BP, k1, [p2, k2] twice.

28th row: [P2, k2] twice, p2, k1, p4, k1, p2, [k2, p2] twice.

29th row: [K2, p2] twice, k2, p1, T2F, T2B, p1, k2, [p2, k2] twice.

30th row: As 2nd row.

31st and 32nd rows: As 1st and 2nd rows.

Rep these 32 rows.

32.11

Multiple of 16 sts + 20.

Special Abbreviations

T6B rib (Twist 6 Back rib) = slip next 3 sts onto cable needle and hold at back of work, k1, p1, k1 from left-hand needle, then k1, p1, k1 from cable needle.

T4R rib (Twist 4 Right rib) = slip next st onto cable needle and hold at back of work, k1, p1, k1 from left-hand needle, then p1 from cable needle.

T4L rib (Twist 4 Left rib) = slip next 3 sts onto cable needle and hold at front of work, p1 from left-hand needle, then k1, p1, k1 from cable needle.

1st row (right side): P7, k1, p1, k2, p1, k1, *p10, k1, p1, k2, p1, k1; rep from * to last 7 sts, p7.

2nd row: K7, p1, k1, p2, k1, p1, *k10, p1, k1, p2, k1, p1; rep from * to last 7 sts, k7.

3rd row: P7, T6B rib, *p10, T6B rib; rep from * to last 7 sts, p7.

4th row: As 2nd row.

5th row: P6, T4R rib, T4L rib, *p8, T4R rib, T4L rib; rep from * to last 6 sts, p6.

6th row: K6, p1, k1, p1, k2, p1, k1, p1, *k8, p1, k1, p1, k2, p1, k1, p1; rep from * to last 6 sts, k6.

7th row: P5, T4R rib, p2, T4L rib, *p6, T4R rib, p2, T4L rib; rep from * to last 5 sts, p5.

8th row: K5, p1, k1, p1, k4, p1, k1, p1, *k6, p1, k1, p1, k4, p1, k1, p1; rep from * to last 5 sts, k5.

9th row: P4, *T4R rib, p4, T4L rib, p4; rep from * to end.

10th row: K4, *p1, k1, p1, k6, p1, k1, p1, k4; rep from * to end.

11th row: P3, *T4R rib, p6, T4L rib, p2; rep from * to last st, p1.

12th row: K3, *p1, k1, p1, k8, p1, k1, p1, k2; rep from * to last st, k1.

13th row: P2, *T4R rib, p8, T4L rib; rep from * to last 2 sts, p2.

14th row: K2, p1, k1, p1, k10, *p1, k1 p2, k1, p1, k10; rep from * to last 5 sts, p1. k1 p1, k2.

15th row: P2, k1, p1, k1, p10, *T6B rib, p10; rep from * to last 5 sts, k1, p1, k1, p2.

16th row: As 14th row.

17th row: P2, k1, p1, k1, p10, *k1, p1, k2, p1, k1, p10; rep from * to last 5 sts, k1, p1, k1, p2.

18th to 20th rows: As 14th to 16th rows.

21st row: P2, *T4L rib, p8, T4R rib; rep from * to last 2 sts, p2.

22nd row: As 12th row.

23rd row: P3, *T4L rib, p6, T4R rib, p2; rep from * to last st, p1.

24th row: As 10th row.

25th row: P4, *T4L rib, p4, T4R rib, p4; rep from * to end.

26th row: As 8th row.

27th row: P5, T4L rib, p2, T4R rib, *p6, T4L rib, p2, T4R rib; rep from * to last 5 sts, p5.

28th row: As 6th row.

29th row: P6, T4L rib, T4R rib, *p8, T4L rib, T4R rib; rep from * to last 6 sts, p6.

30th to 32nd rows: As 2nd to 4th rows.

Rep these 32 rows.

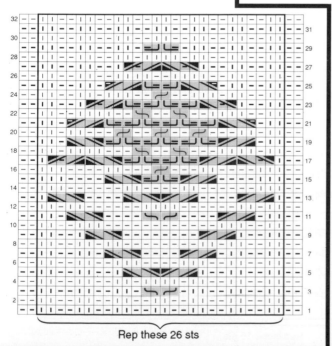

Rep these 26 sts

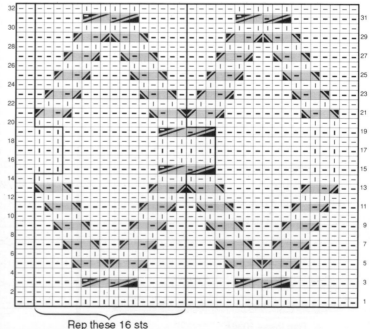

Rep these 16 sts

= C4F.   = T4B.   = T4F.   = T4BP.   = T4FP.

32 Row Repeats

32.12

Multiple of 10 sts + 12.

1st row (right side): P3, T2F, p2, T2B, *p4, T2F, p2, T2B; rep from * to last 3 sts, p3.

2nd row: K4, p1, k2, p1, *k6, p1, k2, p1; rep from * to last 4 sts, k4.

3rd row: P4, T2F, T2B, *p6, T2F, T2B; rep from * to last 4 sts, p4.

4th row: K5, C2BW, *k8, C2BW; rep from * to last 5 sts, k5.

5th row: P4, T2B, T2F, *p6, T2B, T2F; rep from * to last 4 sts, p4.

6th to 13th rows: Rep the last 4 rows twice more.

14th row: As 2nd row.

15th row: P3, T2B, p2, T2F, *p4, T2B, p2, T2F; rep from * to last 3 sts, p3.

16th row: K3, p1, *k4, p1; rep from * to last 3 sts, k3.

17th row: P2, *T2B, p4, T2F, p2; rep from * to end.

18th row: K2, *p1, k6, p1, k2; rep from * to end.

32.13

Multiple of 16 sts + 16.

1st row (right side): P2, k4, *p4, k4; rep from * to last 2 sts, p2.

2nd row: K2, p4, *k4, p4; rep from * to last 2 sts, k2.

3rd row: P2, C4F, p4, C4B, *p4, C4F, p4, C4B; rep from * to last 2 sts, p2.

4th row: As 2nd row.

5th to 8th rows: Rep the last 4 rows once more.

9th row: P1, T3B, T4F, T4B, T3F, *p2, T3B, T4F, T4B, T3F; rep from * to last st, p1.

10th row: K1, p2, k3, p4, k3, p2, *k2, p2, k3, p4, k3, p2; rep from * to last st, k1.

11th row: P1, k2, p3, C4B, p3, k2, *p2, k2, p3, C4B, p3, k2; rep from * to last st, p1.

12th row: As 10th row.

13th row: P1, T3F, T4B, T4F, T3B, *p2, T3F, T4B, T4F, T3B; rep from * to last st, p1.

14th row: As 2nd row.

15th row: P2, C4B, p4, C4F, *p4, C4B, p4, C4F; rep from * to last 2 sts, p2.

16th row: As 2nd row.

17th row: As 1st row.

18th to 24th rows: Rep the last 4 rows once more, then 14th, 15th and 16th rows again.

25th row: P1, T3B, T3F, p2, T3B, *T4F, T4B, T3F, p2, T3B; rep from * to last 4 sts, T3F, p1.

26th row: K1, p2, [k2, p2] twice, *k3, p4, k3, p2, k2, p2; rep from * to last 5 sts, k2, p2, k1.

27th row: P1, k2, [p2, k2] twice, *p3, C4F, p3, k2, p2, k2; rep from * to last 5 sts, p2, k2, p1.

28th row: As 26th row.

29th row: P1, T3F, T3B, p2, T3F, *T4B, T4F, T3B, p2, T3F; rep from * to last 4 sts, T3B, p1.

30th to 32nd rows: As 2nd to 4th rows.

Rep these 32 rows.

19th row: P2, k1, p6, *T2F, T2B, p6; rep from * to last 3 sts, k1, p2.

20th row: K2, p1, k7, C2BW, *k8, C2BW; rep from * to last 10 sts, k7, p1, k2.

21st row: P2, k1, p6, *T2B, T2F, p6; rep from * to last 3 sts, k1, p2.

22nd to 29th rows: Rep the last 4 rows twice more.

30th row: As 18th row.

31st row: P2, *T2F, p4, T2B, p2; rep from * to end.

32nd row: As 16th row.

Rep these 32 rows.

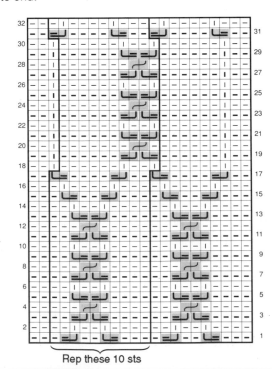

Rep these 10 sts

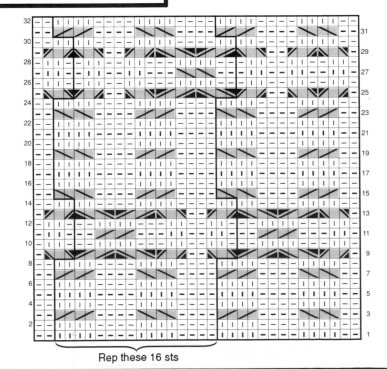

Rep these 16 sts

⊐⊏ = C2BW.　⊒⌐ = T2B.　⌐⊑ = T2F.　⧄ ⧄ = T3B.　◥◤ = T3F.　⧄⧄ = C4B.　◥◤ = C4F.

36.1

Panel of 26 sts on a background of reverse st st.

1st row (right side): P1, T4L, T4R, p8, T4L, T4R, p1.

2nd row: K2, p6, k10, p6, k2.

3rd row: P2, C6F, p10, C6F, p2.

4th row: As 2nd row.

5th row: P1, T4R, T4L, p8, T4R, T4L, p1.

6th row: K1, p3, k2, p3, k8, p3, k2, p3, k1.

7th row: T4R, p2, T4L, p6, T4R, p2, T4L.

8th row: P3, k4, p3, k6, p3, k4, p3.

9th row: K3, p4, T4L, p4, T4R, p4, k3.

10th row: P3, k5, p3, k4, p3, k5, p3.

11th row: T4L, p4, T4L, p2, T4R, p4, T4R.

12th row: K1, p3, k5, p3, k2, p3, k5, p3, k1.

13th row: P1, T4L, p4, T4L, T4R, p4, T4R, p1.

14th row: K2, p3, k5, p6, k5, p3, k2.

15th row: P2, T4L, p4, C6B, p4, T4R, p2.

16th row: K3, p3, k4, p6, k4, p3, k3.

17th row: P3, [T4L, p2, T4R] twice, p3.

18th row: K4, p3, [k2, p3] 3 times, k4.

19th row: P4, T4L, T4R, p2, T4L, T4R, p4.

20th row: K5, p6, k4, p6, k5.

21st row: P5, C6F, p4, C6F, p5.

22nd row: As 20th row.

23rd row: P4, T4R, T4L, p2, T4R, T4L, p4.

24th row: As 18th row.

25th row: P3, [T4R, p2, T4L] twice, p3.

26th row: As 16th row.

27th row: P2, T4R, p4, C6B, p4, T4L, p2.

28th row: As 14th row.

29th row: P1, T4R, p4, T4R, T4L, p4, T4L, p1.

30th row: As 12th row.

31st row: T4R, p4, T4R, p2, T4L, p4, T4L.

32nd row: As 10th row.

33rd row: K3, p4, T4R, p4, T4L, p4, k3.

34th row: As 8th row.

35th row: T4L, p2, T4R, p6, T4L, p2, T4R.

36th row: As 6th row.

Rep these 36 rows.

36.2

Multiple of 24 sts + 2.

1st row (right side): P2, *k2, p2, [k6, p2] twice, k2, p2; rep from * to end.

2nd row: K2, *p2, k2, [p6, k2] twice, p2, k2; rep from * to end.

3rd row: P2, *k2, p2, C6F, p2, C6B, p2, k2, p2; rep from * to end.

4th row: As 2nd row.

5th and 6th rows: As 1st and 2nd rows.

7th to 18th rows: Rep these 6 rows twice more.

19th row: P2, *k6, p2, [k2, p2] twice, k6, p2; rep from * to end.

20th row: K2, *p6, k2, [p2, k2] twice, p6, k2; rep from * to end.

21st row: P2, *C6B, p2, [k2, p2] twice, C6F, p2; rep from * to end.

22nd row: As 20th row.

23rd and 24th rows: As 19th and 20th rows.

25th to 36th rows: Rep 19th to 24th rows twice.

Rep these 36 rows.

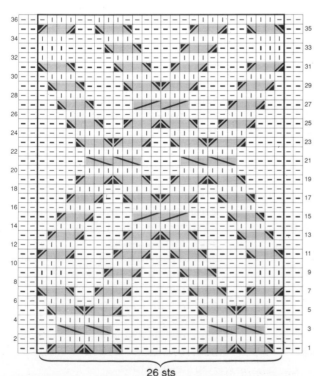

26 sts

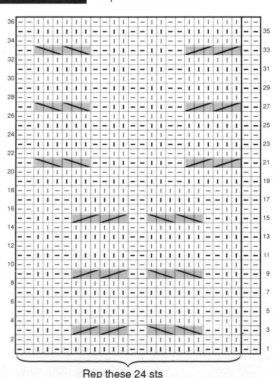

Rep these 24 sts

36 Row Repeats

36.3

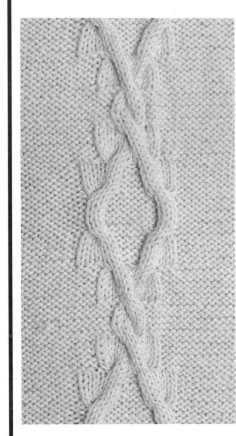

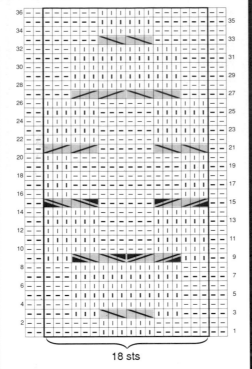

18 sts

Panel of 18 sts on a background of reverse st st.

1st row (right side): P6, k6, p6.
2nd row: K6, p6, k6.
3rd row: P3, k3, C6F, k3, p3.
4th row: K3, p12, k3.
5th row: P3, k12, p3.
6th row: K3, p12, k3.
7th and 8th rows: Rep the last 2 rows once more.
9th row: K3, T6B, T6F, k3.
10th row: P6, k6, p6.
11th row: K6, p6, k6.
12th to 14th rows: Rep the last 2 rows once more then 10th row again.
15th row: T6B, p6, T6F.
16th row: P3, k12, p3.
17th row: K3, p12, k3.
18th to 20th rows: Rep the last 2 rows once more, then 16th row again.
21st row: C6F, p6, C6B.
22nd row: P6, k6, p6.
23rd row: K6, p6, k6.
24th to 26th rows: Rep the last 2 rows once more, then 22nd row again.
27th row: P3, C6F, C6B, p3.
28th row: K3, p12, k3.
29th row: P3, k12, p3.
30th to 32nd rows: Rep the last 2 rows once more, then 28th row again.
33rd row: P6, C6F, p6.
34th row: K6, p6, k6.
35th row: P6, k6, p6.
36th row: K6, p6, k6.
Rep these 36 rows.

36.4

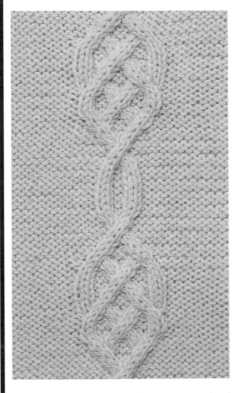

Panel of 16 sts on a background of reverse st st.

1st row (right side): P6, C4B, p6.
2nd row: K6, p4, k6.
3rd row: P4, T4B, T4F, p4.
4th row: K4, [p2, k4] twice.
5th row: P2, C4B, p4, C4F, p2.
6th row: K2, p4, k4, p4, k2.
7th row: [T4B, T4F] twice.
8th row: P2, k4, p4, k4, p2.
9th row: K2, p4, C4B, p4, k2.
10th row: As 8th row.

36.5

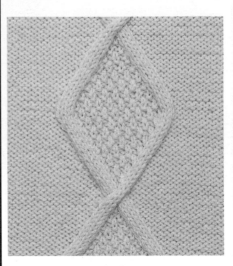

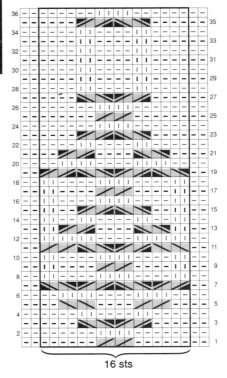

16 sts

11th row: C4F, T4B, T4F, C4B.
12th row: P6, k4, p6.
13th row: K2, T4F, p4, T4B, k2.
14th row: P2, k2, p2, k4, p2, k2, p2.
15th row: K2, p2, T4F, T4B, p2, k2.
16th to 18th rows: As 8th to 10th rows.
19th row: [T4F, T4B] twice.
20th row: As 6th row.
21st row: P2, T4F, p4, T4B, p2.
22nd row: As 4th row.
23rd row: P4, T4F, T4B, p4.
24th row: K6, p4, k6.
25th to 28th rows: As 1st to 4th rows.
29th row: P4, [k2, p4] twice.
30th row: As 4th row.
31st to 34th rows: Rep the last 2 rows twice more.
35th row: As 23rd row.
36th row: K6, p4, k6.
Rep these 36 rows.

☑ = C4B. ☑ = C4F. ☑ = C4R. ☑ = C4L. ☑ = T4B. ☑ = T4F. ☑ = T4R.

Panel of 23 sts on a background of reverse st st.

1st row (right side): P7, C4R, p1, C4L, p7.

2nd row: K7, p4, k1, p4, k7.

3rd row: P6, C4R, p1, k1, p1, C4L, p6.

4th row: K6, p4, k1, p1, k1, p4, k6.

5th row: P5, C4R, p1, [k1, p1] twice, C4L, p5.

6th row: K5, p4, k1, [p1, k1] twice, p4, k5.

7th row: P4, C4R, p1, [k1, p1] 3 times, C4L, p4.

8th row: K4, p4, k1, [p1, k1] 3 times, p4, k4.

9th row: P3, C4R, p1, [k1, p1] 4 times, C4L, p3.

10th row: K3, p4, k1, [p1, k1] 4 times, p4, k3.

11th row: P2, C4R, p1, [k1, p1] 5 times, C4L, p2.

12th row: K2, p4, k1, [p1, k1] 5 times, p4, k2.

13th row: P1, C4R, p1, [k1, p1] 6 times, C4L, p1.

14th row: K1, p4, k1, [p1, k1] 6 times, p4, k1.

15th row: C4R, p1, [k1, p1] 7 times, C4L.

16th row: P4, k1, [p1, k1] 7 times, p4.

17th row: K3, p1, [k1, p1] 8 times, k3.

18th row: P3, k1, [p1, k1] 8 times, p3.

19th row: T4L, p1, [k1, p1] 7 times, T4R.

20th row: K1, p3, k1, [p1, k1] 7 times, p3, k1.

21st row: P1, T4L, p1, [k1, p1] 6 times, T4R, p1.

22nd row: K2, p3, k1, [p1, k1] 6 times, p3, k2.

23rd row: P2, T4L, p1, [k1, p1] 5 times, T4R, p2.

24th row: K3, p3, k1, [p1, k1] 5 times, p3, k3.

25th row: P3, T4L, p1, [k1, p1] 4 times, T4R, p3.

26th row: K4, p3, k1, [p1, k1] 4 times, p3, k4.

27th row: P4, T4L, p1, [k1, p1] 3 times, T4R, p4.

28th row: K5, p3, k1, [p1, k1] 3 times, p3, k5.

29th row: P5, T4L, p1, [k1, p1] twice, T4R, p5.

30th row: K6, p3, k1, [p1, k1] twice, p3, k6.

31st row: P6, T4L, p1, k1, p1, T4R, p6.

32nd row: K7, p3, k1, p1, k1, p3, k7.

33rd row: P7, T4L, p1, T4R, p7.

34th row: K8, p3, k1, p3, k8.

35th row: P8, C7B, p8.

36th row: K8, p7, k8.

Rep these 36 rows.

36.6

Multiple of 16 sts + 18.

1st row (right side): Knit.

2nd and every alt row: Purl.

3rd row: K6, C6B, *k10, C6B; rep from * to last 6 sts, k6.

5th row: K5, C4R, C4L, *k8, C4R, C4L; rep from * to last 5 sts, k5.

7th row: K4, C4R, k2, C4L, *k6, C4R, k2, C4L; rep from * to last 4 sts, k4.

9th row: K3, C4R, k4, C4L, *k4, C4R, k4, C4L; rep from * to last 3 sts, k3.

11th row: *K2, C4R, k6, C4L; rep from * to last 2 sts, k2.

13th row: K1, *C4R, k8, C4L; rep from * to last st, k1.

15th row: K14, *C6B, k10; rep from * to last 4 sts, k4.

17th and 19th rows: Knit.

21st row: As 15th row.

23rd row: K1, *C4L, k8, C4R; rep from * to last st, k1.

25th row: *K2, C4L, k6, C4R; rep from * to last 2 sts, k2.

27th row: K3, C4L, k4, C4R, *k4, C4L, k4, C4R; rep from * to last 3 sts, k3.

29th row: K4, C4L, k2, C4R, *k6, C4L, k2, C4R; rep from * to last 4 sts, k4.

31st row: K5, C4L, C4R, *k8, C4L, C4R; rep from * to last 5 sts, k5.

33rd row: As 3rd row.

35th row: Knit.

36th row: Purl.

Rep these 36 rows.

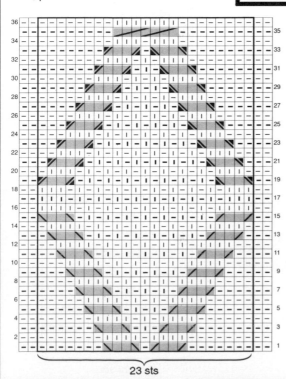

23 sts

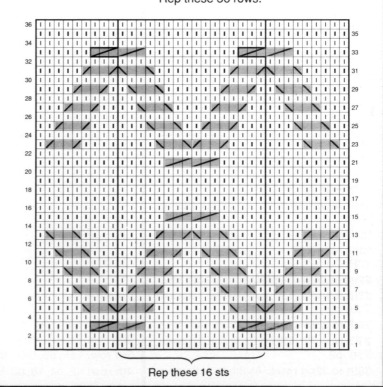

Rep these 16 sts

= T4L. = C6B. = C6F. = T6B. = T6F. = C7B.

40 Row Repeats

40.1

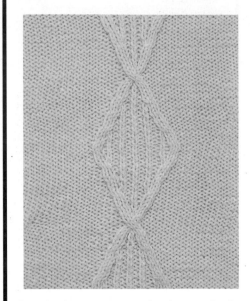

Panel of 15 sts on a background of reverse st st.

Special Abbreviation

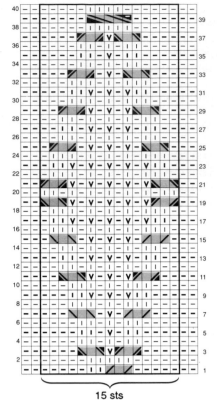

T5LP (Twist 5 Left Purl) = slip next 2 sts onto cable needle and hold at front of work, p1, k2 from left-hand needle, then knit sts from cable needle.

1st row (right side): P5, C3B, k2, p5.
2nd row: K5, p5, k5.
3rd row: P4, T3B, KB1, T3F, p4.
4th row: K4, p2, k1, p1, k1, p2, k4.
5th row: P4, k2, p1, KB1, p1, k2, p4.
6th row: As 4th row.
7th row: P3, C3B, p1, KB1, p1, C3F, p3.
8th row: K3, p3, k1, p1, k1, p3, k3.
9th row: P3, k2, KB1, [p1, KB1] twice, k2, p3.
10th row: As 8th row.
11th row: P2, T3B, KB1, [p1, KB1] twice, T3F, p2.
12th row: K2, p2, k1, [p1, k1] 3 times, p2, k2.
13th row: P2, k2, p1, [KB1, p1] 3 times, k2, p2.
14th row: As 12th row.
15th row: P1, C3B, p1, [KB1, p1] 3 times, C3F, p1.
16th row: K1, p3, k1, [p1, k1] 3 times, p3, k1.
17th row: P1, k2, KB1, [p1, KB1] 4 times, k2, p1.
18th row: As 16th row.
19th row: T3B, KB1, [p1, KB1] 4 times, T3F.
20th row: P2, k1, [p1, k1] 5 times, p2.
21st row: T3F, KB1, [p1, KB1] 4 times, T3B.
22nd to 24th rows: As 16th to 18th rows.
25th row: P1, T3F, p1, [KB1, p1] 3 times, T3B, p1.
26th to 28th rows: As 12th to 14th rows.
29th row: P2, T3F, KB1, [p1, KB1] twice, T3B, p2.
30th to 32nd rows: As 8th to 10th rows.

15 sts

33rd row: P3, T3F, p1, KB1, p1, T3B, p3.
34th to 36th rows: As 4th to 6th rows.
37th row: P4, T3F, KB1, T3B, p4.
38th row: K5, p5, k5.
39th row: P5, T5LP, p5.
40th row: K5, p4, k6.
Rep these 40 rows.

40.2

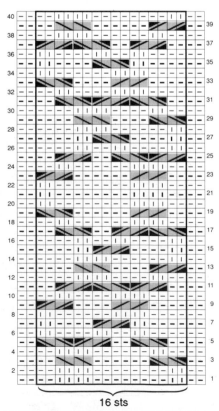

Panel of 16 sts on a background of reverse st st.
1st row (right side): K2, p8, k4, p2.
2nd row: K2, p4, k8, p2.
3rd row: T4F, p6, C4F, p2.
4th row: K2, p4, k6, p2, k2.

5th row: P2, T4F, p2, T4B, T4F.
6th row: P2, k4, p2, k2, p2, k4.
7th row: P4, k2, T4B, p4, k2.
8th row: P2, k6, p4, k4.
9th row: P4, C4B, p4, T4B.
10th row: K2, p2, k4, p4, k4.
11th row: P2, T4B, T4F, T4B, p2.
12th row: K4, p4, k4, p2, k2.
13th row: T4B, p4, C4F, p4.
14th row: K4, p4, k6, p2.
15th row: K2, p4, T4B, k2, p4.
16th row: K4, p2, k2, p2, k4, p2.
17th row: T4F, T4B, p2, T4F, p2.
18th row: K2, p2, k6, p4, k2.
19th row: P2, C4B, p6, T4F.
20th row: P2, k8, p4, k2.
21st row: P2, k4, p8, k2.
22nd row: As 20th row.
23rd row: P2, C4B, p6, T4B.
24th row: As 18th row.
25th row: T4B, T4F, p2, T4B, p2.
26th row: As 16th row.
27th row: K2, p4, T4F, k2, p4.
28th row: As 14th row.
29th row: T4F, p4, C4F, p4.
30th row: As 12th row.
31st row: P2, T4F, T4B, T4F, p2.
32nd row: As 10th row.
33rd row: P4, C4B, p4, T4F.
34th row: As 8th row.
35th row: P4, k2, T4F, p4, k2.
36th row: As 6th row.
37th row: P2, T4B, p2, T4F, T4B.
38th row: As 4th row.
39th row: T4B, p6, C4F, p2.
40th row: K2, p4, k8, p2.
Rep these 40 rows.

16 sts

Y = KB1. = C3B. = C3F. = T3B. = T3F. = C4B. = C4F. = T4B. = T4F.

40.3

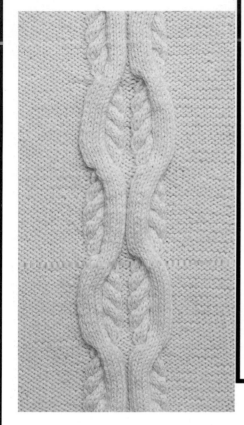

Panel of 27 sts on a background of reverse st st.

1st row (right side): K5, p1, k6, p3, k6, p1, k5.

2nd row: P5, k1, p6, k3, p6, k1, p5.

3rd row: K5, p1, C6B, p3, C6F, p1, k5.

4th row: As 2nd row.

5th to 10th rows: Rep the last 4 rows once more, then 1st and 2nd rows again.

11th row: C12F, p3, C12B.

40.4

12th row: P6, k1, p5, k3, p5, k1, p6.

13th row: K6, p1, k5, p3, k5, p1, k6.

14th row: As 12th row.

15th row: C6F, p1, k5, p3, k5, p1, C6B.

16th to 30th rows: Rep the last 4 rows 3 times more, then 12th, 13th and 14th rows again.

31st row: C12B, p3, C12F.

32nd row: As 2nd row.

33rd to 40th rows: Rep 1st to 4th rows twice.

Rep these 40 rows.

Panel of 20 sts on a background of reverse st st.

1st row (right side): P8, C4B, p8.

2nd row: K8, p4, k8.

3rd row: P6, T4BP, T4FP, p6.

4th row: K6, [p2, k1] twice, p2, k6.

5th row: P6, [k2, p1] twice, k2, p6.

6th to 12th rows: Rep the last 2 rows 3 times more, then 4th row again.

13th row: P6, T4F, T4B, p6.

14th row: K8, p4, k8.

15th and 16th rows: As 1st and 2nd rows.

17th row: P6, C4B, C4F, p6.

18th row: K6, p8, k6.

19th row: P4, T4B, k4, T4F, p4.

20th row: K4, p2, k2, p4, k2, p2, k4.

21st row: P2, T4B, C4B, C4F, T4F, p2.

22nd row: K2, p2, k2, p8, k2, p2, k2.

23rd row: [T4B] twice, C4B, [T4F] twice.

24th row: [P2, k2] twice, p4, [k2, p2] twice.

25th row: K2,T4B, p2, k4, p2, T4F, k2.

26th row: [P4, k4] twice, p4.

27th row: C4F, [p4, C4B] twice.

28th row: As 26th row.

29th row: K2, T4F, p2, k4, p2, T4B, k2.

30th row: As 24th row.

31st row: [T4F] twice, C4B, [T4B] twice.

32nd row: As 22nd row.

33rd row: P2, [T4F] twice, [T4B] twice, p2.

34th row: As 20th row.

35th row: P4, T4F, k4, T4B, p4.

36th row: K6, p8, k6.

37th and 38th rows: As 13th and 14th rows.

39th and 40th rows: As 1st and 2nd rows. Rep these 40 rows.

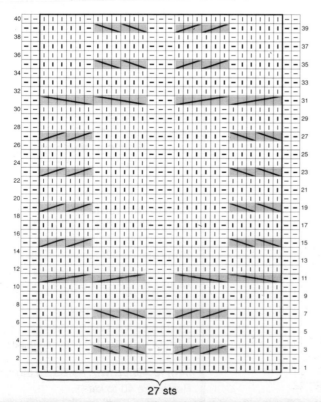

27 sts

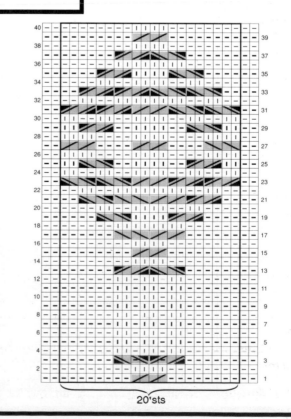

20 sts

= T4BP.   = T4FP.   = C6B.   = C6F.   = C12B.   = C12F.

40 Row Repeats

40.5

Multiple of 12 sts + 20.

Special Abbreviation

Bind 2 = yarn over needle to make a st, p2, pass new st over the 2 purl sts.

1st row (right side): P7, *T3F, T3B, p6; rep from * to last st, p1.

2nd row: K8, *bind 2, p2, k8; rep from * to end.

3rd row: P8, *C4B, p8; rep from * to end.

4th row: K8, *[bind 2] twice, k8; rep from * to end.

5th row: P7, *T3B, T3F, p6; rep from * to last st, p1.

6th row: K7, *bind 2, k2, bind 2, k6; rep from * to last st, k1.

7th row: P7, *k2, p2, k2, p6; rep from * to last st, p1.

8th and 9th rows: Rep the last 2 rows once more.

10th row: As 6th row.

11th to 16th rows: As 1st to 6th rows.

17th row: P6, *T3B, p2, T3F, p4; rep from * to last 2 sts, p2.

18th row: K6, *bind 2, k4; rep from * to last 2 sts, k2.

19th row: P5, *T3B, p4, T3F, p2; rep from * to last 3 sts, p3.

20th row: K5, *bind 2, k6, bind 2, k2; rep from * to last 3 sts, k3.

21st row: P4, *T3B, p6, T3F; rep from * to last 4 sts, p4.

22nd row: K4, bind 2, k8, *p2, bind 2, k8; rep from * to last 6 sts, bind 2, k4.

23rd row: P3, T3B, p8, *C4F, p8; rep from * to last 6 sts, T3F, p3.

24th row: K3, bind 2, k9, *[bind 2] twice, k8; rep from * to last 6 sts, k1, bind 2, k3.

25th row: P2, T3B, p8, *T3B, T3F, p6; rep from * to last 7 sts, p2, T3F, p2.

26th row: K2, bind 2, k9, *bind 2, k2, bind 2, k6; rep from * to last 7 sts, k3, bind 2, k2.

27th row: P2, k2, p9, *k2, p2, k2, p6; rep from * to last 7 sts, p3, k2, p2.

28th and 29th rows: Rep the last 2 rows once more.

30th row: As 26th row.

31st row: P2, T3F, p8, *T3F, T3B, p6; rep from * to last 7 sts, p2, T3B, p2.

32nd row: K3, bind 2, k9, *p2, bind 2, k8; rep from * to last 6 sts, k1, bind 2, k3.

33rd row: P3, T3F, p8, *C4F, p8; rep from * to last 6 sts, T3B, p3.

34th row: K4, bind 2, k8, *[bind 2] twice, k8; rep from * to last 6 sts, bind 2, k4.

35th row: P4, *T3F, p6, T3B; rep from * to last 4 sts, p4.

36th row: As 20th row.

37th row: P5, *T3F, p4, T3B, p2; rep from * to last 3 sts, p3.

38th row: As 18th row.

39th row: P6, *T3F, p2, T3B, p4; rep from * to last 2 sts, p2.

40th row: As 6th row.

Rep these 40 rows.

40.6

Multiple of 18 sts + 19.

1st row (right side): P2, [k3, p3] twice, *k9, p3, k3, p3; rep from * to last 5 sts, k3, p2.

2nd row: K2, [p3, k3] twice, *p9, k3, p3, k3; rep from * to last 5 sts, p3, k2.

3rd row: P2, k3, [p3, k3] twice, *C6F, [p3, k3] twice; rep from * to last 2 sts, p2.

4th row: As 2nd row.

5th and 6th rows: As 1st and 2nd rows.

7th row: P2, [k3, p3] twice, *C6B, [k3, p3] twice; rep from * to last 5 sts, k3, p2.

8th row: As 2nd row.

9th row: P2, T4L, p2, k3, *p2, T4R, k3, T4L, p2, k3; rep from * to last 8 sts, p2, T4R, p2.

10th row: K3, p3, [k2, p3] twice, *[k1, p3] twice, [k2, p3] twice; rep from * to last 3 sts, k3.

11th row: P3, T4L, p1, k3, p1, T4R, *p1, k3, p1, T4L, p1, k3, p1, T4R; rep from * to last 3 sts, p3.

12th row: K4, p3, [k1, p3] twice, *[k2, p3] twice, [k1, p3] twice; rep from * to last 4 sts, k4.

13th row: P4, T4L, k3, T4R, *p2, k3, p2, T4L, k3, T4R; rep from * to last 4 sts, p4.

14th row: K5, p9, *k3, p3, k3, p9; rep from * to last 5 sts, k5.

15th row: P5, k3, C6F, *[p3, k3] twice, C6F; rep from * to last 5 sts, p5.

16th row: As 14th row.

17th row: P5, k9, *p3, k3, p3, k9; rep from * to last 5 sts, p5.

18th row: As 14th row.

19th row: P5, C6B, *[k3, p3] twice, C6B; rep from * to last 8 sts, k3, p5.

20th row: As 14th row.

21st row: As 17th row.

22nd to 28th rows: As 14th to 20th rows.

29th row: P4, T4R, k3, T4L, *p2, k3, p2, T4R, k3, T4L; rep from * to last 4 sts, p4.

30th row: As 12th row.

31st row: P3, T4R, p1, k3, p1, T4L, *p1, k3, p1, T4R, p1, k3, p1, T4L; rep from * to last 3 sts, p3.

32nd row: As 10th row.

33rd row: P2, T4R, p2, k3, p2, T4L, *k3, T4R, p2, k3, p2, T4L; rep from * to last 2 sts, p2.

34th to 40th rows: As 2nd to 8th rows.

Rep these 40 rows.

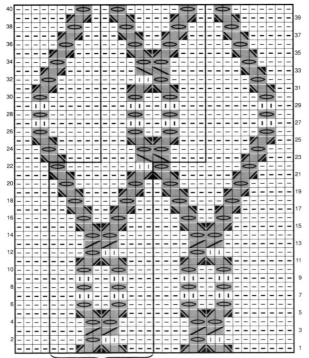

Rep these 12 sts

 = T3B. = T3F. = C4B. = C4F. = C4R. = C4L.

48.1

Panel of 29 sts on a background of reverse st st.

1st row (right side): P10, C4R, p1, C4L, p10.

2nd row: K10, p4, k1, p4, k10.

3rd row: P9, C4R, p1, k1, p1, C4L, p9.

4th row: K9, p4, k1, p1, k1, p4, k9.

5th row: P8, C4R, p1, [k1, p1] twice, C4L, p8.

6th row: K8, p4, k1, [p1, k1] twice, p4, k8.

7th row: P7, C4R, p1, [k1, p1] 3 times, C4L, p7.

8th row: K7, p4, k1, [p1, k1] 3 times, p4, k7.

9th row: P6, C4R, p1, [k1, p1] 4 times, C4L, p6.

10th row: K6, p4, k1, [p1, k1] 4 times, p4, k6.

11th row: P5, C4R, p1, [k1, p1] 5 times, C4L, p5.

12th row: K5, p4, k1, [p1, k1] 5 times, p4, k5.

13th row: P4, C4R, p1, [k1, p1] 6 times, C4L, p4.

14th row: K4, p4, k1, [p1, k1] 6 times, p4, k4.

15th row: P3, C4R, p1, [k1, p1] 7 times, C4L, p3.

16th row: K3, p4, k1, [p1, k1] 7 times, p4, k3.

17th row: P2, C4R, p1, [k1, p1] 8 times, C4L, p2.

18th row: K2, p4, k1, [p1, k1] 8 times, p4, k2.

19th row: P1, C4R, p1, [k1, p1] 9 times, C4L, p1.

20th row: K1, p4, k1, [p1, k1] 9 times, p4, k1.

21st row: C4R, p1, [k1, p1] 10 times, C4L.

22nd row: P4, k1, [p1, k1] 10 times, p4.

23rd row: K3, p1, [k1, p1] 11 times, k3.

24th row: P3, k1, [p1, k1] 11 times, p3.

25th row: T4L, p1, [k1, p1] 10 times, T4R.

26th row: K1, p3, k1, [p1, k1] 10 times, p3, k1.

27th row: P1, T4L, p1, [k1, p1] 9 times, T4R, p1.

28th row: K2, p3, k1, [p1, k1] 9 times, p3, k2.

29th row: P2, T4L, p1, [k1, p1] 8 times, T4R, p2.

30th row: K3, p3, k1, [p1, k1] 8 times, p3, k3.

31st row: P3, T4L, p1, [k1, p1] 7 times, T4R, p3.

32nd row: K4, p3, k1, [p1, k1] 7 times, p3, k4.

33rd row: P4, T4L, p1, [k1, p1] 6 times, T4R, p4.

34th row: K5, p3, k1, [p1, k1] 6 times, p3, k5.

35th row: P5, T4L, p1, [k1, p1] 5 times, T4R, p5.

36th row: K6, p3, k1, [p1, k1] 5 times, p3, k6.

37th row: P6, T4L, p1, [k1, p1] 4 times, T4R, p6.

38th row: K7, p3, k1, [p1, k1] 4 times, p3, k7.

39th row: P7, T4L, p1, [k1, p1] 3 times, T4R, p7.

40th row: K8, p3, k1, [p1, k1] 3 times, p3, k8.

41st row: P8, T4L, p1, [k1, p1] twice, T4R, p8.

42nd row: K9, p3, k1, [p1, k1] twice, p3, k9.

43rd row: P9, T4L, p1, k1, p1, T4R, p9.

44th row: K10, p3, k1, p1, k1, p3, k10.

45th row: P10, T4L, p1, T4R, p10.

46th row: K11, p3, k1, p3, k11.

47th row: P11, C7B, p11.

48th row: K11, p7, k11.

Rep these 48 rows.

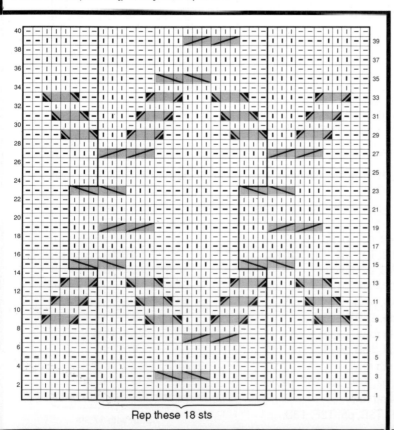

Rep these 18 sts

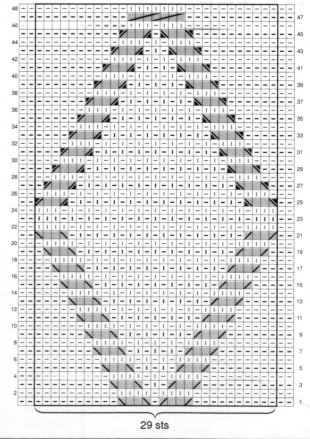

29 sts

= T4R. = T4L. = C6B. = C6F. = C7B.

48-52 Row Repeats

48.2

Panel of 16 sts on a background of reverse st st.

1st row (right side): P4, T3B, k2, T3F, p4.
2nd row: K4, p2, [k1, p2] twice, k4.
3rd row: P3, T3B, p1, k2, p1, T3F, p3.
4th row: K3, p2, [k2, p2] twice, k3.
5th row: P2, T3B, p2, k2, p2, T3F, p2.
6th row: K2, p2, [k3, p2] twice, k2.
7th row: P2, T3F, p2, k2, p2, T3B, p2.
8th row: As 4th row.
9th row: P3, T3F, p1, k2, p1, T3B, p3.
10th row: As 2nd row.
11th row: P4, T3F, k2, T3B, p4.
12th row: K5, p6, k5.
13th row: P5, k2, C4B, p5.
14th row: K5, p6, k5.
15th row: P5, C4F, k2, p5.

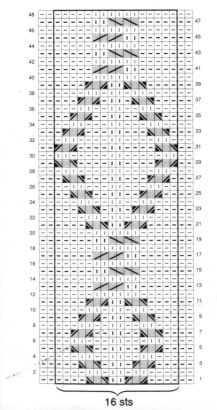

16 sts

16th to 20th rows: Rep the last 4 rows once more, then 12th row again.
21st to 26th rows: As 1st to 6th rows.
27th row: P1, T3B, p3, k2, p3, T3F, p1.
28th row: K1, p2, [k4, p2] twice, k1.
29th row: T3B, p4, k2, p4, T3F.
30th row: P2, [k5, p2] twice.
31st row: T3F, p4, k2, p4, T3B.
32nd row: As 28th row.
33rd row: P1, T3F, p3, k2, p3, T3B, p1.
34th to 48th rows: As 6th to 20th rows.
Rep these 48 rows.

52.1

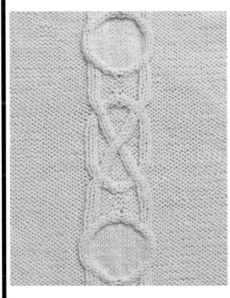

Panel starts with 17 sts and is worked on a background of reverse st st. The number of sts within the panel varies, therefore work between markers.

Special Abbreviations

Work 5 tog (work 5 sts together) = with yarn at back of work, slip 3 sts purlwise, *pass 2nd st on right-hand needle over 1st (centre) st, slip centre st back to left-hand needle, pass 2nd st on left-hand needle over*, slip centre st back to right-hand needle; rep from * to * once more, purl centre st.

M1K, M3, M1K = see abbreviations on pages 20 and 21.

1st row (right side): T3B, T3F, p5, T3B, T3F.
2nd row: P2, k2, p2, k5, p2, k2, p2.
3rd row: K2, p2, T3F, p3, T3B, p2, k2.
4th row: P2, [k3, p2] 3 times.
5th row: K2, p3, T3F, p1, T3B, p3, k2.
6th row: P2, k4, p2, k1, p2, k4, p2.
7th row: K2, p4, T5BP, p4, k2.
8th row: As 6th row.
9th row: K2, p3, T3B, p1, T3F, p3, k2.
10th row: As 4th row.
11th row: K2, p2, T3B, p3, T3F, p2, k2.
12th row: As 2nd row.
13th row: T3F, T3B, p5, T3F, T3B.

14th row: K1, p4, k7, p4, k1.
15th row: P1, C4B, p7, C4F, p1.
16th row: As 14th row.
17th row: T3B, T5F, p1, T5B, T3F.
18th row: As 6th row.
19th row: K2, p4, work 5 tog, p4, k2. (13 sts)
20th row: P2, k9, p2.
21st row: K2, p9, k2.
22nd row: P2, k9, p2.
23rd row: K2, p4, M1K, M3, M1K, p4, k2. (17 sts)
24th row: P2, k4, p5, k4, p2.
25th row: K2, p1, C5B, k1, C5F, p1, k2.
26th row: P2, k1, p11, k1, p2.
27th row: K1, C4B, k7, C4F, k1.
28th row: P17.
29th row: C3B, k11, C3F.
30th row: P17.
31st row: K17.
32nd row: P17.
33rd to 36th rows: Rep the last 2 rows twice more.
37th row: C3F, k11, C3B.
38th row: P17.
39th row: K1, T4FP, k7, T4BP, k1.
40th row: As 26th row.
41st row: K2, p1, T5F, k1, T5B, p1, k2.
42nd row: As 24th row.
43rd to 47th rows: As 19th to 23rd rows.
48th row: As 6th row.
49th row: T3F, T5B, p1, T5F, T3B.
50th row: As 14th row.
51st row: P1, C4F, p7, C4B, p1.
52nd row: As 14th row.
Rep these 52 rows.

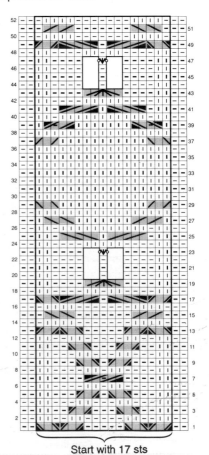

Start with 17 sts

= T4BP. = T4FP. = C5F. = C5B. = T5B. = T5F. = T5BP.

His and Her Aran Sweater

To Fit

Bust/Chest sizes

	85/90	95/100	105/110	cm
	34/36	38/40	42/44	ins

Finished measurement

	104	114	126	cm
	$41^{1}/_{2}$	$45^{1}/_{2}$	$50^{1}/_{2}$	ins

Length to shoulder

	64	68	72	cm
	$25^{1}/_{4}$	$26^{3}/_{4}$	$28^{1}/_{4}$	ins

Sleeve length

	45	47	48	cm
	$17^{3}/_{4}$	$18^{1}/_{2}$	19	ins

Shown in 95/100 cm [38/40 inch] size.

Materials

Aran type (Worsted Weight) knitting yarn

	1000	1200	1400	grams
	36	43	50	ounces

Pair needles each size 5mm (UK 6, USA 8) and 4mm (UK 8, USA 6).
Cable needle.

The quantities of yarn stated are based on average requirements and are therefore approximate.

For abbreviations see pages 20 and 21.

Instructions are given for the smallest size; larger sizes are given in ( )s. Figures or instructions given in [ ]s should be repeated as stated after the brackets. Where only one figure is given this applies to all sizes.

Tension

19 sts and 26 rows = 10 cm [4 ins] square measured over double moss stitch using larger needles.

Special Abbreviations

C6B or C6F (Cable 6 Back or Cable 6 Front) = slip next 3 sts on to cable needle and hold at back or front of work, knit next 3 sts from left hand needle, then knit sts from cable needle.

C4B or C4F (Cable 4 Back or Cable 4 Front) = slip next 2 sts on to cable needle and hold at back or front of work, knit next 2 sts from left hand needle, then knit sts from cable needle.

T4B (Twist 4 Back) = slip next 2 sts on to cable needle and hold at back of work, knit next 2 sts from left hand needle, then purl sts from cable needle.

T4F (Twist 4 Front) = slip next 2 sts on to cable needle and hold at front of work, purl next 2 sts from left hand needle, then knit sts from cable needle.

C4R (Cross 4 Right) = slip next st on to cable needle and hold at back of work, knit next 3 sts from left hand needle, then knit st from cable needle.

C4L (Cross 4 Left) = slip next 3 sts on to cable needle and hold at front of work, knit next st from left hand needle, then knit sts from cable needle.

T4R (Twist 4 Right) = slip next st on to cable needle and hold at back of work, knit next 3 sts from left hand needle, then purl st from cable needle.

T4L (Twist 4 Left) = slip next 3 sts on to cable needle and hold at front of work, purl next st from left hand needle, then knit sts from cable needle.

C7B (Cable 7 Back) = slip next 4 sts on to cable needle and hold at back of work, knit next 3 sts from left hand needle, then knit sts from cable needle.

Slip marker = make a slip knot in a short length of contrasting yarn and place on needle where indicated. On the following rows slip the marker from one needle to the other until pattern is established and marker is no longer required.

Diamond Panel

(Worked across 25 sts between markers).

1st row (right side): P8, C4R, p1, C4L, p8.
2nd row: K8, p4, k1, p4, k8.
3rd row: P7, C4R, p1, k1, p1, C4L, p7.
4th row: K7, p4, k1, p1, k1, p4, k7.
5th row: P6, C4R, p1, [k1, p1] twice, C4L, p6.
6th row: K6, p4, k1, [p1, k1] twice, p4, k6.
7th row: P5, C4R, p1, [k1, p1] 3 times, C4L, p5.
8th row: K5, p4, k1, [p1, k1] 3 times, p4, k5.
9th row: P4, C4R, p1, [k1, p1] 4 times, C4L, p4.
10th row: K4, p4, k1, [p1, k1] 4 times, p4, k4.
11th row: P3, C4R, p1, [k1, p1] 5 times, C4L, p3.
12th row: K3, p4, k1, [p1, k1] 5 times, p4, k3.

13th row: P2, C4R, p1, [k1, p1] 6 times, C4L, p2.
14th row: K2, p4, k1, [p1, k1] 6 times, p4, k2.
15th row: P2, k3, p1, [k1, p1] 7 times, k3, p2.
16th row: K2, p3, k1, [p1, k1] 7 times, p3, k2.
17th row: P2, T4L, p1, [k1, p1] 6 times, T4R, p2.
18th row: K3, p3, k1, [p1, k1] 6 times, p3, k3.
19th row: P3, T4L, p1, [k1, p1] 5 times, T4R, p3.
20th row: K4, p3, k1, [p1, k1] 5 times, p3, k4.
21st row: P4, T4L, p1, [k1, p1] 4 times, T4R, p4.
22nd row: K5, p3, k1, [p1, k1] 4 times, p3, k5.
23rd row: P5, T4L, p1, [k1, p1] 3 times, T4R, p5.
24th row: K6, p3, k1, [p1, k1] 3 times, p3, k6.
25th row: P6, T4L, p1, [k1, p1] twice, T4R, p6.
26th row: K7, p3, k1, [p1, k1] twice, p3, k7.
27th row: P7, T4L, p1, k1, p1, T4R, p7.
28th row: K8, p3, k1, p1, k1, p3, k8.
29th row: P8, T4L, p1, T4R, p8.
30th row: K9, p3, k1, p3, k9.
31st row: P9, C7B, p9.
32nd row: K9, p7, k9.

These 32 rows form the Diamond Panel.

Back

Using smaller needles cast on 85(95-105) sts.

1st row (right side): K1, *p1, k1; rep from * to end.
2nd row: P1, *k1, p1; rep from * to end.

Rep the last 2 rows until rib measure 8 cm [3 ins] ending with a right side row.

Next row (increase): Rib 1(5-8), *inc in each of next 2 sts, rib 1; rep from * to last 3(6-10) sts, inc in next st, rib to end. 140(152-164) sts.

Change to larger needles and commence pattern.

1st row: [P1, k1] 7(8-11) times, p1, *k6, slip marker, work 1st row of Diamond Panel across next 25 sts, slip marker, k6*, p4, [C4B, p4] 4(5-5) times; rep from * to *, p1, [k1, p1] 7(8-11) times.

2nd row: [K1, p1] 7(8-11) times, k1, *p6, work 2nd row of Diamond Panel, p6*, k4, [p4, k4] 4(5-5) times; rep from * to *, k1, [p1, k1] 7(8-11) times.

3rd row: [K1, p1] 6(7-10) times, k1, p2, C6B, work 3rd row of Diamond Panel, C6B, p2, [T4B, T4F] 4(5-5) times, p2, C6F, work 3rd row of Diamond Panel, C6F, p2, k1, [p1, k1] 6(7-10) times.

4th row: [P1, k1] 6(7-10) times, p1, *k2, p6, work 4th row of Diamond Panel, p6, k2*, p2, k4, [p4, k4] 3(4-4) times, p2; rep from * to *, p1, [k1, p1] 6(7-10) times.

His and Her Aran Sweater

These 4 rows form double moss st and cables at either side of Diamond Panels.

5th row: [P1, k1] 7(8-11) times, p1, *k6, work 5th row of Diamond Panel, k6*, p2, k2, p4, [C4F, p4] 3(4-4) times, k2, p2; rep from * to *, p1, [k1, p1] 7(8-11) times.

6th row: [K1, p1] 7(8-11) times, k1, *p6, work 6th row of Diamond Panel, p6*, k2, p2, k4, [p4, k4] 3(4-4) times, p2, k2; rep from * to *, k1, [p1,k1] 7(8-11) times.

7th row: [K1, p1] 6(7-10) times, k1, p2, C6B, work 7th row of Diamond Panel, C6B, p2, [T4F, T4B] 4(5-5) times, p2, C6F, work 7th row of Diamond Panel, C6F, p2, k1, [p1, k1] 6(7-10) times.

8th row: [P1, k1] 6(7-10) times, p1, k2, *p6, work 8th row of Diamond Panel, p6*, k4, [p4, k4] 4(5-5) times; rep from * to *, k2, p1, [k1, p1] 6(7-10) times.

These 8 rows form the trellis pattern at centre.

Keeping the 32 rows of Diamond Panel correct on sts between markers, continue in pattern as set until back measures 64(68-72) cm [25(26-28) ins] or required length to shoulder ending with a wrong side row.

Shape Shoulders

Next row: Cast off 47(52-56) sts, work until there are 46(48-52) sts on right-hand needle, cast off remaining 47(52-56) sts.

Slip remaining 46(48-52) sts on to a holder for neckband.

Front

Work as given for Back until front is 23(27-31) rows shorter than back to shoulder, thus ending with a right side row.

Shape Neck

Next row: Work 58(64-69) sts, turn and complete this side first.

★ Keeping pattern correct, dec 1 st at neck edge on next 7 rows, then following 4(5-6) alt rows. 47(52-56) sts remain. Work 7(9-11) rows straight thus ending with a wrong side row. Cast off.

Slip next 24(24-26) sts at centre on to a holder for neckband. With wrong side facing rejoin yarn to neck edge of remaining 58(64-69) sts and work to end.

Complete as given for first side from ★ to end.

Sleeves

Using smaller needles cast on 41(47-51) sts and work 8 cm [3 ins] in k1, p1 rib as given for Back ending with a right side row.

Next row (increase): Rib 1(6-2), *inc in each of next 2(2-1) sts, rib 1; rep from * to last 4(8-3) sts, inc in each of next 2(2-1) sts, rib to end. 67(71-75) sts.

Change to larger needles and commence pattern.

1st row: [P1, k1] 7(8-9) times, p1, k6, slip marker, work 1st row of Diamond Panel across next 25 sts, k6, p1, [k1, p1] 7(8-9) times.

2nd row: [K1, p1] 7(8-9) times, k1, p6, work 2nd row of Diamond Panel, p6, k1, [p1, k1] 7(8-9) times.

3rd row: [K1, p1] 6(7-8) times, k1, p2, C6B, work 3rd row of Diamond Panel, C6F, p2, k1, [p1, k1] 6(7-8) times.

4th row: [P1, k1] 6(7-8) times, p1, k2, p6, work 4th row of Diamond Panel, p6, k2, p1, [k1, p1] 6(7-8) times.

These 4 rows form double moss st and cables at either side of Diamond Panel. Keeping the cables and 32 rows of Diamond Panel correct as set and bringing extra sts into double moss st, inc 1 st

at each end of next and every following 5th(4th-4th) row until there are 101(91-121) sts.

2nd size only: Inc 1 st at each end of every following 5th row until there are 111 sts.

All sizes: Work straight until sleeve measures 45(47-48) cms [17(18-19) ins] or required length ending with a wrong side row. Cast off.

Finishing and Neckband

Block and press pieces according to instructions on ball band. Join left shoulder seam.

Neckband

Using smaller needles and with right side facing, work across sts on holder at back neck as follows: K2(3-2), *[k2tog] twice, k1; rep from * to last 4(4-5) sts, k2tog, knit to end. Pick up and k20(23-26) sts down left front slope, work across sts on holder at front neck as follows: K2(2-3), *[k2tog] twice, k1; rep from * to last 7(7-8) sts, [k2tog] twice, knit to end, then pick up and k20(23-26) sts up right front slope. 85(93-103) sts.

Starting with a 2nd row work 8 cm [3 ins] in k1, p1 rib as given for Back. Slip sts on to a length of yarn.

Join right shoulder seam and ends of neckband. Fold neckband in half to inside and slip stitch **loosely** in place allowing for stretch and taking care to catch every stitch.

Fold sleeves in half lengthways and mark centre of cast off edge. Sew sleeve to side edge placing centre at shoulder seam. Note: armhole should measure approximately 23(25-28) cm [9(10-11) ins].

Join side and sleeve seams.

Press seams if required.

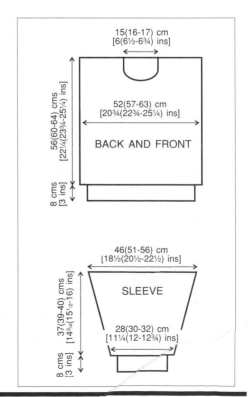

Aran Combinations

I. Panel of 64 sts on a background of reverse st st.

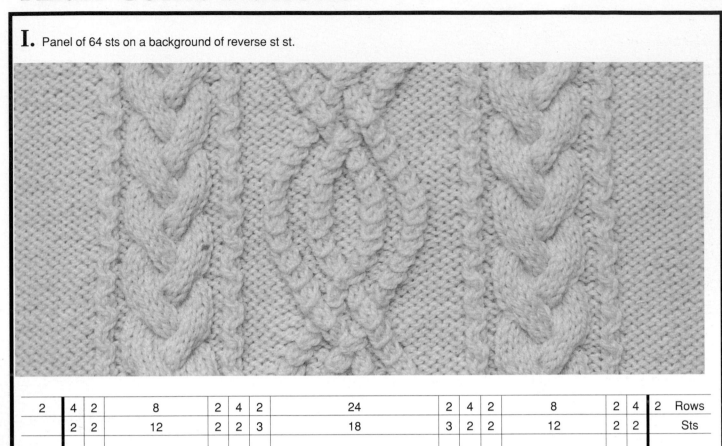

2	4	2	8	2	4	2	24	2	4	2	8	2	4	2	Rows
	2	2	12	2	2	3	18	3	2	2	12	2	2		Sts
★	4.1	★	8.6	★	4.1	★	24.14	★	4.1	★	8.6	★	4.1	★	

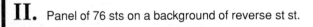

64 sts

★ = reverse st st.

II. Panel of 76 sts on a background of reverse st st.

2	4	2	24	2	4	2	24	2	4	2	24	2	4	2	Rows
	4	2	16	2	4	2	16	2	4	2	16	2	4		Sts
★	4.2	★	24.7 (start 13th row)	★	4.2	★	24.7 (start 1st row)	★	4.3	★	24.7 (start 13th row)	★	4.3	★	

76 sts

★ = reverse st st.

III. Panel of 84 sts on a background of st st.

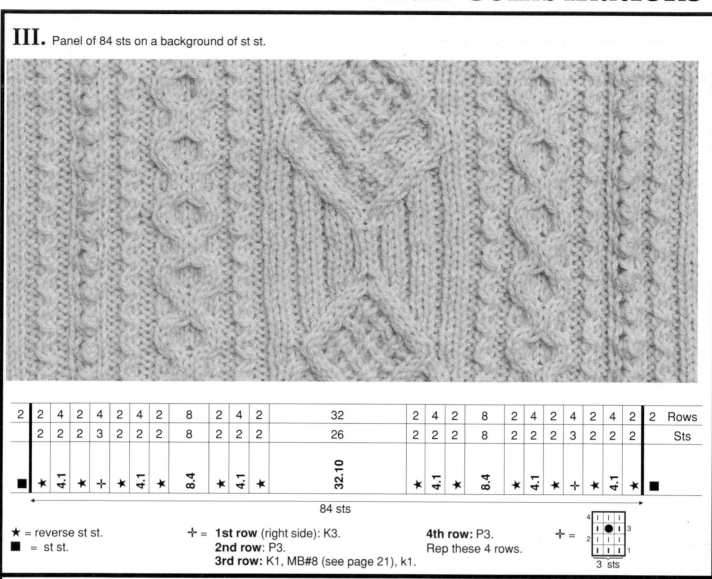

2	2	4	2	4	2	4	2	8	2	4	2	32	2	4	2	8	2	4	2	4	2	4	2	2	Rows
	2	2	2	3	2	2	2	8	2	2	2	26	2	2	2	8	2	2	2	3	2	2	2		Sts
■	★	4.1	★	+	★	4.1	★	8.4	★	4.1	★	32.10	★	4.1	★	8.4	★	4.1	★	+	★	4.1	★	■	

◀——————————————— 84 sts ———————————————▶

★ = reverse st st.
■ = st st.

+ = **1st row** (right side): K3.
2nd row: P3.
3rd row: K1, MB#8 (see page 21), k1.
4th row: P3.
Rep these 4 rows.

+ = 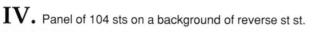 3 sts

---

IV. Panel of 104 sts on a background of reverse st st.

2	8	2	16	2	8	2	8	2	8	2	16	2	8	2	Rows
	4	2	22	2	4	1	34	1	4	2	22	2	4		Sts
★	8.5 (start 5th row)	★	16.11 (start 9th row)	★	8.5 (start 5th row)	★	8.24 Work edge sts in reverse st st	★	8.5 (start 1st row)	★	16.11 (start 1st row)	★	8.5 (start 1st row)	★	

◀——————————————— 104 sts ———————————————▶

★ = reverse st st.   Work each **16.11** between markers.

V. Panel of 88 sts on a background of double moss st (4.21).

4	16	2	2	8	2	8	2	8	2	2	16	4	Rows
	14	4	2	16	2	12	2	16	2	4	14		Sts
4.21	16.18 (start 1st row)	2.7	★	8.9	★	8.11	★	8.9	★	2.7	16.18 (start 9th row)	4.21	

88 sts

★ = reverse st st.

VI. Panel of 82 sts on a background of reverse st st.

2	6	2	18	2	6	2	18	2	6	2	18	2	6	2	Rows
	6	2	12	2	6	2	22	2	6	2	12	2	6		Sts
★	6.2	★	18.4	★	6.2	★	18.6	★	6.1	★	18.4	★	6.1	★	

82 sts

★ = reverse st st.

VII. Panel of 88 sts on a background of rice st (2.10).

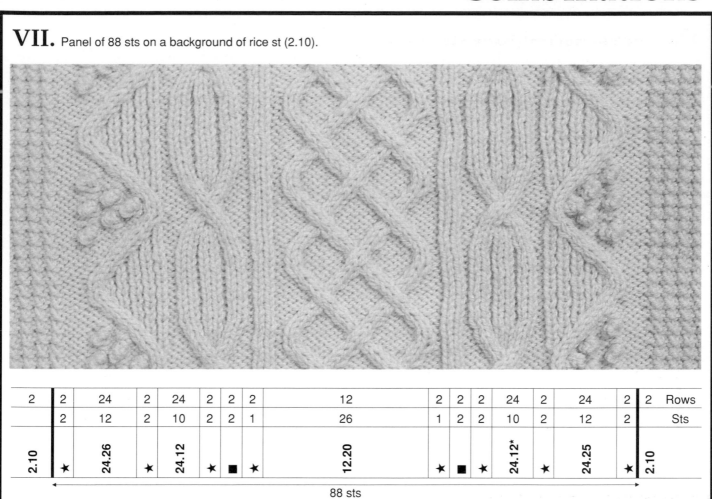

2	2	24	2	24	2	2	2	12	2	2	2	24	2	24	2	2	Rows
	2	12	2	10	2	2	1	26	1	2	2	10	2	12	2		Sts
2.10	★	24.26	★	24.12	★	■	★	12.20	★	■	★	24.12*	★	24.25	★	2.10	

← 88 sts →

★ = reverse st st.   ■ = stocking st.   *Substitute C4B for C4F when working panel **24.12** on right of central panel (**12.20**).

VIII. Panel of 114 sts on a background of reverse st st.

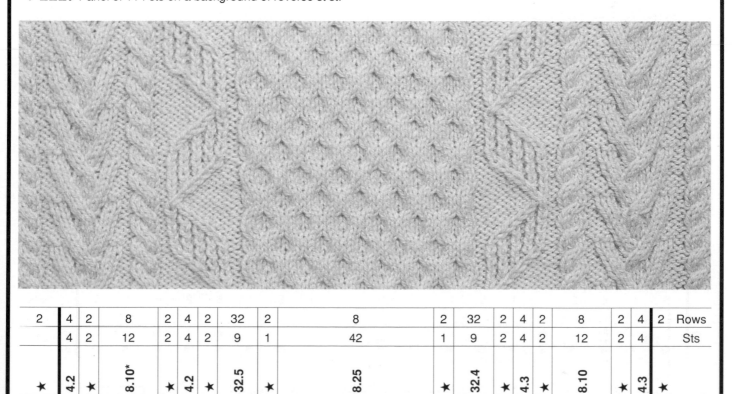

2	4	2	8	2	4	2	32	2	8	2	32	2	4	2	8	2	4	2	Rows
	4	2	12	2	4	2	9	1	42	1	9	2	4	2	12	2	4		Sts
★	4.2	★	8.10*	★	4.2	★	32.5	★	8.25	★	32.4	★	4.3	★	8.10	★	4.3	★	

← 114 sts →

★ = reverse st st.   *Substitute C4F for C4B when working panel **8.10** on left of central panel (**8.25**).

Aran Combinations

IX. Panel of 84 sts on a background of reverse st st.

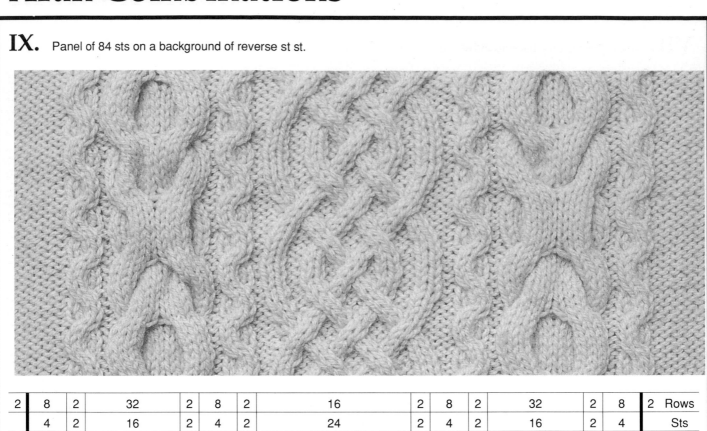

2	8	2	32	2	8	2	16	2	8	2	32	2	8	2 Rows
	4	2	16	2	4	2	24	2	4	2	16	2	4	Sts
★	8.5	★	32.1	★	8.5	★	16.14	★	8.5	★	32.1	★	8.5	★

84 sts

★ = reverse st st.

X. Panel of 75 sts on a background of rice st (2.10).

2	2	2	16	2	16	2	2	2	8	2	2	2	16	2	16	2	2	2 Rows
	5	1	6	2	6	1	5	1	21	1	5	1	6	2	6	1	5	Sts
2.10	✪	★	4.13*	★	4.13*	★	✪	★	8.8	★	✪	★	4.12*	★	4.12*	★	✪	2.10

75 sts

★ = reverse st st.

✪ = **1st row** (right side): P1, [KB1, p1] twice.
2nd row: K1, [p1, k1] twice.
Rep these 2 rows.

✪ =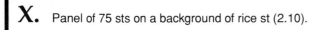

5 sts

*On **4.12** and **4.13** cross cables on 3rd and every following 16th row, working extra rows in st st.

XI.
Panel of 118 sts on a background of rice st (2.10).

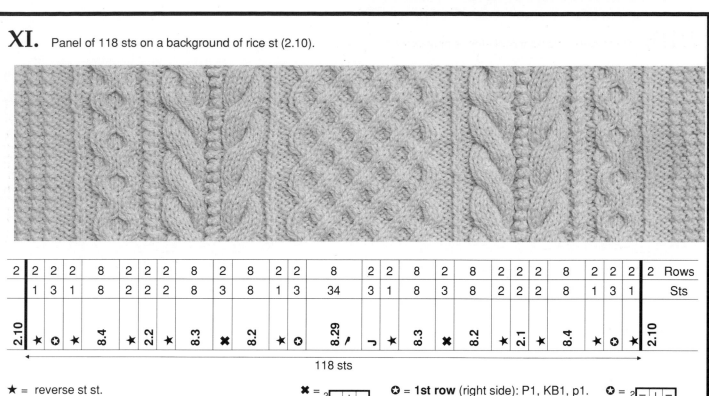

2	2	2	2	8	2	2	2	8	2	8	2	2	8	2	2	8	2	8	2	2	2	8	2	2	2	2	Rows
	1	3	1	8	2	2	2	8	3	8	1	3	34	3	1	8	3	8	2	2	2	8	1	3	1		Sts
2.10	★	✪	★	8.4	★	2.2	★	8.3	✖	8.2	★	✪	8.29 ╱	J	★	8.3	✖	8.2	★	2.1	★	8.4	★	✪	★	2.10	

← 118 sts →

★ = reverse st st.
✖ = **1st row** (right side): P1, MB#1 (see page 21), p1.
2nd row: K1, p1, k1.
Rep these 2 rows.

✪ = **1st row** (right side): P1, KB1, p1.
2nd row: K1, p1, k1.
Rep these 2 rows.

XII.
Panel of 103 sts on a background of double moss st (4.21).

4	2	6	2	24	2	6	2	48	2	6	2	24	2	6	2	4	Rows
	2	6	2	17	2	6	2	29	2	6	2	17	2	6	2		Sts
4.21	★	6.2	★	24.9	★	6.2	★	48.1	★	6.1	★	24.9	★	6.1	★	4.21	

← 103 sts →

★ = reverse st st.

Aran Combinations

XIII.
Panel of 100 sts on a background of double moss st (4.21).

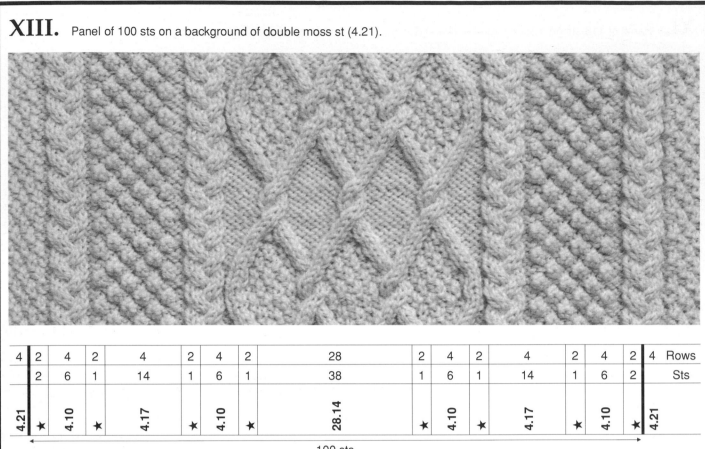

4	2	4	2	4	2	4	2	28	2	4	2	4	2	4	2	4	Rows
	2	6	1	14	1	6	1	38	1	6	1	14	1	6	2		Sts
4.21	★	4.10	★	4.17	★	4.10	★	28.14	★	4.10	★	4.17	★	4.10	★	4.21	

100 sts

★ = reverse st st.

XIV.
Panel of 64 sts on a background of double moss st (4.21).

4	2	2	2	2	2	8	2	24	2	8	2	2	2	2	2	4	Rows
	1	2	2	2	2	6	2	30	2	6	2	2	2	2	1		Sts
4.21	★	2.2	★	2.2	★	6.1*	★	24.18	★	6.2*	★	2.1	★	2.1	★	4.21	

64 sts

★ = reverse st st.   *On **6.1** and **6.2** cross cables on 3rd and every following 8th row, working extra rows in st st.

FAIR ISLE
KNITTING

FAIR ISLE KNITTING

Fair Isle Knitting is the combination of design repeats and motifs using a selection of pattern and background colours. While Aran knitting combines panels of stitches for its texture and effect, Fair Isle knitting uses stocking stitch with bands and blocks of variable coloured designs to create an original design. The actual patterns are made up of either vertical or horizontal sections which are made to relate.

The objective of this book is not to provide a myriad of knitted patterns which can be slavishly copied, but to give the knitter inspiration, remove the fear of experimentation and provide examples of how colour changes a pattern design. The book indicates what ingredients are necessary for the knitter to create a recipe to their own taste. The knitter can become a designer and, with a blank piece of graph paper, draw a freestyle design. This needs confidence, but no formal training.

The approach in this book is to show that Fair Isle designs are combinations of bricks (the borders) and mortar (the peeries) that can be built into patterns. The process is simple if certain steps are followed. There is a catalogue of peeries, borders, patterns and motifs that can be developed and coloured to change even simple patterns of the same design.

The book explains the history of Fair Isle knitting and the specific techniques required, such as stranded and circular knitting, but above all it concentrates on patterns and designs, both horizontal and vertical. The pages 120 to 122 should be studied very carefully because they explain how a pattern is built by combining bands of knitting. These bands are created from motifs, and their repeats, peeries, which are strips of repeats, and borders, which are blocks of repeats all of which can be edged with seeding patterns. Understand the principle of developing a pattern using these building blocks and Fair Isle design is simple.

The basic stitch is simple and constant. The book, therefore, uses charts with occasional photographs to demonstrate the relationship to the actual piece of knitting. As Fair Isle is about design and the use of colour, we have shown how garments can be 'built', how colour can change a pattern and that background and main colours can be planned and varied according to taste.

Historical Fair Isle designs were limited by the technology that could not create fast colour dyes, and the geography of an isolated island population living on the cultural fringe of the North Sea! Designs, however, are unlimited and, today, colour is only controlled by 'what goes with what', and what is available.

We have used colour charts, black and white charts with symbols and photography. We have given examples of patterns, a 'traditional beret' worked in rounds, a lady's top, where we have also shown how the pattern was 'built', and a man's sleeveless pullover in muted the colours which were so typical of the designs made famous in the 1920's and 1930's by the Prince of Wales and the fashionable 'golfing set'.

Fair Isle Knitting

Origins of Fair Isle Knitting

The history of Fair Isle or stranded knitting is not quite so straightforward to trace as that of Aran knitting. Much mystery surrounds the development of the distinctive patterns that take their name from the tiny island of Fair Isle, the southernmost of the Shetland Isles. A rugged and windswept group of over 100 islands situated about 200 miles off the northeast tip of Scotland and 180 miles from the west coast of Norway.

While the location may seem remote the Shetlands are actually at a crossroads for trading fleets from the North and Baltic seas. These routes along with the rich fishing grounds have made the Islands a convenient and frequently visited maritime trading centre since the Vikings took temporary control in the ninth century.

The Shetland Islands were annexed into Scottish rule by James II in the mid seventeenth century. It is probably from this time that knitting flourished into a major cottage industry. Sheep native to the Shetlands tend to be small and sturdy, producing soft fine wool ideal for hand knitted hosiery.

Cottage industries continued to thrive until the advent of the industrial revolution in the early 1800's when the hand knitted stocking and hosiery trade went into decline. It is well recorded that the Shetlanders were forced to develop lace knitting, which had been evolving for some time. But what was happening on Fair Isle?

We know Fair Isle knitting existed on the island as early as 1681 from coins designs discovered in knitting preserved in a peat bog. What is still not known is whether this was brought to the island by a traveller, trader or local islander and why there is no mention of the distinctive and colourful patterning until 1856.

Although romantic theories suggested a link with Spain, from the shipwreck of a Spanish Armada in 1588. It is probable that early pieces where brought to the islands from the Baltic States where the craft of stranded knitting was already more advanced and colour dyes more readily available. These could then have been copied by the islanders.

There was also a colour explosion and rapid development of stranded knitting in the Baltic region around 1800 which coincided with an upsurge in trade between the Baltic countries and the Shetlands. Open work techniques that had appeared so frequently in Baltic stranded knitting before 1850, also started to disappear.

If we acknowledge the influence of foreign sources and the islanders own propensity and self sufficiency, it seems more likely that colour stranded knitting evolved as a natural progression of Fair Isle which went unrecorded due to concentration on lace knitting throughout the Shetlands.

Although the earliest museum pieces of Fair Isle, dated 1850, are all highly developed and liberally coloured there is evidence of experimentation and they are not knitted in Shetland yarn. Later pieces, however, display clear evidence of pattern and colour experimentation, and were knitted in Shetland wool. The Shetlanders, with their history of a hand knitting industry, added to their later developed knowledge of lacemaking, had come to dislike repetition. They took the oxo, star, tree (not a natural choice for the windswept islanders) from Russia, Estonia and Norway. They created lozenge shapes and circular patterned yokes but altered them by preserving the complexity of design while elaborating the colours in the centre. Changing colours within the design became a hallmark of Fair Isle.

By the end of the 19th century the knitters of Fair Isle had worked their patterns into the traditional loose gansey. This was the step that enabled the knitters of Fair Isle to supply a new fashion market. The demand for hand knitted lace was dwindling as machines were developed. By 1910 stranded knitting had become increasingly popular with the Edwardians. All over Shetland the old patterns of Fair Isle were being copied and passed from croft to croft. The style became both fashionable and distinctive.

The 1920's were a period of innovation and development with the Shetland and Fair Isle knitters continuing to experiment with patterns and colours. In line with fundamental change in fashion after The Great War, in favour of more practical and liberated styles, the most important development was the arrival of the fisherman's working jersey or gansey as a fashion garment for the wealthy and middle classes.

In 1921, the Prince of Wales wore a Fair Isle pullover, presented to him by James Smith, a Lerwick draper, which he wore to play golf at St. Andrews. The popularity of the Prince and his travels guaranteed that the Fair Isle sweater or cardigan would become very fashionable clothing.

Techniques

Circular Knitting

Circular knitting or knitting in the round produces a seamless fabric. Stitches cast on and knitted in the round continuously on a circular needle (twin-pin) or set of 4 needles without shaping will produce a tubular fabric.

There are many advantages to working in the round. It is much quicker since the knitting is never turned at the end of each row. The right side of the work is always facing you and **every** row is knitted when working in stocking stitch. The number of rows worked for the back and front will always be the same, and there are fewer seams to join.

Colour and texture patterns are easier too. By looking at the right side all the time you can see how the pattern is developing. For Fair Isle designs the colour not in use is always at the back of the work and colours are always in the correct position at the start of a round when they are next needed, thereby avoiding breaking off the yarns.

Until the end of the 19th century almost all knitting was worked in the round. However today, it is not so popular except for traditional garments and items like hats and berets. These are cast on at the lower edge and decreased in to the centre with regular decrease rounds. The shape of the top of the hat is governed by the number of stitches decreased in a round, and the number of rounds between each decrease round.

Patterns for socks and gloves worked in the round on sets of 4 needles are also available. These are ideal for circular knitting as seams are often bulky and uncomfortable in such small items.

Using a Circular Needle

A circular needle or twin pin, has two pointed ends joined by a length of flexible nylon. This kind of needle comes in a range of sizes, from 40 cm [16 ins] to 120 cm [47 ins]. For each size there is a minimum number of stitches required - those which, at a given tension, will fit around the needle without stretching. Many more than this minimum will, however, fit on the needle.

1. To start work, cast on to one point the number of stitches required. It is a good idea to wind an elastic band around the other point to prevent the stitches from slipping off.

2. Spread the stitches along the whole length of the needle and check to make sure that they are not twisted. This step is **vital**; once the work is joined into a circle the stitches cannot be untwisted.

3. Hold the needle so that the point with the first cast-on stitch is in your left hand, with the ball end of the yarn on the right-hand point. Place a marker over the right-hand point and work the first stitch on the left-hand point, pulling the yarn firmly to prevent a gap.

4. Work around to the marker to complete one round. Slip the marker and continue with the next round. Proceed in this manner, always slipping the marker at the beginning of a round and pulling the yarn firmly at this point.

Using Double- pointed Needles

Double-pointed needles must be used if you have only a few stitches. These are most commonly available in sets of four. The stitches are divided evenly on to three of the needles and the remaining needle is used for the knitting. As each needle becomes free, it becomes the working needle.

1. Cast the required number of stitches on to an ordinary needle or circular needle, then slip one-third of them on to each double-pointed needle. (This is easier than casting on to the double-pointed needles).

2. Make sure that the stitches are not twisted, then draw the needles into a triangular shape as shown. Place a marker on the needle holding the last cast-on stitch, then use the free needle to work the first stitch to the left. Pull the yarn across tightly to prevent a gap.

3. When you have finished working all the stitches on one needle, continue with those on the next. At the end of the round slip the marker and begin the next round.

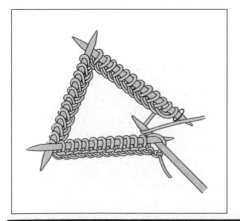

> ☆ **TIP** ☆
>
> The nylon joining the two points of a circular needle should be straightened before use. Immerse the needle in a bowl of hot water for ten to fifteen minutes, then straighten it out by pulling.

Slip Markers

A slip marker is required to mark the beginning of a round in circular knitting or certain parts of a pattern. Plastic ring markers can be used, or you can make one by tying a loop in a short piece of contrasting yarn. The marker is placed on the left-hand needle where indicated and is slipped onto the right-hand needle on every row or round.

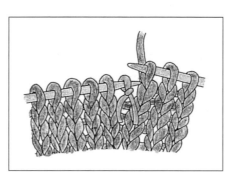

Steek

This is an old Scottish word that means to close or fasten. It is used to describe the methods of joining armholes and fronts of cardigans while knitting in the round. There are several methods of working steeks and it is worth experimenting before embarking on a garment. In all cases it is necessary to work an extra stitch on either side of the steek. These edge stitches are then used when picking up the sleeves and front bands.

Knitted steeks are worked by casting on an extra eight to ten stitches at the opening, which are then knitted in alternate colours. The first and last of these stitches are edge stitches. When the knitting is finished cut up the centre of the steek.

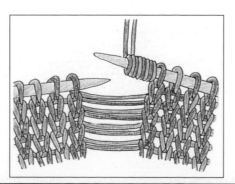

Wound steeks are formed winding the pattern and background yarns loosely around the right-hand needle. On the following round these loops are dropped off the needle and another set are made.

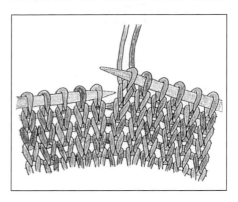

This method results in a wide ladder which is then cut up the middle.

Finishing Steeks

Once the sleeves and bands have worked the steeks have to be finished. Each of the yarn ends for a wound have to be darned in. Knitted steeks should be trimmed so that two stitches are left inside the edge stitch. These are then folded back and slip stitched in place, taking care to catch every stitch.

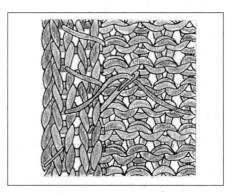

Stranded Knitting

'Fair Isle' has become the general term for multi-coloured stocking stitch patterns in which two or more colours are worked across a single row of knitting. Traditional patterns however only use two colours in any row or round. By changing the colour of the pattern stitches on some rows you can make the work more colourful. This can also be achieved by changing the background stitches, or ultimately both sets of stitches, (see 6.11 on page 137).

For stranded knitting the colour not in use is carried **loosely** across the wrong side of the work. If strands must be carried over more than six stitches, there is a danger that they could be pulled when the garment is put on or taken off. To avoid this you should twist together the yarn being used with the yarn not in use every third or fourth stitch.

As well as mastering the technique of

Techniques

working with two colours, it is vital to watch out for problems with the tension. The yarn must be stranded very loosely - loosely enough to maintain the elasticity of the fabric; this is difficult to achieve until you have practised the techniques involved and feel relaxed with the work. If you pull the strands even slightly you will buckle the work, giving the finished fabric a puckered, uneven appearance, and thus making the piece too small.

1. On a knit row, hold the first colour in your right hand and the second colour in your left hand. Work as normal with the first colour carrying the second loosely across the wrong side of the work.

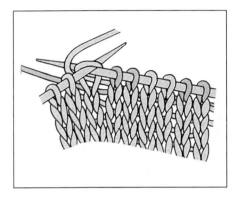

2. When the second colour is required, insert the right-hand needle into the next stitch and draw through a loop of the left-hand yarn; carry the yarn in the right hand loosely across the wrong side until next required.

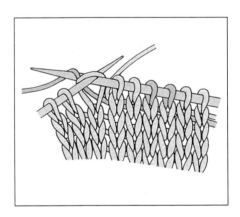

For Flat knitting:

3. On a purl row, work as usual with the first colour held in the right hand, holding the second colour in the left hand.

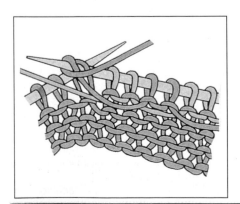

4. To purl a stitch in the second colour, insert the right-hand needle purlwise into the next stitch and draw through a loop of the left-hand yarn.

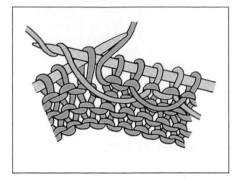

Stranded knitting should look neat on the wrong side as well as the right. Always keep each colour in the same hand throughout and take both of them to the end of the rows. Twisting them together once at the end of the row to keep them in place, helps to give the fabric a professional appearance.

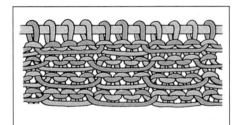

If you find it awkward to hold the yarns in both hands, simply work as usual, dropping the yarn not in use and picking it up again when required, making sure to keep it loose. Always carry the same colour across the top throughout the round or row for a neat appearance on the wrong side and to prevent the yarns from becoming twisted.

Weaving

Weaving in yarns should only be done if there are more than six stitches worked in one colour. The yarns can be crossed over each other on every third or fourth stitch to avoid long, loose strands or 'floats'. Simply lay the colour not in use across the yarn being used before working the next stitch.

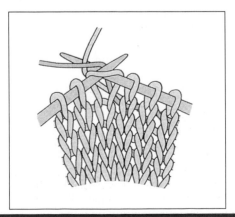

If this is done on every stitch it creates a woven effect on the wrong side of the work. The back of a woven fabric looks extremely neat but this method distorts the shape of the stitches and alters the tension. Unless the pattern specifically states that this method should be used, **do not** weave the yarn in but follow the stranding method. Weaving also tends to create a solid, less elastic fabric than the stranding method.

Two Colour Ribbing

Many Fair Isle garments feature two colour or corrugated ribbing. When working k2, p2 rib with right side facing all the knit stitches are worked in one colour and the purl stitches in another. The yarn not in use is always stranded across the wrong side of the work.

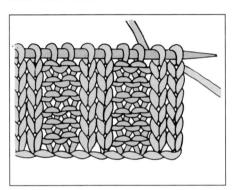

Joining in New Yarn

Always join in a new ball of yarn at the start of a row wherever possible. As a general guide, for a stocking stitch or fairly plain fabric, you can estimate whether there is sufficient yarn remaining in the old ball to complete a row of knitting. Lay the knitting flat and see if the yarn reaches at least three times across the width - that is the length you need to finish a stocking stitch row. If in doubt join in the new ball at the start of the row to avoid the frustration of running out of yarn in the middle of a row and having to unpick the stitches worked.

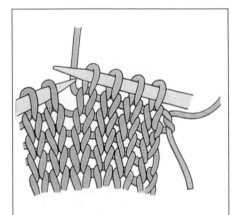

To make a perfect join at the edge of the work, simply drop the old yarn and start working the row with the new yarn. After a few stitches, tie the old and new ends in a loose knot. The ends can be darned into the seam at a later stage.

For circular knitting, when it is impossible to avoid joining in the middle of a round, just drop the old yarn leaving sufficient length to sew in, pick up the new yarn leaving sufficient length and continue knitting with it. After a few more rows have been completed, the ends of yarn should be darned in to secure them.

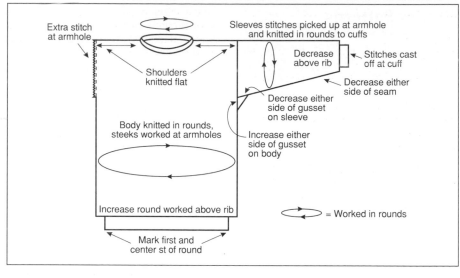

Securing Ends

An end of yarn simply woven around the stitches will soon work itself loose once the garment is worn. To secure the end properly, weave the yarn loosely around a few stitches, then double back on the woven-in end splitting those stitches already worked, use a sharp needle (easier for splitting the yarn) rather than the blunt-ended needle necessary for seaming. Make sure the yarn is not pulled tightly as it will distort the knitting. Stretch the fabric before fastening off the yarn to loosen the woven in end. Make sure also that the woven in end is not visible from the right side.

Never tie knots in the yarn as these will almost invariably come undone or work their way through to the right side. Any knots found in the yarn should also be undone.

Tension/Gauge

Knitting tension/gauge refers to the number of stitches and rows in a given area. If you are adding a Fair Isle pattern to a stocking stitch garment, bear in mind that the tension will probably not be the same. Generally the stitches tend to be 'squarer' than in plain stocking stitch; in other words, the number of stitches to 10 cm [4 ins] is often the same as the number of rows to the same measurement, whereas in plain stocking stitch there are more rows than stitches. Always work a tension piece beforehand, as tension can vary enormously between different Fair Isle patterns.

Constructing a Fair Isle Sweater

Traditionally garments were knitted in such a way that there are no seams to be joined.

Firstly, the body is worked in the round, increasing directly after the rib, up to just below the armholes. An underarm gusset is then worked by regular increases either side of the seam stitches. The gusset stitches are placed on holders until the sleeves are worked. An extra stitch is

then cast on at the armhole edges and 'steeks' (see page 117) are worked between them. The body is continued in the round until the neck opening is reached. The neck stitches are put on a holder, then the shoulders are knitted flat using double pointed needles and working from the right side only. These stitches are then cast off or grafted together. The stitches for the neckband are picked up and worked in the round. The 'steeks' are cut and then the sleeves are picked up through the edge stitch and worked downwards, creating a gusset at the top edge of the underarm by decreasing more frequently either side of the seam stitch at the top of the sleeve, then more gradually to the cuff. A decrease round is then worked above the cuff, which is ribbed and then cast off. All the loose ends then have to be finished off on the wrong side of the garment.

For a jacket, the body is still worked in the round, with a 'steek' at the centre front, which is cut before the front bands are worked. The neckband, button and buttonhole bands are all worked flat.

Many patterns can be adapted for circular knitting by simply casting on the back and front stitches together. Remember to reverse the instructions for the wrong side rows (i.e. knit instead of purl and vice versa). The work will have to be divided at the armholes and worked in rows as the pattern instructions. For the sleeves, cast on the number of stitches stated and join into a ring, working the increases at the underarm edge (i.e. the beginning and end of each round). Remember when working in rib that the same stitches are knitted and purled on every round.

Patterns and Design

There are several features that are typical of Fair Isle knitting. Firstly no more than two colours, which change frequently, are used in any one row and secondly that the patterns contains diagonal lines. These

are particularly important because they keep the fabric elastic as the change over positions constantly change. If the colour changes are in the same position vertically the fabric tends to be less elastic and weaker at the change over point.

Another characteristic of this type of knitting is the symmetry within the patterns. Symetrical patterns are easy to remember, and therefore quicker to produce. Once the first line has been completed it acts as a guide for the following rows. Lozenges and crosses are two shapes that have four or more lines of symmetry, they also fit together well to form the basic OXO pattern that features so prominently in Fair Isle knitting. The patterning possibilities of the OXO is endless, and only the smallest changes need to be made to create another patterns.

Asymmetrical patterns and patterns with no symmetry can also feature in Fair Isle knitting, however they have disadvantages, firstly the patterning may not be regular, therefore more difficult to remember and more time consuming to knit, and secondly the use of colour is more limited (see Knitting with Colour on page 123).

Types of Patterns

Fair Isle designs generally are made up of horizontal bands of patterning. These bands can vary from as little as one row to thirty or more rows. Other designs can be made of panels of patterning, or alternatively all-over patterns. The patterns can be grouped together by the number of rows each uses.

Peeries

Peeries patterns have between one and seven rows, and they are used to separate the larger bands of patterning. In addition they can be worked vertically and placed between patterns worked as panels (see page 121).

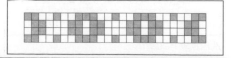

Patterns and Design

Border Patterns

These are patterns that have nine to fifteen rows. Border patterns are very versatile, they can be worked at the edges of garments or combined with peeries and Large Fair Isle Patterns to produce all-over designs.

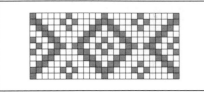

Large Fair Isle Patterns

These have more than fifteen rows and are generally based on the OXO.

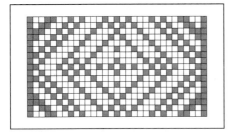

Norwegian Stars

This category of stitch is based on star patterns which have the same number of stitches and rows. They can be worked singly as motifs, repeated across the width of the fabric in bands or repeated in depth as panels.

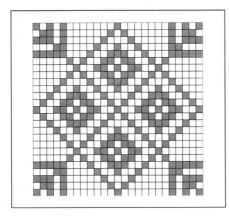

All-over Patterns

As the name suggests the patterns is repeated across the full width and depth of the knitting. Rather than giving a separate category for this type of stitch, we

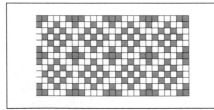

All-over Pattern

have illustrated many of the stitches in the other sections as all-over patterns. Small repeats or seeding patterns are useful as filling stitches between panels and bands.

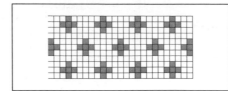

Seeding Pattern

Working from Charts

Knitting instructions for a Fair Isle pattern are usually given in **chart form**. This gives a visual impression of how the design will look when knitted. A single pattern repeat of the complete design (which must be worked across the width of the fabric) is shown as a chart on a squared grid. The colours in the pattern are represented either by symbols identified in an adjacent key, or by colours corresponding to the yarns. The Fair Isle charts in this book use colour to indicate the pattern, see the Colour Chart on page 123 for the selection of colours used.

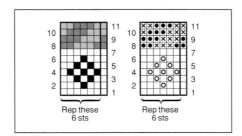

Each square on the chart represents a single stitch; each horizontal line of squares, a row of knitting. The details of how to follow a chart are usually given with the pattern but generally the following rules apply.

Rows

For stocking stitch, work across a line of squares from right to left for the knit rows, then follow the line immediately above from left to right for the purl rows. Odd numbers - 1, 3, 5, etc - at the right-hand edge usually indicate the knit rows, while even numbers - 2, 4, 6, etc - at the left-hand edge denote the purl rows. For a completely symmetrical pattern or if working in the round, every row may be read from right to left. To make following a chart easier, use a row counter or place a ruler above the row being worked and move the ruler up as each row is completed.

Stitches

Usually only one repeat of the pattern is given in the chart and must be repeated across the width of the material. This section is usually contained within bold vertical lines with a bracketed indication that it is to be repeated across the row. There may be extra stitches at either end

which are edge stitches worked at the beginning and end of rows to complete the pattern so that the rows are symmetrical or 'balanced'. **Note:** For each chart in this book the repeat has given, in addition a bigger area has been shown, to illustrate the effect of the pattern. In many cases the pattern has been repeated vertically as well as horizontally, so it appears as an all-over pattern.

Patterns Arrangements

The simplest form of Fair Isle knitting is to repeat a single pattern over the entire width and depth of the fabric. However more interesting effects can be achieved by adding different stitch patterns. By combining peerie and border patterns the design potential increases, from alternating a peerie and border pattern to more complicated arrangements.

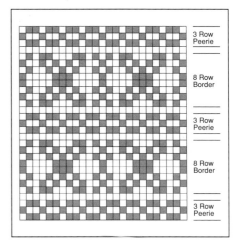

Alternating peerie and border patterns

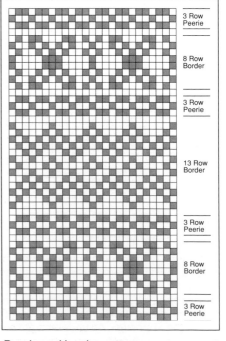

Peerie and border patterns arrangement

Another way of arranging patterns is in vertical panels (see next page). A typical

Patterns and Design

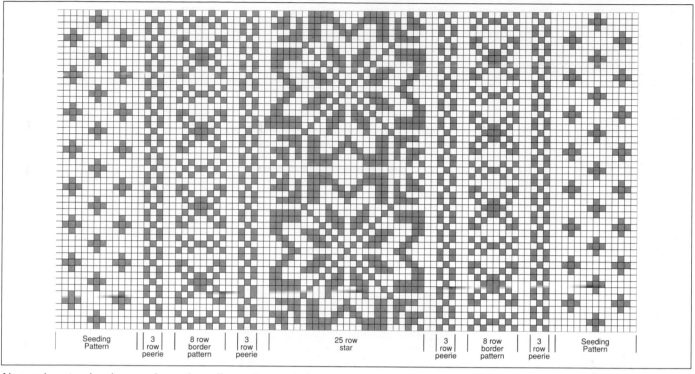

Norwegian star, border, peerie, and seeding pattern panel arrangement

arrangement would have a central panel of a Norwegian star, with peeries, borders and seeding patterns either side.

When combining patterns it is necessary to consider the stitch repeat and position of each of the individual elements as well as the method of knitting. For circular knitting the total number of stitches in the round **must** be divisible by the number of stitches in the repeat and that the balancing stitches are **not** required. For flat knitting the stitches at either side edge should be the same, therefore the balancing stitches are required.

Plan the finished pattern on graph paper. The main feature should be at the horizontal centre of the fabric and repeated outwards. To achieve this the central stitch of the pattern has to be identified - in most cases this is the middle stitch of the chart given. Once the main feature has been positioned the other patterns can be added. Choose stitches that have compatible stitch repeats, for example if the central pattern has a twelve stitch repeat choose bands with two, three, four or six stitch repeats. The position of these should also be considered, in relation to

the main feature and the centre of the fabric. The illustration below left has each stitch pattern centred horizontally, these are within the bold lines and would be repeated across the whole width (or round) of the fabric, working the balancing stitch or stitches as required.

Centre Stitches

Some patterns can be centred on more than one point and it may be preferable to change the centre of subsequent patterns. In the illustration below the original

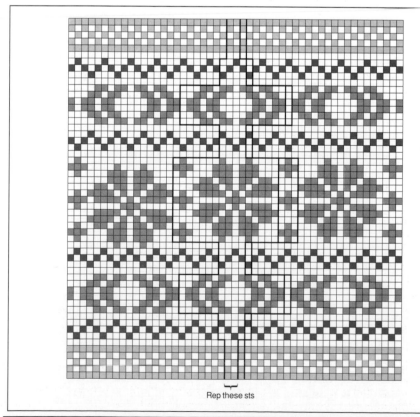

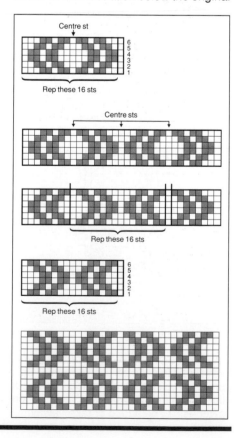

Patterns and Design

chart has been repeated, the additional centre points indicated and from this a new repeat has been given. By changing the centre of a stitch the number of design options available is greatly increased.

Creating Patterns

It is very easy to create a different pattern in Fair Isle knitting. Firstly by combining different peeries and borders etc, secondly by changing the starting point of individual patterns and combining them, and thirdly by altering an existing pattern.

When working in the round the total number of stitches must be divisible by the stitch repeat. It may therefore be necessary to adjust the repeat of a pattern, OXO's are particularly suitable for increasing or decreasing. More or less stitches can be worked between the individual elements, and these can be worked as background or pattern depending on the effect required. In the illustration below four variations of the original repeat have been given, in each case the X has remained the same and the space between or the O have been adjusted

Rep these 12 sts

Rep these 14 sts

Rep these 14 sts

Rep these 10 sts

Rep these 8 sts

In addition to adjusting the repeat, small variations to patterns can be made. Solid areas of colour can be replaced with outlines, outlines can be filled and pattern stitches can be added or taken away.

Once you become familiar with varying something that exists, the next step is to start experimenting and create your own patterns. Start by drawing a basic shape, a cross for example, on graph paper and then add, or take away pattern stitches. It is important remember to change from background to pattern and vis versa frequently and avoid too many change overs in vertical lines. The diagram on the right is an example of a geometric progression, this method of work can be done with any shape. Only by experimentation can the full possibilities of Fair Isle patterning be attained, so don't be afraid to try!

The source of a pattern can come from anywhere, from plants and flowers, carvings and architecture, or even the design on a carpet. The inspiration can be a shape or the starting point to an all-over pattern. Just put the initial idea down on graph paper and let it progress geometrically.

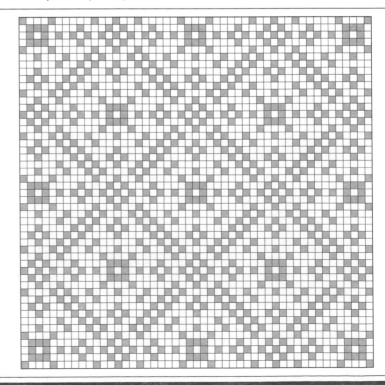

A middle eastern carpet, the inspiration for the all-over pattern (below).

A geometric progression

Knitting with Colour

Traditional Fair Isle knitting only uses two colours in any row. This may sound limiting but it is not. The background and pattern colours can both change on every row to give a multitude of colour schemes. However this is not necessary to acheive colourful garments.

In traditional Fair Isle garments the colour changes reflect the symmetry of the patterns, both the pattern and the background colours can be mirrored either side of the centre row. In many cases the colours are shaded from light to dark, and then back to light agian, using subtle changes. The patterns on pages 164 to 173 have been worked in this way, they also illustrate that the colours used and their relationship to one and other can completely alter the patterns appearance.

The use of colour can be very daunting and it can be easier to opt for colours that someone else has put together rather than chosing new ones. Anyone can put colours together, it is just a matter of experimentation and patience until you get the required result. A large selection of different coloured and toned yarns makes the task easier, also a good colour range of coloured pencils or felt pens can help. Start by colouring the pattern on gragh paper with the intial choice of colours. From this visual impression you can see whether the pattern looks balanced, and the colours work well together if not try other colour combinations. Once you have a pleasing result, devise ways of improving it, try reversing some of the background and pattern colours or working from light to dark to light, or vise versa.

It then helps to actually knit swatches of some of the pleasing effects, and then make improvements to these. The more colour samples and swatches you do and the easier it will become.

Simple colour schemes, using shades of a colour rather than different hues, can be very effective. More interest can be given by having a light background in some areas and dark in others.

Take inspiration from your surroundings, autumn trees, spring flowers, brick walls, anything that is coloured can be a starting point and can encourage you to mix colours that do not appear to work.

To help you begin each of the stitches on the following pages has different colourways given in chart form. These are just suggestions of what can be done and illustrate how you can plan other schemes. All the charts and knitted samples have all been worked in a range of 22 colours and these have been shown in the table below.

The knitted swatches have often been extensions of the original pattern with peeries added, the starting point changed or the rows of the chart worked in reverse order.

☆ TIPS ☆

If you are working out your own fair Isle pattern for flat knitting, make sure that colours are joined in at the same edge each time to avoid breaking the yarns unnecessarily.

For very small areas of colour, you may find it easier and neater to swiss darn (or duplicate) the stitches rather than knitting them in (see page 124).

Finishing Touches

Knitted garments and accessories may be further embellished with various trimmings sewn or tied in place.

Fringing

Fringing is often worked along the edge of a scarf or shawl.

Simple Fringe

Cut the required number of lengths for each group; the number of strands in each group determines the thickness of the fringe as well as the distance between each tassel. The strands should measure slightly more than twice the length of the finished fringe. Fold the strands in half and draw the folded end through the edge of the knitted fabric using a crochet hook. Draw the loose ends of yarn through the loop and pull them up firmly to form a knot. Trim the ends to neaten them.

Knotted fringe

With two or more rows of additional knots a fringe can be quite elegant. Fewer strands per group are required than for the simple fringe but they must be longer, about 13 cm [5 ins] is the minimum depth, so for this length cut the strands 27-28 cm [10½-11ins] long.

1. Knot the strands on to the edge of the knitting as for a simple fringe.

2. On the next row knot together half the strands from each two adjacent groups. This will leave half a group free at each end.

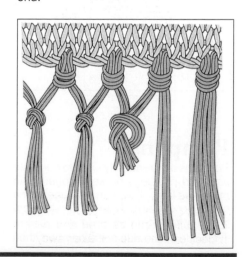

A	■	BLACK	L	□	WHITE
B	▨	DARK GREY	M	▨	LIGHT GREY
C	▨	BROWN	N	▨	OATMEAL
D	▨	MUSTARD	O	▨	PRIMROSE
E	▨	CREAM	P	■	DARK GREEN
F	▨	LIGHT GREEN	Q	▨	PALE GREEN
G	▨	JADE	R	■	NAVY BLUE
H	▨	AIRFORCE	S	▨	LIGHT BLUE
I	■	MAUVE	T	■	ROSE
J	▨	LILAC	U	■	CHERRY
K	■	RED	V	▨	PINK

Finishing Touches

3. On the next row knot half the strands from each two adjacent groups (those formed in step 2), thus bringing the outer strands into the pattern.

Add more rows of knots as required.

Tassels

Tassels are often used to decorate hats and novelty items.

1. Cut a rectangle of cardboard as wide as the length of the finished tassel. Wind the yarn around the cardboard until the required thickness is reached. Break the yarn, thread it through a sewing needle and pass the needle under all the loops. Do not remove the needle.

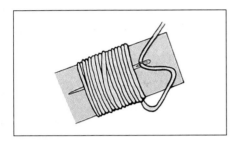

2. Tie the end of the yarn firmly around the loops, remove the card and cut through the loops at the end opposite the knot.

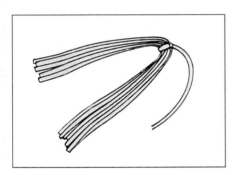

3. Wind the end of yarn around all the loops below the fold and fasten it securely. Pass the needle through the top and use the end to sew the tassel in place. Trim the ends neatly.

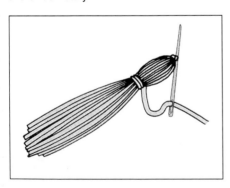

Pompons

Pompons are frequently used to decorate hats and may also be sewn together to make soft toys. They can be made in one colour or several and can vary in size from very tiny to quite large.

1. Decide on the size of the pompon, then cut two circles of cardboard with a diameter slightly bigger than the size of the finished pompon. Cut a smaller hole in the centre of each circle, about half the size of the original diameter. The larger this hole is, the fuller the pompon will be, but if you make it too large the pompon will be oval instead of round! Cut a hole in one circle, then use the opening as a template for drawing and cutting the other to ensure the holes are equal and aligned.

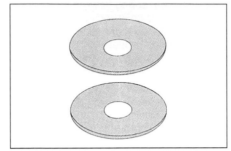

2. Holding the two circles together, wind the yarn around the ring (using several strands at a time for speed) until the ring is completely covered. As the hole in the centre gets smaller you will need to use a tapestry needle to pass the yarn through.

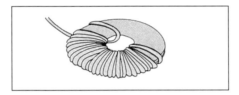

3. Cut all around the yarn at the outside edge between the two circles using a pair of sharp scissors. Make sure that all the yarn has been cut.

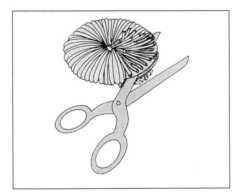

4. Separate the two circles slightly, wind a length of yarn between them and tie it **firmly** in a knot, leaving an end long enough to sew the pompon in place. Pull the two circles apart and fluff out the pompon to cover the centre join. Trim around the ends of yarn to produce a smooth shape.

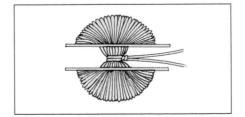

Swiss darning

A Swiss darned or duplicate stitch covers an individual knit stitch, giving the appearance that the design has been knitted in. Swiss darning can be used in conjunction with multi-coloured knitting - for example, to introduce a third colour to a row of Fair Isle knitted in two colours, or to work very thin vertical or diagonal stripes in a plaid or diamond pattern.

Always match your tension to that of the knitting - too loose and the stitches will not be covered; too tight and the work will pucker. If the yarn used for embroidery is finer than the knitted yarn it may not cover the knitted stitch completely.

Swiss darning horizontally

Work from right to left. Thread a tapestry needle with the embroidery yarn and weave in the yarn invisibly at the back of the work. Bring the needle out at the base of the first stitch, take it around the top of the stitch, then insert the needle back through the base of the same stitch, thus covering the original stitch completely. For the next stitch bring the needle through at the base of the next stitch to the left. Continue in this way until the appropriate stitches have been covered.

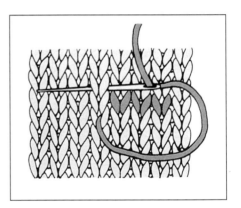

Swiss darning vertically

Work from bottom to top. Bring the needle out at the base of the first stitch, then take it around the top of the stitch. Insert the needle back through the base of the **same** stitch, then bring it up through the base of the stitch above, thus forming a vertical chain.

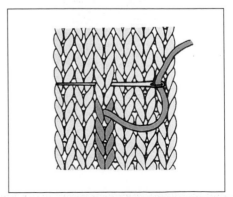

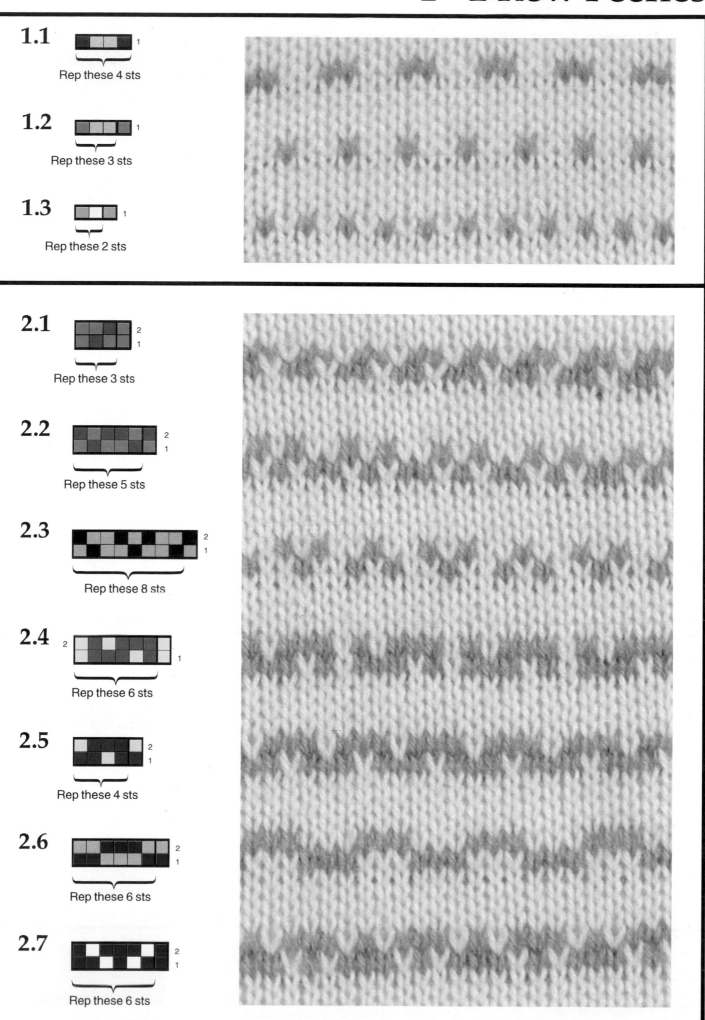

1.1

Rep these 4 sts

1.2

Rep these 3 sts

1.3

Rep these 2 sts

2.1

Rep these 3 sts

2.2

Rep these 5 sts

2.3

Rep these 8 sts

2.4

Rep these 6 sts

2.5

Rep these 4 sts

2.6

Rep these 6 sts

2.7

Rep these 6 sts

3 Row Peeries

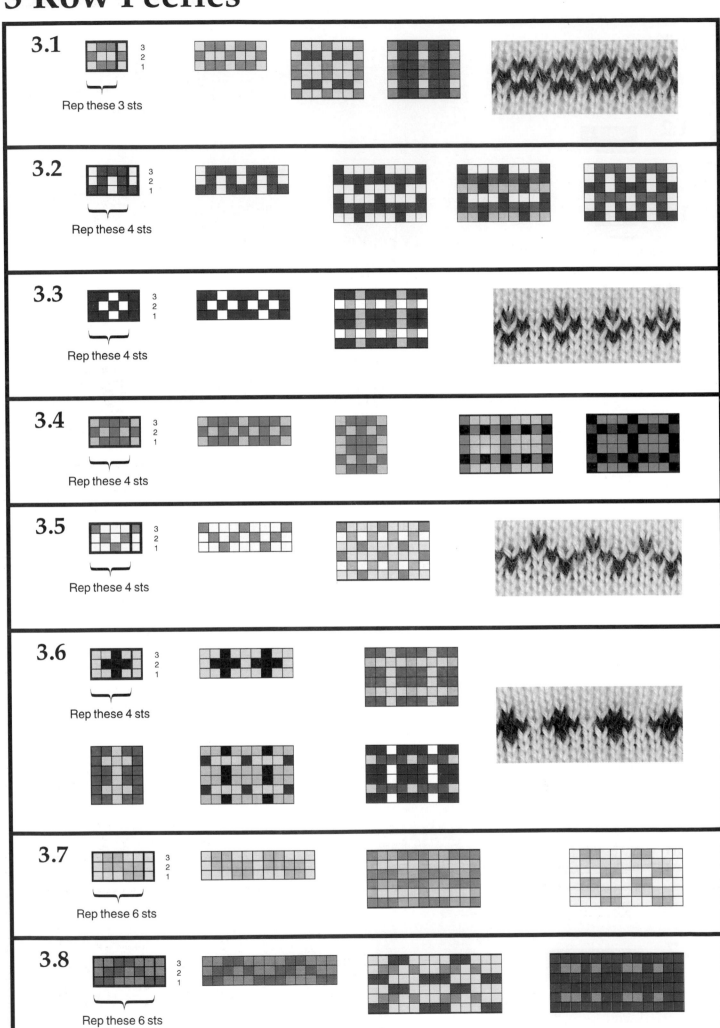

3.1 Rep these 3 sts

3.2 Rep these 4 sts

3.3 Rep these 4 sts

3.4 Rep these 4 sts

3.5 Rep these 4 sts

3.6 Rep these 4 sts

3.7 Rep these 6 sts

3.8 Rep these 6 sts

4 Row Peeries

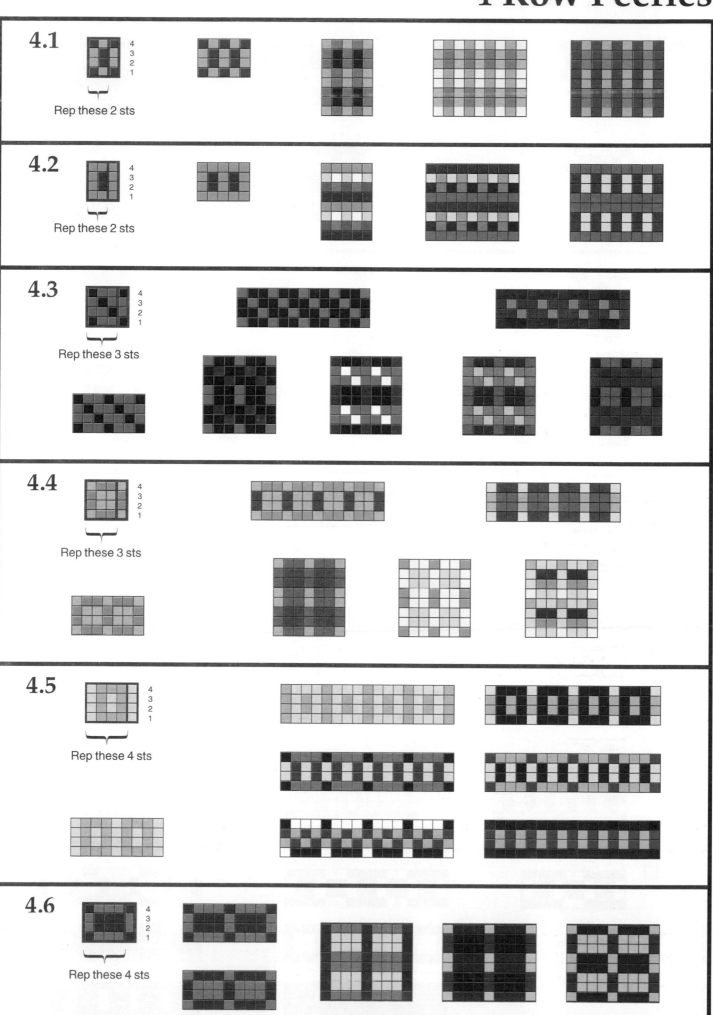

4.1
Rep these 2 sts

4.2
Rep these 2 sts

4.3
Rep these 3 sts

4.4
Rep these 3 sts

4.5
Rep these 4 sts

4.6
Rep these 4 sts

4 Row Peeries

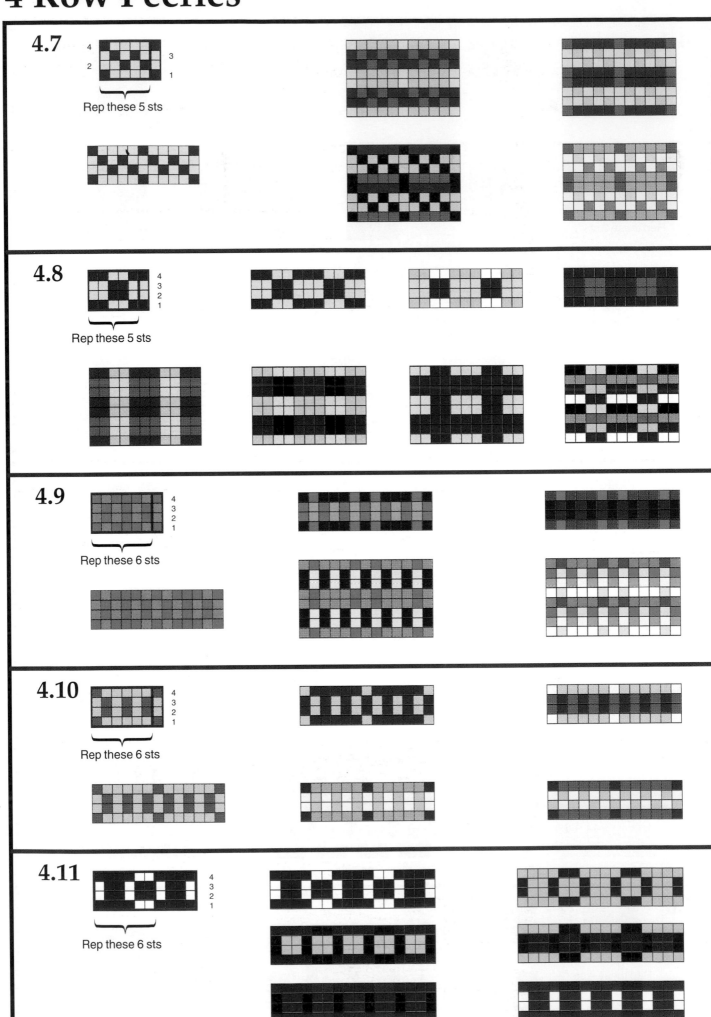

4.7

4 3
2 1

Rep these 5 sts

4.8

4
3
2
1

Rep these 5 sts

4.9

4
3
2
1

Rep these 6 sts

4.10

4
3
2
1

Rep these 6 sts

4.11

4
3
2
1

Rep these 6 sts

4 Row Peeries

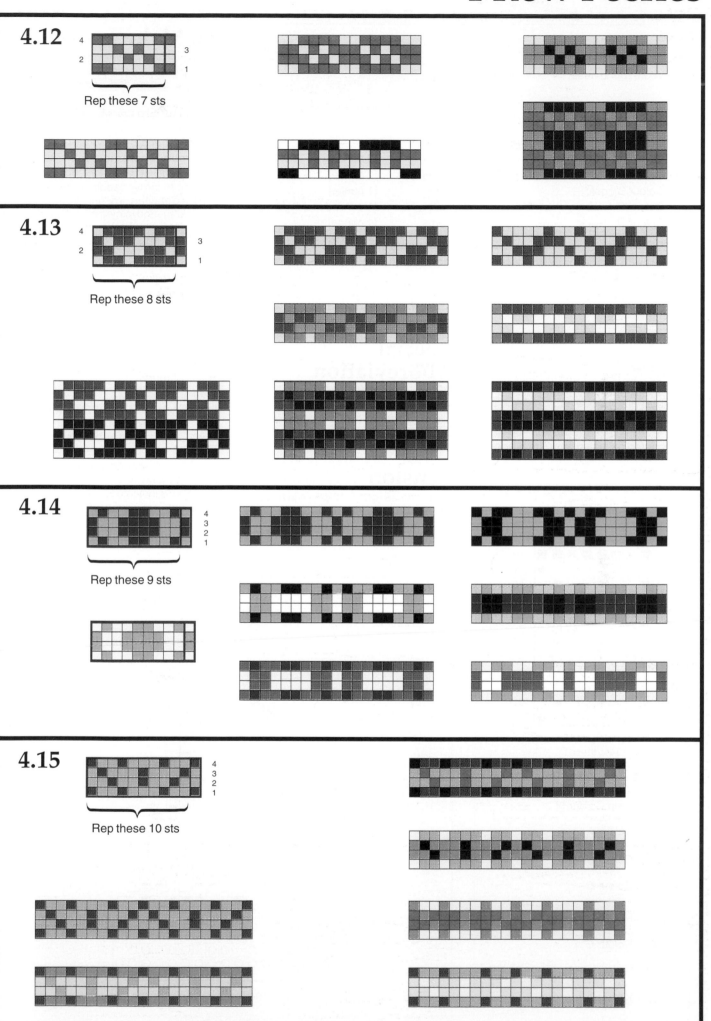

4.12 Rep these 7 sts

4.13 Rep these 8 sts

4.14 Rep these 9 sts

4.15 Rep these 10 sts

Fair Isle Beret

Measurement

Width round head: 56 cm   [2½ ins]

Materials

Double Knitting (Sports Weight) yarn

Main Colour (M) - dark green:	50 grams	[2 ounces]
Colour A - yellow:	25 grams	[1 ounce]
Colour B - gold:	25 grams	[1 ounce]
Colour C - red:	25 grams	[1 ounce]
Colour D - black:	25 grams	[1 ounce]
Colour E - white:	25 grams	[1 ounce]

Set of 4 needle each size 3¼mm (UK 10, USA 3 or 4) and 4mm (UK 8, USA 6).

The quantities of yarn stated are based on average requirements and are therefore approximate.

For abbreviations see pages 20 and 21.

Figures or instructions given in [ ]s should be repeated as stated after the brackets.

Special Abbreviation

Slip marker = make a slip knot in a short length of contrasting yarn and plance on needle where indicated. On the following rounds slip the marker from one needle to the other.

Tension

26 sts and 26 rows = 10 cm [4 ins] square measured over Fair Isle pattern using larger needles.

To Make

Using smaller needles and M, cast on 120 sts. Making sure that work is not twisted, join into a ring and work in rounds as follows:

1st round: Slip marker, *k2, p2; rep from * to end.

Rep this round 8 times more.

Next round (increase): *Rib 4, inc in next st; rep from * to end. 144 sts.

Change to larger needle and knit 1 round in M. Continue working in st st (every round knit), and joining in and breaking off colours as required, work 24 rounds of Chart 1. (18 pattern repeats).

Shape Crown

Work 2 rounds of Chart 2, (8 pattern repeats). Keeping chart correct work double decreases as follows:

3rd round (decrease): K2tog, work 15 sts, *sl 1, k2tog, psso, work 15 sts; rep from * to last st, sl 1, pass slipped st over first st of round.

Work 2 rounds.

6th round (decrease): K2tog, work 13 sts, *sl 1, k2tog, psso, work 13 sts; rep from * to last st, sl 1, pass slipped st over first st of round.

Keeping chart correct, work 18 more rows, working double decreases as before where indicated.

Break yarn, thread through remaining 16 sts, draw up firmly and fasten off.

Chart 1

(rows numbered 1–12)

```
Rep these
23 sts
```

☐ = Main Colour M

☒ = Colour A

⊙ = Colour B

— = Colour C

● = Colour D

■ = Colour E

§ = Sl 1

▨ = K2tog

Chart 2

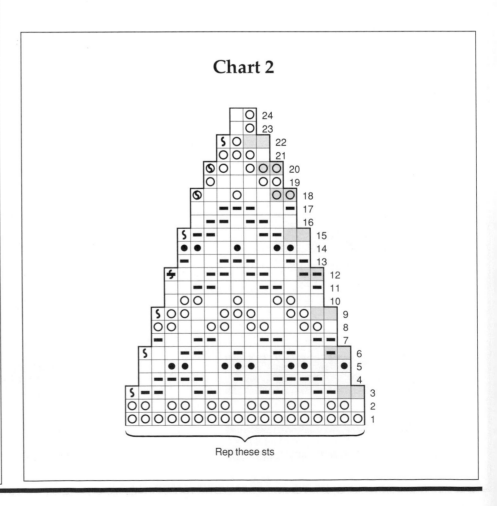

Rep these sts

Fair Isle Beret

For instructions for Gloves see page 162

5 Row Peeries

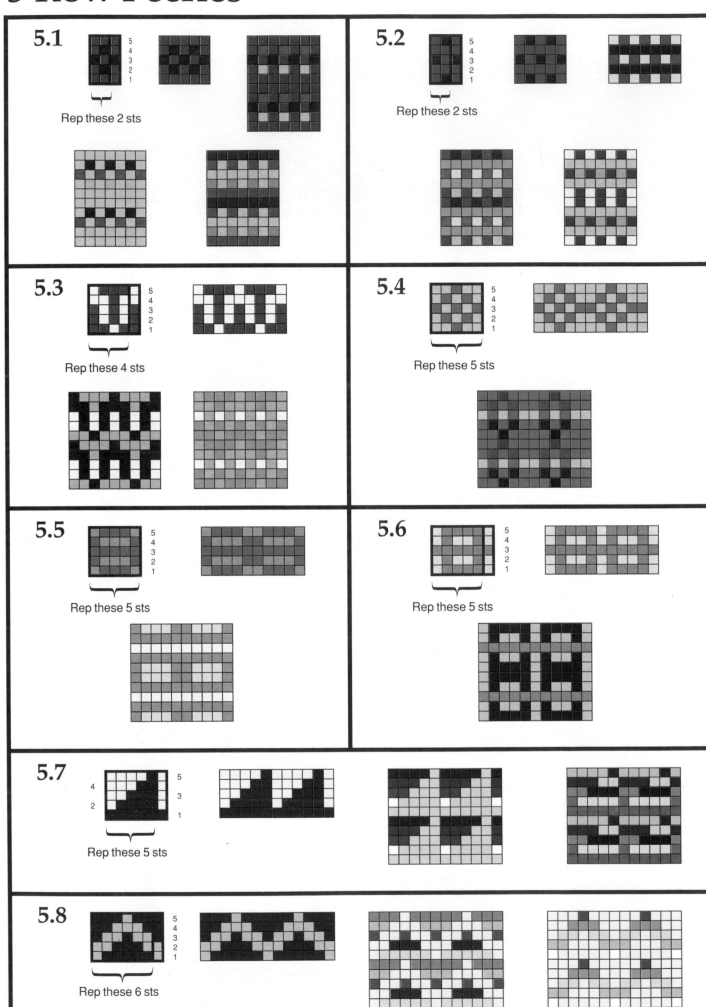

5.1 Rep these 2 sts

5.2 Rep these 2 sts

5.3 Rep these 4 sts

5.4 Rep these 5 sts

5.5 Rep these 5 sts

5.6 Rep these 5 sts

5.7 Rep these 5 sts

5.8 Rep these 6 sts

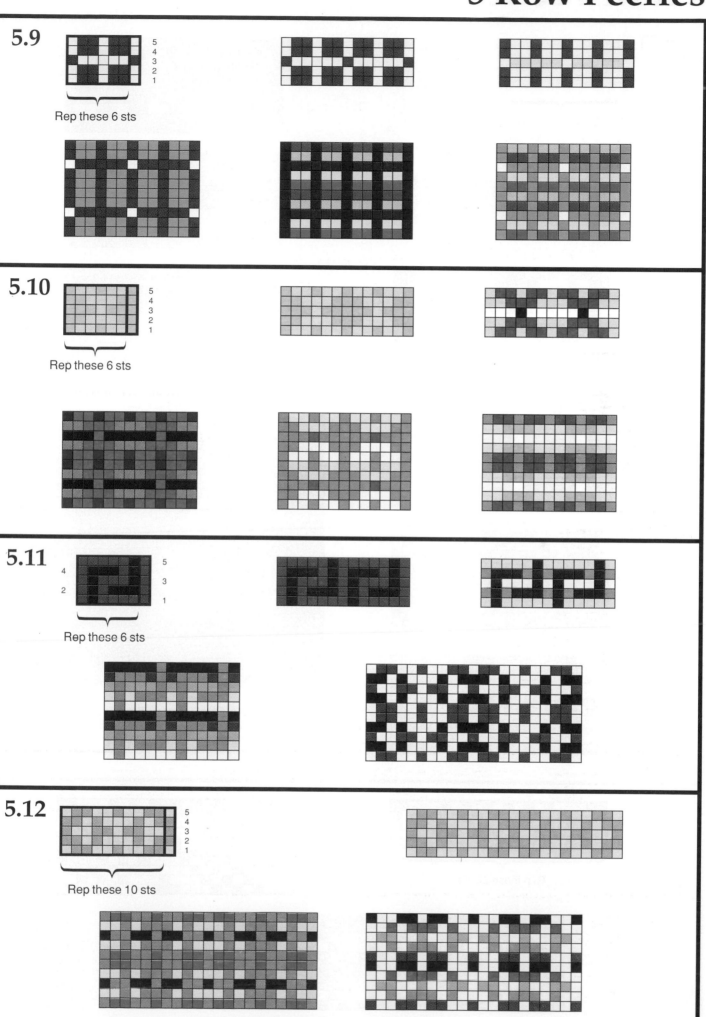

5.9

Rep these 6 sts

5.10

Rep these 6 sts

5.11

Rep these 6 sts

5.12

Rep these 10 sts

5 Row Peeries

5.13

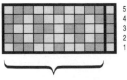

Rep these 10 sts

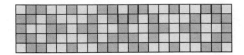

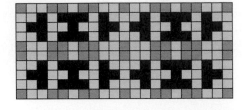

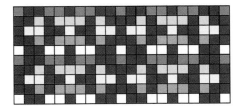

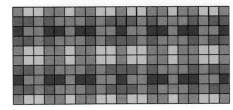

5.14

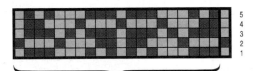

Rep these 20 sts

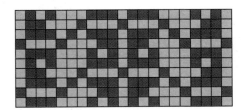

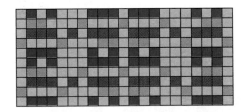

Worked as an all-over pattern.
Background colour: All rows = B.
Pattern colour: Rows 1 and 2 = I,   3-5 = K.

5.15

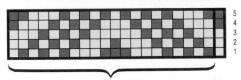

Rep these 20 sts

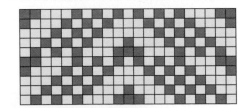

134

6 Row Peeries

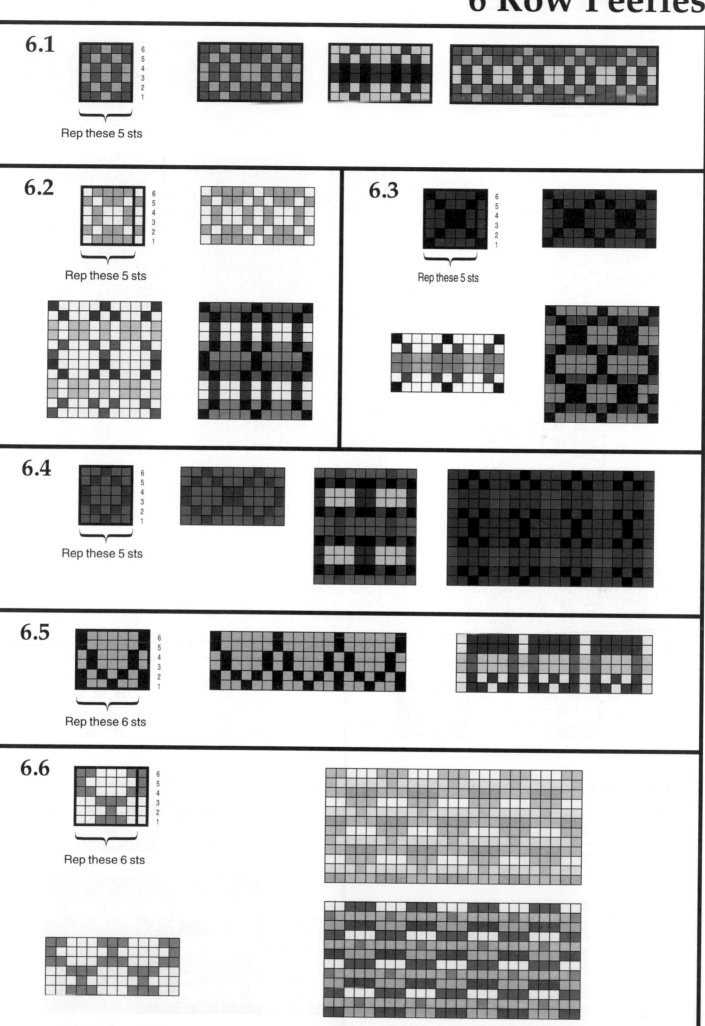

6.1
Rep these 5 sts

6.2
Rep these 5 sts

6.3
Rep these 5 sts

6.4
Rep these 5 sts

6.5
Rep these 6 sts

6.6
Rep these 6 sts

6 Row Peeries

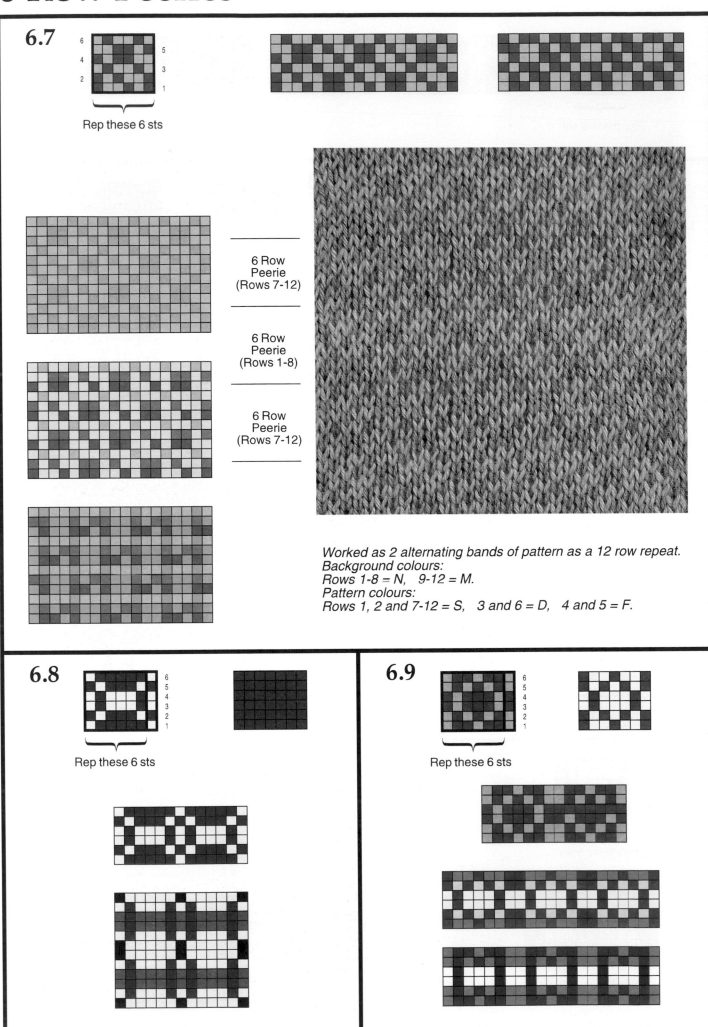

6.7

Rep these 6 sts

6 Row Peerie (Rows 7-12)

6 Row Peerie (Rows 1-8)

6 Row Peerie (Rows 7-12)

Worked as 2 alternating bands of pattern as a 12 row repeat.
Background colours:
Rows 1-8 = N,   9-12 = M.
Pattern colours:
Rows 1, 2 and 7-12 = S,   3 and 6 = D,   4 and 5 = F.

6.8

Rep these 6 sts

6.9

Rep these 6 sts

6.10

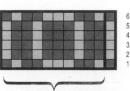

Rep these 10 sts

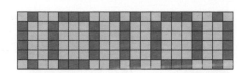

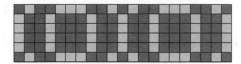

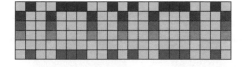

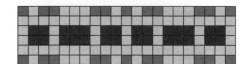

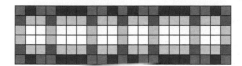

6.11

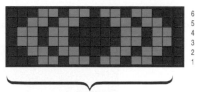

Rep these 16 sts

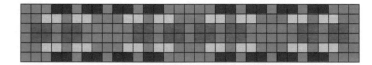

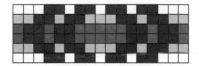

6 Row
Peerie
(Rows 8-13)

6 Row
Peerie
(Rows 1-6)

6 Row
Peerie
(Rows 8-13)

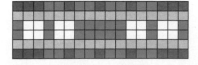

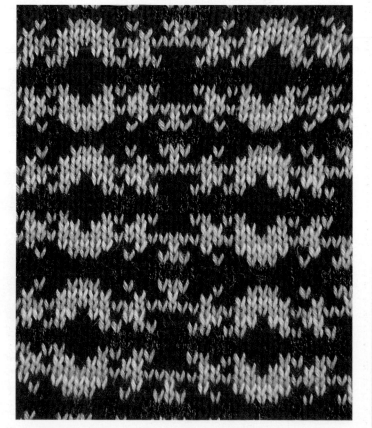

Worked as 2 bands of pattern as a 14 row repeat. On rows 8-13 the pattern is worked from the 9th (centre) stitch (see page 121).
Background colours:
Rows 1 and 6 = L,   2, 5, 7 and 14 = M,   3 and 4 = B,   8-13 = U.
Pattern colours:
Rows 1-6 = U,   8 and 13 = L,   9 and 12, = M, 10 and 11 = B.

7 Row Peeries

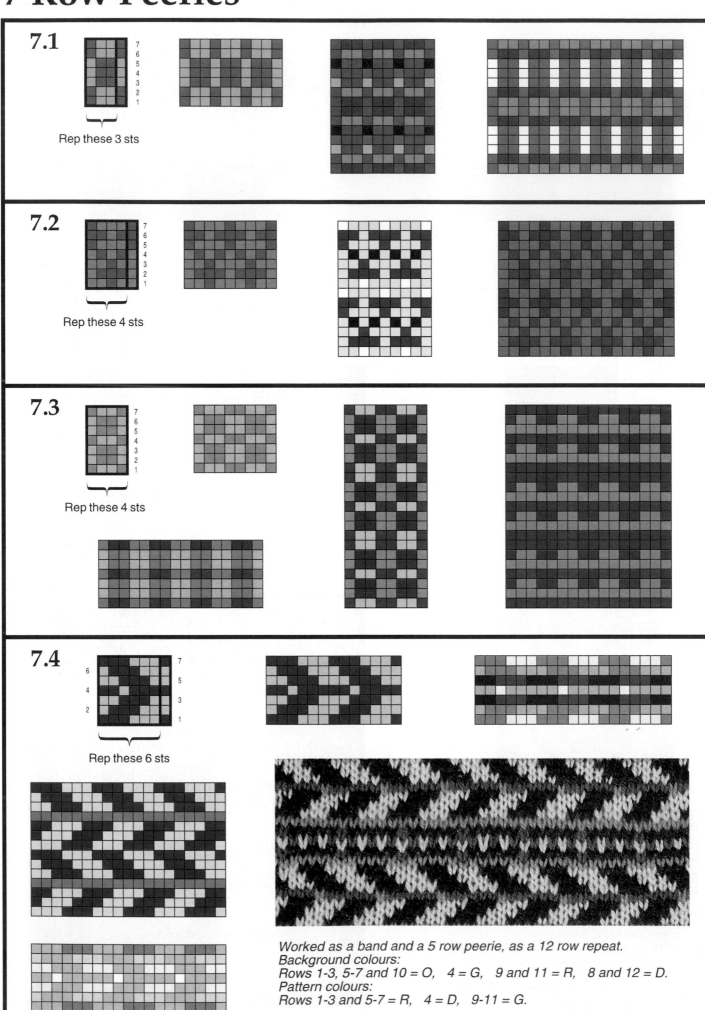

7.1 Rep these 3 sts

7.2 Rep these 4 sts

7.3 Rep these 4 sts

7.4 Rep these 6 sts

Worked as a band and a 5 row peerie, as a 12 row repeat.
Background colours:
Rows 1-3, 5-7 and 10 = O,   4 = G,   9 and 11 = R,   8 and 12 = D.
Pattern colours:
Rows 1-3 and 5-7 = R,   4 = D,   9-11 = G.

7.5

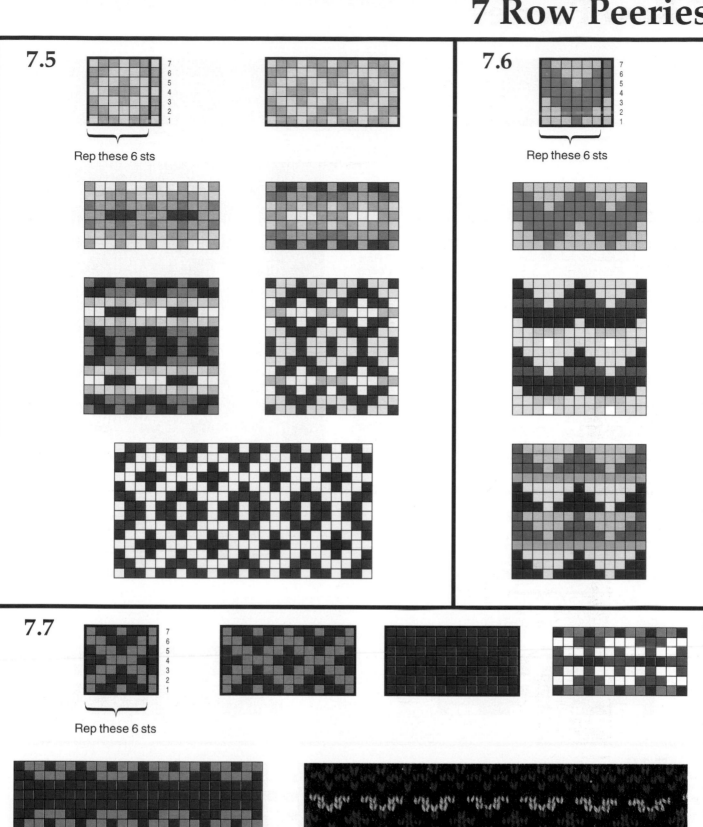

Rep these 6 sts

7.6

Rep these 6 sts

7.7

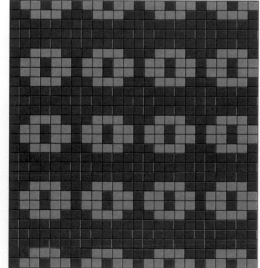

Rep these 6 sts

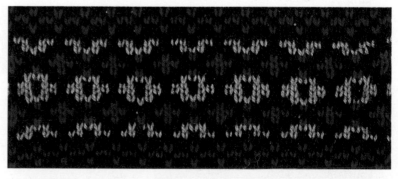

Worked as a band of 14 rows and a 5 row peerie, as a 19 row repeat.
Background colours:
All rows = A.
Pattern colours:
Rows 1, 2, 13, 14 and 6-9 = D,   3-5, 10-12 and 16-18 = K.

7 Row Peeries

7.8

Rep these 10 sts

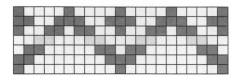

Worked as an 18 row repeat of 2 bands and 2 peeries. Rows 1-7 as chart followed by a 1 row peerie. Rows 9-15 as chart but with rows worked in reverse order, followed by a 3 row peerie.
Background colours:
Rows 1-7 and 9-15 = J, 8, 16, 17 and 18 = S.
Pattern colours:
Rows 1, 15 and 17 = I, 2, 5, 11 and 14 = S, 3, 6, 10 and 13 = H, 4, 7, 9 and 12 = R, 8, 16 and 18 = J,

7 Row
Peerie
(Rows 9-15)
_____
_____
7 Row
Peerie
(Rows 1-7)
_____
3 Row
Peerie
_____
7 Row
Peerie
(Rows 9-15)
_____
_____
7 Row
Peerie
(Rows 1-7)

7.9

Rep these 10 sts

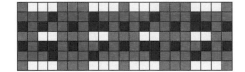

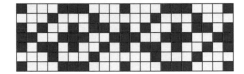

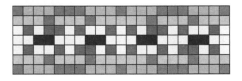

7.10

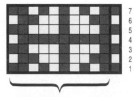

Rep these 10 sts

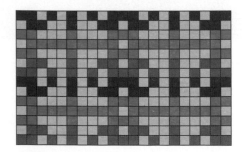

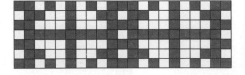

Worked as a 20 row repeat with first 7 rows as chart followed by a 3 row Peerie, then rows 11-17 as chart but worked from 6th (centre) stitch (see page 121), then a 3 row peerie.
Background colours:
Rows 1-3, 5-8, 10-13, and 15-18 and 20 = M, 4, 9, 14 and 19 = R.
Pattern colours:
1, 7, 11 and 17 = I, 2, 6, 12 and 16 = K, 3, 5, 13 and 15 = D, 4, 9, 14 and 19 = G.

7.11

Rep these 12 sts

7.12

Rep these 12 sts

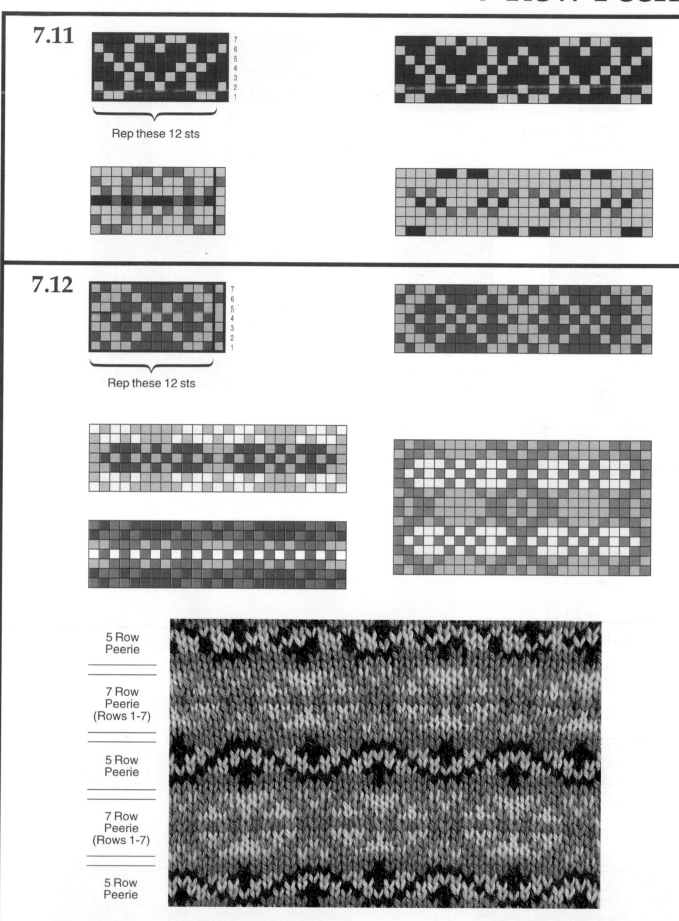

5 Row
Peerie

7 Row
Peerie
(Rows 1-7)

5 Row
Peerie

7 Row
Peerie
(Rows 1-7)

5 Row
Peerie

Worked as a 28 row repeat, first 7 rows as chart, 1 row, a 5 row peerie, 1 row, then next 7 rows as chart but worked from 7th (centre) stitch (see page 121). Rows 22-28 as rows 8-14 but worked in reverse order.
Background colours:
Rows 1-8, 14-22 and 28 = S,   9, 13, 23 and 27 = T,   10, 12, 24 and 26 = V,   11 and 25 = E.
Pattern colours:
Rows 1-3, 5-7, 15-17 and 19-21 = E,   4 and 18 = D,   9-13 and 23-27 = H.

8 Row Borders

8.1

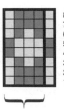

Rep these 4 sts

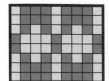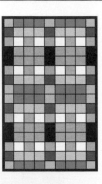

8.2

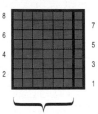

Rep these 6 sts

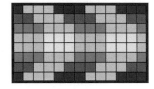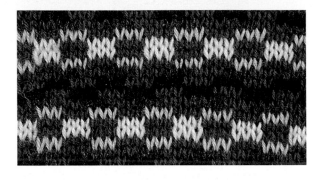

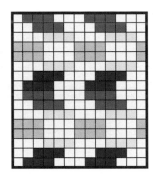

Worked as a 16 row repeat with first 8 rows as chart. Rows 9-16 as chart but worked from 4th (centre) stitch (see page 121).
Background colours:
All rows = G.
Pattern colours:
Rows 1, 8, 9 and 16 = A,   2, 7, 10 and 15 = B, 3, 6, 11 and 14 = M,   4, 5, 12 and 13 = L.

8.3

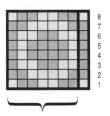

Rep these 7 sts

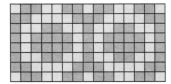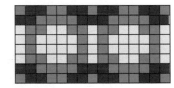

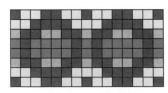

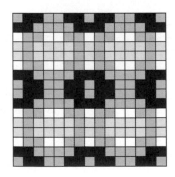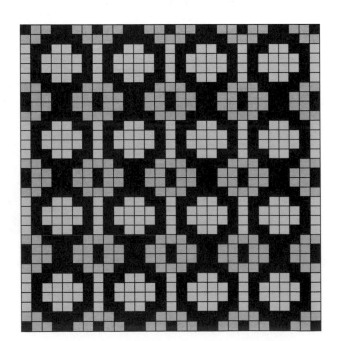

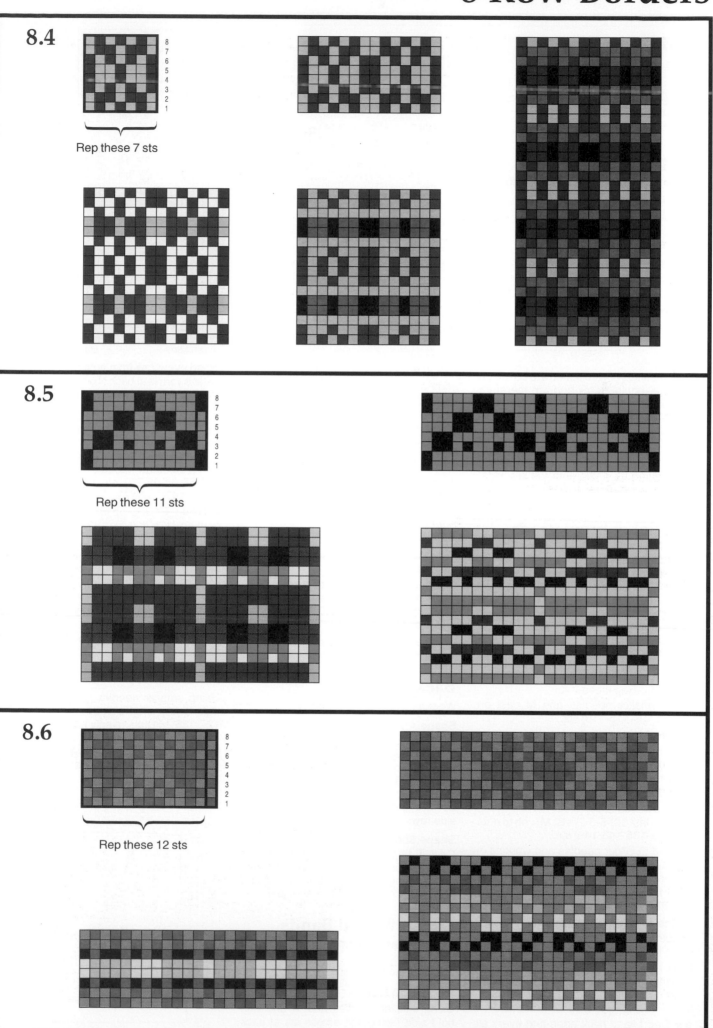

8.4

Rep these 7 sts

8.5

Rep these 11 sts

8.6

Rep these 12 sts

Man's Fair Isle Slipover

Measurements

To fit chest sizes

90	95	100	105	110	cm
36	38	40	42	44	ins

Finished measurement

94	100	104	110	114	cm
37	39½	41	43½	45	ins

Materials

Double Knitting (Sports Weight) yarn

Main Colour (M)	200	250	250	300	300	grams
(Dark Grey)	7	9	9	11	11	ounces
Colour A	50	100	100	100	100	grams
(Cherry)	3	4	4	4	4	ounces
Colour B	50	100	100	100	100	grams
(Airforce Blue)	3	4	4	4	4	ounces
Colour C	50	50	50	100	100	grams
(Navy Blue)	3	3	3	4	4	ounces

Pair of needles each size 4mm (UK8, USA6) and 3¼mm (UK7, USA7).

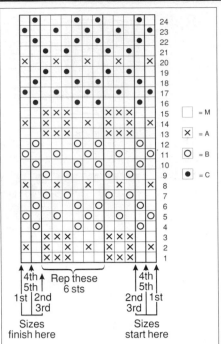

4th 5th 1st 2nd 3rd / Rep these 6 sts / 4th 5th 1st 2nd 3rd

Sizes finish here — Sizes start here

= M
⊠ = A
○ = B
● = C

Read every row from right to left. Do not weave yarn in at back of work, carry colour not in use **loosely** across back of work.

The quantities of yarn stated are based on average requirements and are therefore approximate.

For abbreviations see pages 20 and 21.

Instructions are given for the smallest sizes; larger sizes are given in ( )s. Figures or instructions given in [ ]s should be repeated as stated after the brackets. Where only one figure is given this applies to all sizes.

Special abbreviations

M1 = (Make 1) Make a st by picking up strand of yarn lying between last st worked and next st and working into the back of it.

Tension

26 sts and 26 rows = 10 cm [4 ins] square measured over Fair Isle pattern using larger needles.

Front

Using smaller needles and M cast on 97(103-109-115-119) sts.

1st row (right side): K1, *p1, k1; rep from * to end.

2nd row: P1, *k1, p1; rep from * to end.

Rep the last 2 rows until rib measures 7 cm [2¾ ins] ending with a right side row.

Next row: Rib 2(1-4-4-1), *M1, rib 4; rep from * to last 3(2-5-3-2) sts, M1, rib to end. 121(129-135-143-149) sts.

Change to larger needles and working in st st starting knit, work the 24 rows of chart until front measures 34 cm [13½ ins] or required length to armholes, ending with a wrong side row ★.

Shape Armholes and Divide for Neck

Keeping pattern correct cast off 3(4-4-5-5) sts at beg of next row.

Next row: Cast off 3(4-4-5-5) sts, work until there are 57(60-63-66-69) sts on right hand needle, turn and complete this side first.

★★ Dec 1 st at neck edge and every alt row, **at the same time** dec 1 st at armhole edge on next 3 rows, then every alt row until 32(31-32-33-34) sts remain. Keeping armhole edge straight continue to dec 1 st at neck edge on every alt row until, 28(28-29-30-32) sts remain then every following 4th row until 25(25-25-26-27) sts remain.

Work 8 rows straight (work 1 row less here for 2nd side), thus ending at armhole edge.

Shape Shoulder

Cast off 12(12-12-13-13) sts at beg of next row. Work 1 row. Cast off remaining 13(13-13-13-14)sts.

Slip next st at centre onto a safety pin. With wrong side facing rejoin yarn to neck edge of remaining 57(60-63-66-69) sts and work to end.

Complete as given for first side from ★★ to end working 1 row less where indicated.

Back

Work as given for front to ★.

Shape Armholes

Keeping pattern correct cast off 3(4-4-5-5) sts at beg of next 2 rows. Dec 1 st at each end of next 3 rows then every alt row until 89(91-95-99-103) sts remain. Work straight until back measures same as front to shoulder ending with a wrong side row.

Shape Shoulders

Cast off 12(12-12-13-13) sts at beg of next 2 rows, then 13(13-13-13-14) sts at beg of following 2 rows. Slip remaining 39(41-45-47-49) sts onto a st holder.

Finishing and Bands

Press pieces according to instructions on ball band.
Join left shoulder seam.

Neckband

Using smaller needles and M and with right side facing knit across sts at back neck decreasing 1 st at centre, pick up and k54(58-64-66-70) sts down left side of neck, knit st from safety (mark this st with a coloured thread), and pick up and k54(58-64-66-70) sts up right side of neck. 147(157-173-179-189) sts.

1st row: *P1, k1; rep from * to 2 sts before marked st, p2tog, p1, p2togtbl, **k1, p1; rep from ** to end.

2nd row: K1, *p1, k1; rep from * to 2 sts before marked st, sl 1, k1, psso, k1, k2tog, k1, **p1, k1; rep from ** to end.

Rep these 2 rows twice more then 1st row again. Cast off in rib decreasing on this row also.

Join right shoulder seam and ends of neckband.

Armbands

Using smaller needles and M and with right side facing, pick up and k109(117-127-135-141) sts evenly around armhole edge.

Work 7 rows in k1, p1 rib as given for Front starting with a 2nd row. Cast off in rib.

Join side seams and ends of armbands.

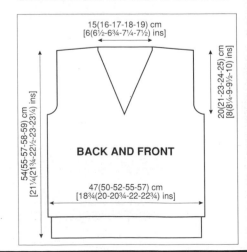

15(16-17-18-19) cm
[6(6½-6¾-7¼-7½) ins]

20(21-23-24-25) cm
[8(8¼-9-9½-10) ins]

54(55-57-58-59) cm
[21¼(21¾-22½-23-23¼) ins]

BACK AND FRONT

47(50-52-55-57) cm
[18¾(20-20¾-22-22¾) ins]

9 Row Borders

9.1

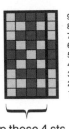

9
8
7
6
5
4
3
2
1

Rep these 4 sts

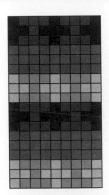

9.2

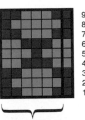

9
8
7
6
5
4
3
2
1

Rep these 6 sts

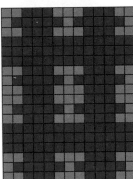

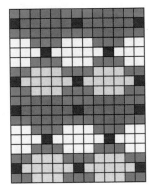

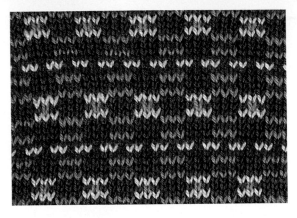

Worked as a band and a 3 row peerie as a 12 row repeat.
Background colours:
Rows 1-9 = G,   10-12 = C.
Pattern colours:
Rows 1, 3, 5, 7 and 9 = D,   2 and 8 = C,   4, 6 and 11 = E.

9.3

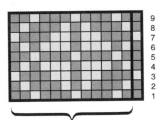

9
8
7
6
5
4
3
2
1

Rep these 12 sts

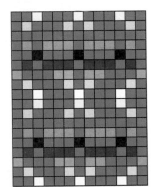

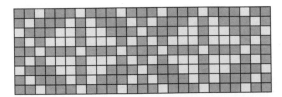

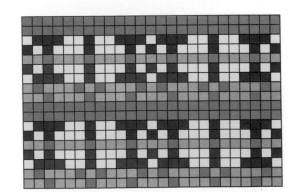

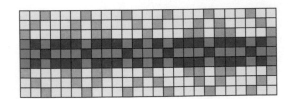

9.4

Rep these 14 sts

9.5

Rep these 14 sts

9 Row
Border
(Rows 11-19)

9 Row
Border
(Rows 11-19)

Worked as 2 bands worked as a 20 row repeat. Rows 1-9 as chart, 11-19 as chart but worked from 8th (centre) stitch.
Background colours:
Rows 1, 9-11, 19 and 20 = L, 2, 8, 12 and 18 = Q, 3, 7, 13 and 17 = S, 4, 6, 14 and 16 = H, 5 and 15 = R.
Pattern colours:
Rows 1-9 and 11-19 = D.

10 Row Borders

10.1

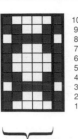

Rep these 5 sts

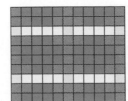

10.2

Rep these 6 sts

10.3

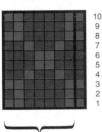

Rep these 7 sts

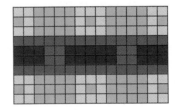

10.4

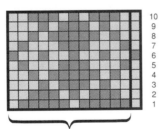

Rep these 12 sts

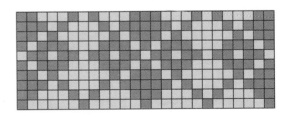

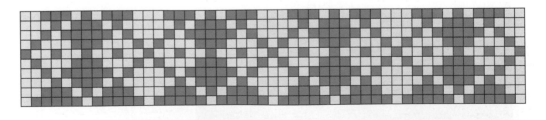

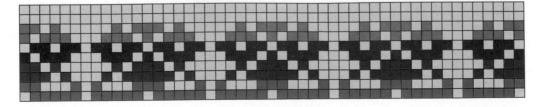

10 - 12 Row Borders

10.5

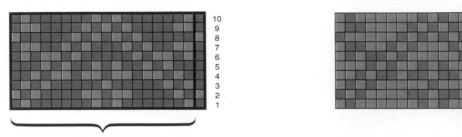

Rep these 18 sts

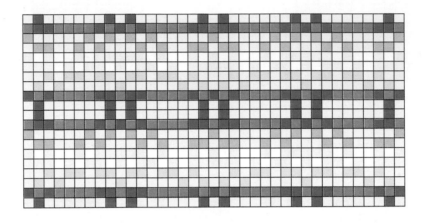

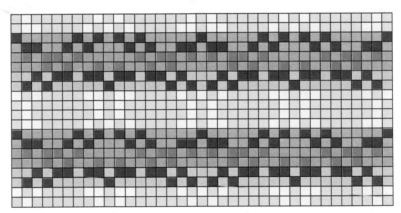

12.1

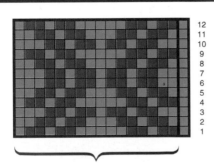

Rep these 16 sts

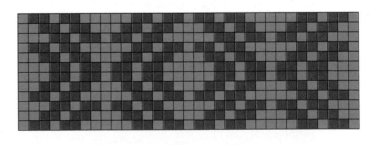

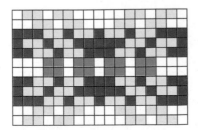

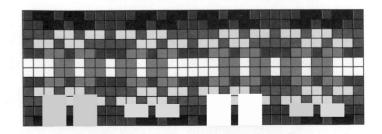

13.1

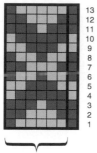

13
12
11
10
9
8
7
6
5
4
3
2
1

Rep these 6 sts

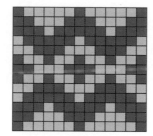

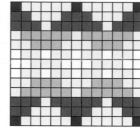

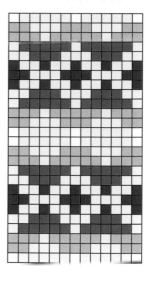

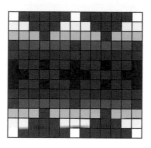

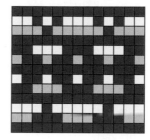

13.2

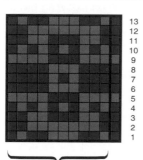

13
12
11
10
9
8
7
6
5
4
3
2
1

Rep these 10 sts

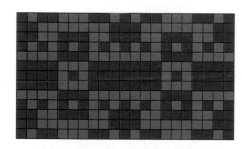

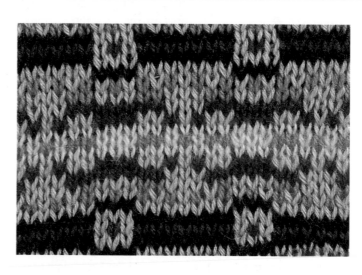

Worked as a band with a 3 row peerie, as a 16 row repeat.
Background colours:
Rows 1-4, 10-13 = N,   5, 6, 8 and 9 = R,   7 = C,   14-16 = E.
Pattern colours:
Rows 1, 2, 12 and 13 = C,   3, 4, 10, 11 and 15 = D,   5-9 = N.

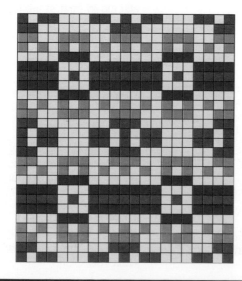

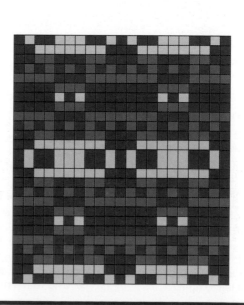

Fair Isle Top

Measurements

To fit bust size

	80/85	90/95	100/105	cm
	32/34	36/38	40/42	ins

Finished measurement

	103	119	135	cm
	41	47	54	ins

Length to shoulder (approximately)

	58	59	60	cm
	23	23½	24	ins

Sleeve length (approximately)

	28	28	28	cm
	11	11	11	ins

Shown in 90/95 cm [36/38 inch] size.

Materials

Double Knitting (Sports Weight) yarn

Main Colour (M)	450	500	600	grams
(pale blue)	16	18	22	ounces
Contrast Colour A	100	100	100	grams
(pale pink)	4	4	4	ounces
Contrast Colour B	100	150	150	grams
(sand)	4	6	6	ounces
Contrast Colour C	50	100	100	grams
(white)	2	4	4	ounces
Contrast Colour D	50	50	50	grams
(coral)	2	2	2	ounces

Pair needles each size 3¼mm (UK 10, USA 3 or 4), 4mm (UK 8, USA 6) and 4½mm (UK 7, USA 7).
Cable needle.

The quantities of yarn stated are based on average requirements and are therefore approximate.

For abbreviations see pages 20 and 21.

Instructions are given for the smallest size; larger sizes are given in ( )s. Figures or instructions given in [ ]s should be repeated as stated after the brackets. Where only one figure is given this applies to all sizes.

Tension

22 sts and 30 rows = 10 cm [4 ins] square measured over st st using middle size needles.

Special Abbreviation

C12F (Cable 12 Front) = slip next 6 sts on to cable needle and hold at front of work, knit next 6 sts from left-hand needle, then knit sts from cable needle.

Note: Do not weave yarn in at back of work. Carry colour not in use **loosely** across back of work twisting yarns together at each colour change to avoid making a hole.

Charts 1 and 3: Read odd number (knit) rows from right to left and even number (purl) rows from left to right.

Chart 2: Read odd number (purl) rows from left to right and even number (knit) rows from right to left.

Back

Using middle size needles and M, cast on 113(131-149) sts, and starting knit, work 14(18-20) rows in st st, thus ending with a purl row.

Commence pattern.

★**Next row:** K1, *k2tog, yf, k1; rep from * to last st, k1.

Next row: Purl.

★★Change to largest needles and, joining in and breaking off colours as required, work the 9 rows of chart 1, thus ending with a knit row. ★★★

Change to middle size needles and working in M only, continue as follows:

Next row: Purl.

Next row: K1, *k2tog, yf, k1; rep from * to last st, k1. ★★★★

Starting purl, work 19 rows in st st, thus ending with a purl row.

Rep from ★ to ★★★.

Joining in and breaking off colours as required, work the 25 rows of chart 2, thus ending with a purl row.

Rep from ★★ to ★★★★.

Starting purl, work 19 rows in st st, thus ending with a purl row.

Rep from ★ to ★★★★.

Starting purl, work 25(25-27) rows in st st, thus ending with a purl row.

Shape Shoulders

Cast off 18(23-26) sts at beg of next 2 rows, then 19(23-26) sts at beg of following 2 rows. Slip remaining 39(39-45) sts on to a holder.

Front

Work as given for Back until front is 22(22-24) rows shorter than back to start of shoulder shaping, thus ending with a purl row.

Shape Neck

Next row: K47(56-63), turn and complete this side first.

Dec 1 st at neck edge on next 4(4-8) rows, then on following 6(6-3) alt rows. 37(46-52) sts remain. Work 5(5-9) rows straight (work 1 row more here for 2nd side), thus ending at side edge.

Shape Shoulder

Cast off 18(23-26) sts at beg of next row. Work 1 row. Cast off remaining 19(23-26) sts.

With right side of work facing, slip centre 19(19-23) sts on to a holder, rejoin M to remaining 47(56-53) sts, knit to end. Complete to match first side, reversing shapings by working 1 row more where indicated.

Sleeves

Using smallest needles and M, cast on 63(67-75) sts.

1st row (right side): K1, *p1, k1; rep from * to end.

2nd row: P1, *k1, p1; rep from * to end.

Rep the last 2 rows until rib measures 5 cm [2 ins], ending with a right side row.

Next row (increase): Rib 5(3-4), *inc in next st, rib 3(3-5); rep from * to last 6(4-5) sts, inc in next st, rib to end. 77(83-87) sts.

Change to middle size needles and starting knit, work 6 rows in st st, increasing 1 st at each end of 3rd row. 79(85-89) sts.

Next row: Inc in first st, k1(1-0), k2tog, yf, *k1, k2tog, yf; rep from * to last 3(3-2) sts, k1(1-0), inc in next st, k1. 81(87-91) sts.

Next row: Purl.

Change to largest needles and, joining in and breaking off colours as required, work the 43 rows of chart 3, increasing 1 st at each end of 3rd and every following 4th row as indicated until there are 103(109-113) sts.

Change to middle size needles and continue in M only.

Next row: Purl.

Fair Isle Top

Next row: K2(2-1), *k2tog, yf, k1; rep from * to last 2(2-1) sts, k2(2-1).

Next row: Purl.

Knit 1 row increasing 1 st at each end of next row. 105(111-115) sts. Continuing in st st, work 5 rows straight, thus ending with a purl row. Cast off **loosely**.

Finishing and Edgings

Block, but do not press.

Join right shoulder seam.

Neckband

With right side facing, using smallest needles and M, pick up and k24(24-26) sts down left front slope, knit across sts on holder at front neck, pick up and k24(24-26) sts up right front slope, then knit across sts on holder at back neck decreasing 1 st at centre. 105(105-119) sts.

Starting with a 2nd row, work 3 cm [1¼ ins] in k1, p1 rib as given for Sleeves. Cast off in rib.

Join left shoulder seam and ends of neckband. Fold each sleeve in half lengthways and mark centre of cast off edge. Sew each sleeve to a side edge placing centre at shoulder seam. Join side and sleeve seams.

Lower Border

Using middle size needles and M, cast on 13 sts and commence pattern.

1st row (right side): Knit.

2nd row: P12, k1.

3rd to 6th rows: Rep 1st and 2nd rows twice more.

7th row: K1, C12F.

8th row: As 2nd row.

9th to 16th rows: Rep 1st and 2nd rows 4 times.

These 16 rows form the pattern. Continue in pattern until strip fits from left side seam all round lower edge. Sew in place as illustrated. Join border edges.

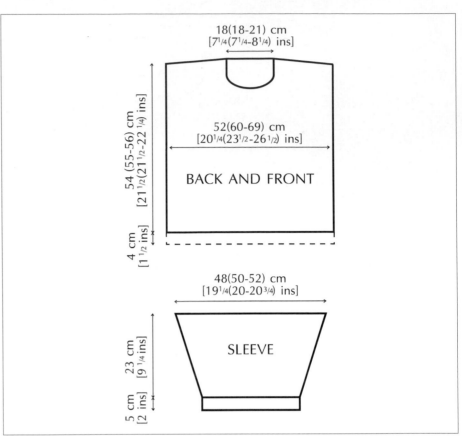

Chart 1   Chart 2

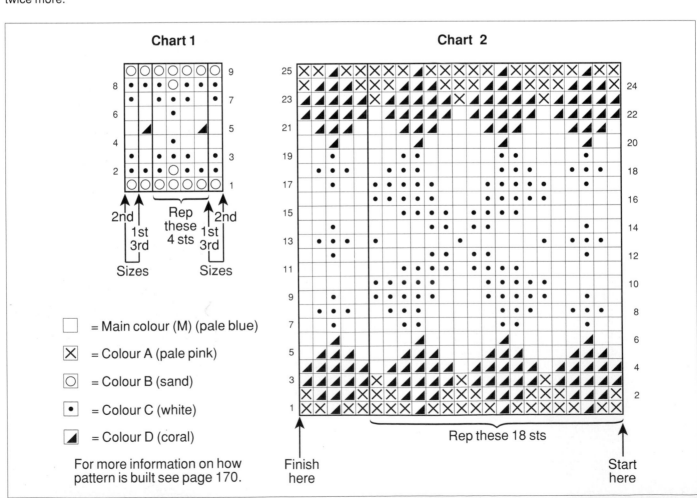

☐ = Main colour (M) (pale blue)

⊠ = Colour A (pale pink)

⊘ = Colour B (sand)

• = Colour C (white)

◤ = Colour D (coral)

For more information on how pattern is built see page 170.

Chart 3

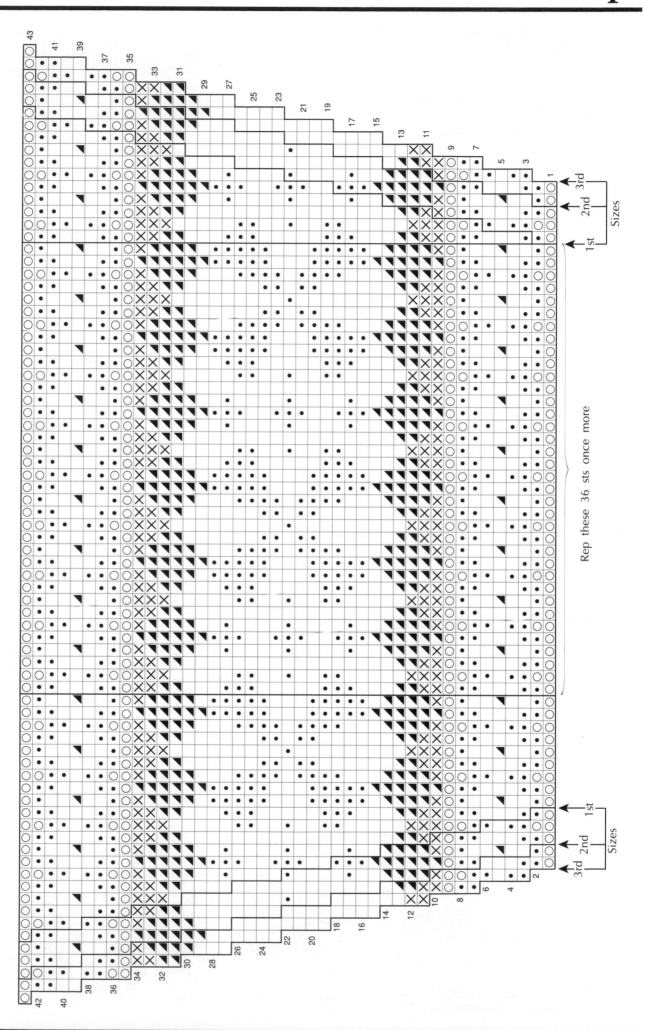

Rep these 36 sts once more

13 Row Borders

13.3

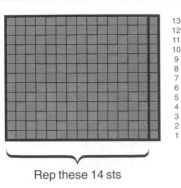

13
12
11
10
9
8
7
6
5
4
3
2
1

Rep these 14 sts

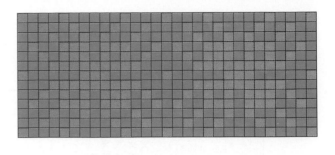

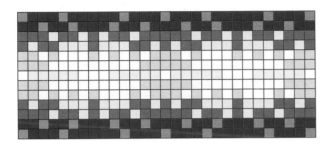

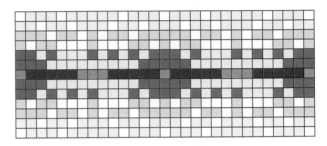

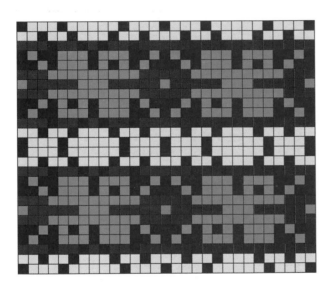

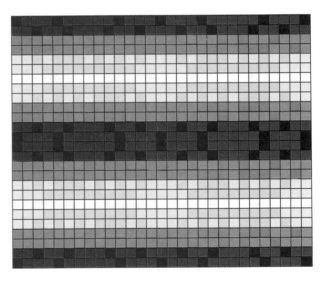

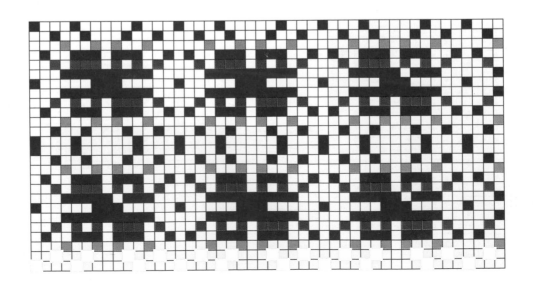

15.1

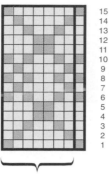

15
14
13
12
11
10
9
8
7
6
5
4
3
2
1

Rep these 7 sts

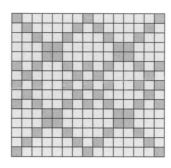

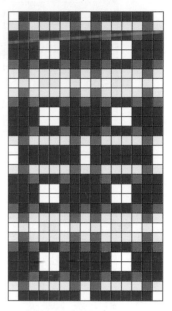

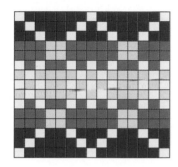

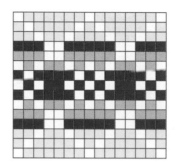

15.2

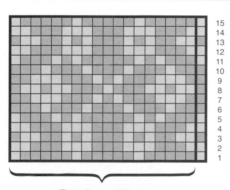

15
14
13
12
11
10
9
8
7
6
5
4
3
2
1

Rep these 18 sts

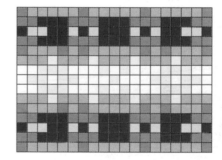

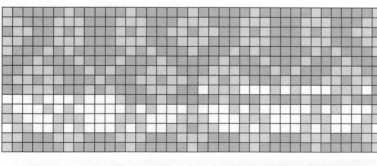

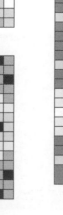

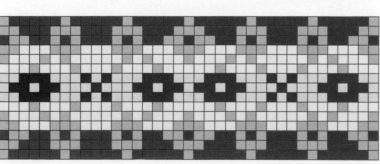

16 - 18 Row Patterns

16.1

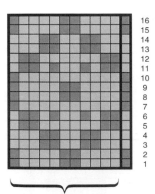

16
15
14
13
12
11
10
9
8
7
6
5
4
3
2
1

Rep these 11 sts

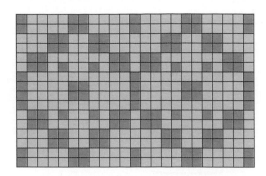

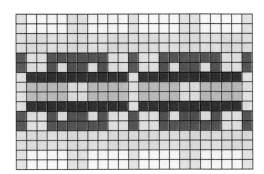

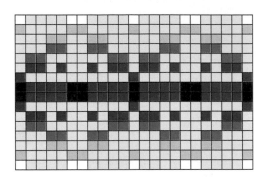

18.1

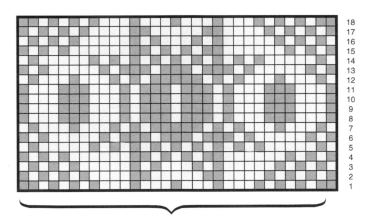

18
17
16
15
14
13
12
11
10
9
8
7
6
5
4
3
2
1

Rep these 31 sts

Worked as a 58 row repeat of 2 bands and 2 borders. Rows 1-18 as chart, then an 11 row border. Rows 30-47 as chart but worked from 16th (centre) stitch (see page 121), then an 11 row border.

Background colours:
Rows 1-4, 15-18, 30-33 and 44-47 = E,   5-7, 12-14, 34-36 and 41-43 = N,   8-11 and 37-40 = D,   19-29 and 48-58 = F.

Pattern colours:
Rows 1-4, 15-18, 24, 30-33, 44-47 and 53 = D,   5-8, 11-14, 34-37 and 40-43 = C,   9, 10, 20-23, 25-28, 38, 39, 49-52, 54-57 = G.
For more information on how pattern is built see page 172.

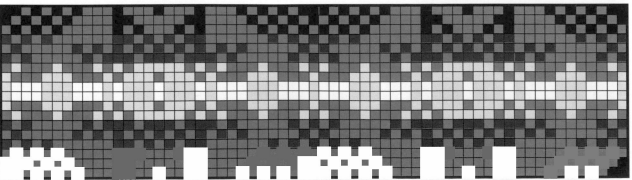

18.2

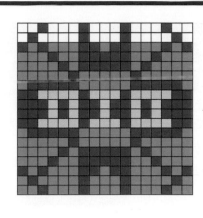

18
17
16
15
14
13
12
11
10
9
8
7
6
5
4
3
2
1

Rep these 17 sts

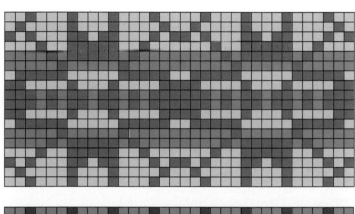

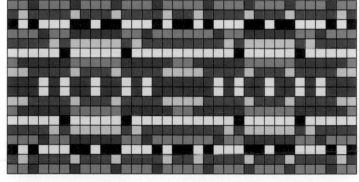

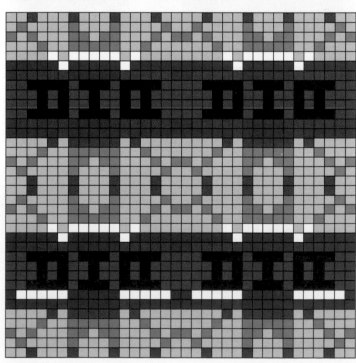

19 Row Patterns

19.1

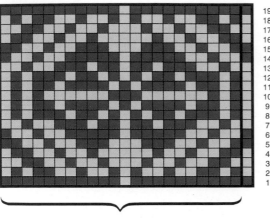

19
18
17
16
15
14
13
12
11
10
9
8
7
6
5
4
3
2
1

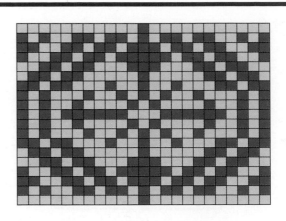

Rep these 22 sts

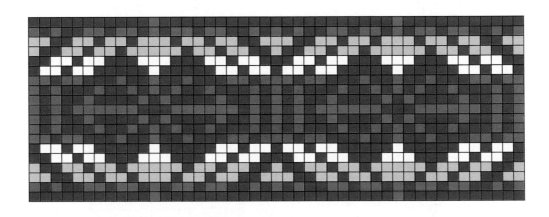

19.2

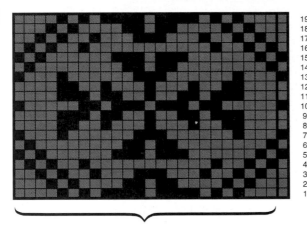

19
18
17
16
15
14
13
12
11
10
9
8
7
6
5
4
3
2
1

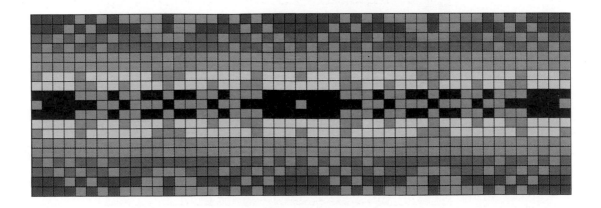

Rep these 24 sts

25.1

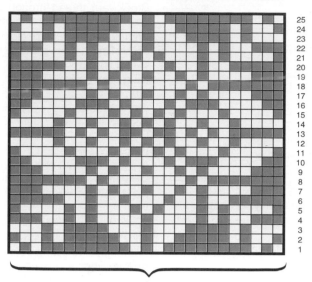

25
24
23
22
21
20
19
18
17
16
15
14
13
12
11
10
9
8
7
6
5
4
3
2
1

Rep these 25 sts

Worked as a band with a 9 row border as a 34 row repeat.
Background colours:
Rows 1-25, 27-29, 31-33 = I,   26 and 34 = D,   30 = J.
Pattern colours:
Rows 1 and 25 = H,   2-4 and 22-24 = G,   5-8 and 18-21 = F,   9-12 and 14-17 = Q,   13 = L,   27,
28, 32 and 33 = D,   13 and 29-31 = E.

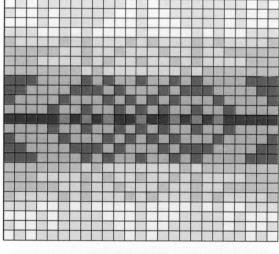

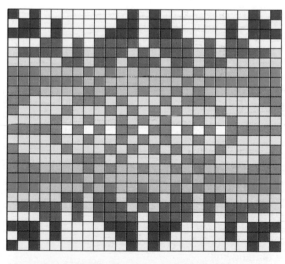

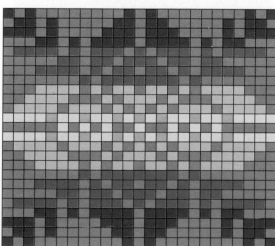

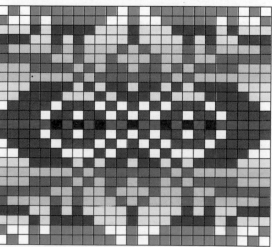

Fair Isle Gloves

Measurements

Width round palm 21 cm [8½ ins]

Materials

Double Knitting (Sports Weight) yarn

Main Colour (M) (dark green) 50 grams [2 ounces].

Oddments each in Colours A (yellow), B (gold), C (red), D (white).

Pair needles each size 3¼mm (UK 10, USA 3 or 4) and 4mm (UK 8, USA 6).

The quantities of yarn stated are based on average requirements and are therefore approximate.

For abbreviations see pages 20 and 21.

Figures or instructions given in [ ]s should be repeated as stated after the brackets.

Special Abbreviations

M1 (Make 1 stitch) = pick up the strand of yarn lying between last st worked and next st and knit into back of it.

Slip marker = make a slip knot in a short length of contrasting yarn and plance on needle where indicated. On the following rounds slip the marker from one needle to the other until the pattern is established and the marker is no longer required.

Tension

22 sts and 30 rows = 10 cm [4 ins] square measured over st st using larger needles.

Right Hand

Using smaller needles and M, cast on 46 sts.

1st row (right side): K2, *p2, k2; rep from * to end.

2nd row: P2, *k2, p2; rep from * to end.

Rep these 2 rows until rib measures 5 cm [2 ins] ending with a 2nd row, increasing 1 st at beg of last row. (47 sts).

Change to larger needles and work 4 rows in st st starting knit.

Shape Thumb Gusset

1st row: K25, M1, k3, M1, k19. 49 sts.

2nd row: Purl.

3rd row: K1, slip marker (see Special Abbreviations), work 1st row of chart across next 23 sts, slip marker, knit to end.

4th row: P25, work 2nd row of chart, p1.

Keeping Fair Isle pattern correct on sts between markers continue as follows:

5th row: Work 25 sts, M1, k5, M1, k19. 51 sts.

Work 3 rows straight.

9th row: Work 25 sts, M1, k7, M1, k19. 53 sts.

Work 1 row straight.

Keeping continuity of chart correct on sts between markers until completed and then continuing in M only, inc 2 sts in this way on next and following 2 alt rows. 59 sts.

Work 1 row straight thus ending with a wrong side row.

Divide for Thumb

Next row: Work 40 sts, turn.

★ **Next row:** Inc in first st, p13, inc in next st, turn.

Work 14 rows in st st on these 17 sts starting knit.

Next row: K2tog, *k1, k2tog; rep from * to end.

Next row: P1, *p2tog; rep from * to end.

Break yarn, thread through remaining sts, draw up firmly and fasten off ★.

With right side facing, rejoin yarn at base of thumb, pick up and k3 sts from base of thumb, k19. 47 sts.

Keeping pattern and st st correct as set, work 10 rows straight thus ending with a right side row.

Next row (decrease): P26, *p2tog, p6; rep from * to last 5 sts, p2tog, purl to end. 44 sts remain.

★★ Divide for Fingers

Next row: K28, turn.

Next row: Inc in first st, p11, inc in next st, turn.

Work 20 rows in st st on these 15 sts for first finger.

Next row: *K1, k2tog; rep from * to end.

Next row: *P2tog; rep from * to end.

Break yarn, thread through remaining sts, draw up firmly and fasten off.

With right side facing, rejoin yarn at base of first finger, pick up and k2 sts from base of first finger, k6, turn.

Next row: Inc in first st, p11, inc in next st, turn.

Work 22 rows in st st on these 15 sts for second finger. Complete as given for first finger.

With right side facing, rejoin yarn at base of second finger, pick up and k2 sts from base of second finger, k5, turn.

Next row: Inc in first st, p10, inc in next st, turn.

Work 20 rows in st st on these 14 sts for third finger. Complete as given for thumb.

With right side facing, rejoin yarn at base of third finger, pick up and k2 sts from base of third finger, knit to end.

Work 15 rows in st st on these 12 sts for fourth finger. Complete as given for first finger.

Left Hand

Using smaller needles and M, cast on 46 sts and work 5 cm [2 ins] in rib as given for Right Hand ending with 2nd row, increasing 1 st at end of last row. (47 sts).

Change to larger needles and work 4 rows in st st starting knit.

Shape Thumb Gusset

1st row: K19, M1, k3, M1, knit to end. 49 sts.

2nd row: Purl.

3rd row: K25, slip marker, work 1st row of chart across next 23 sts, slip marker, knit to end.

4th row: P1, work 2nd row of chart, purl to end.

Keeping Fair Isle pattern correct on sts between markers continue as follows:

5th row: K19, M1, k5, M1, work to end. 51 sts.

Work 3 rows straight.

9th row: K19, M1, k7, M1, work to end. 53 sts.

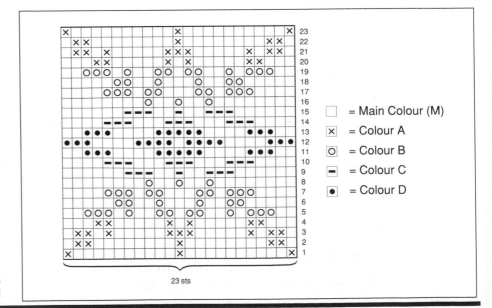

23 sts

☐ = Main Colour (M)

☒ = Colour A

⊙ = Colour B

— = Colour C

● = Colour D

Work 1 row straight.

Keeping continuity of chart correct on sts between markers until completed and then continuing in M only, inc 2 sts in this way on next and following 2 alt rows. 59 sts.

Work 1 row straight thus ending with a wrong side row.

Divide for Thumb

Next row: K34, turn.

Complete as given for Thumb of Right Hand from ★ to ★.

With right side facing rejoin yarn at base of thumb, pick up and k3 sts from base of thumb, work in pattern to end. 47 sts.

Keeping pattern and st st correct as set, work 10 rows straight thus ending with a right side row.

Next row (decrease): P3, p2tog, [p6, p2tog] twice, purl to end. 44 sts remain.

Complete as given for Right Hand from ★★ to end.

To Finish

Do not press. Join all seams.

For instructions for Beret see page 130.

30 Row Motifs

30.1

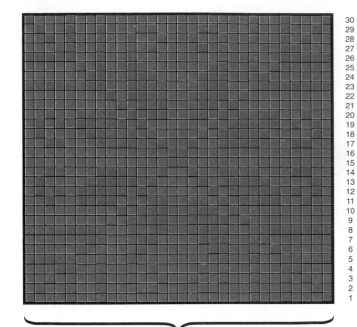

30
29
28
27
26
25
24
23
22
21
20
19
18
17
16
15
14
13
12
11
10
9
8
7
6
5
4
3
2
1

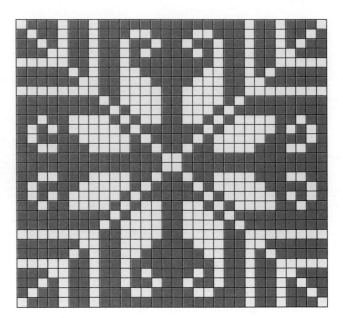

Rep these 30 sts

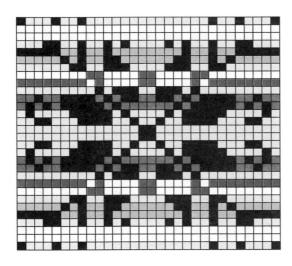

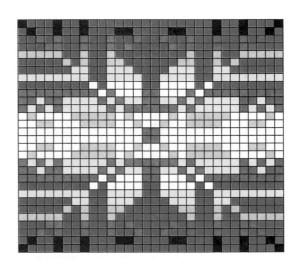

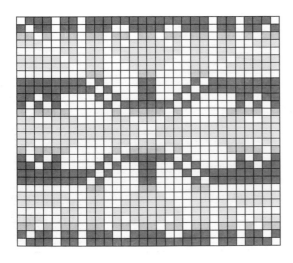

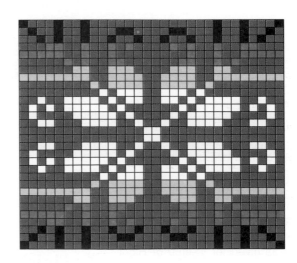

30.2

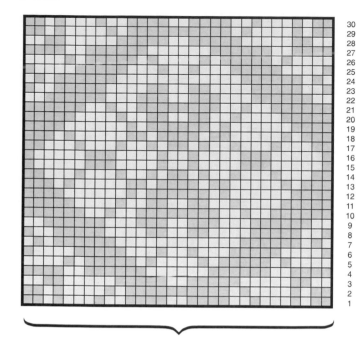

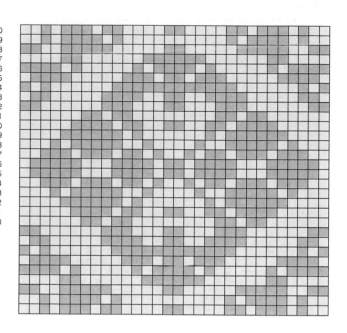

30
29
28
27
26
25
24
23
22
21
20
19
18
17
16
15
14
13
12
11
10
9
8
7
6
5
4
3
2
1

Rep these 30 sts

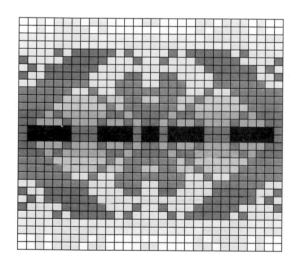

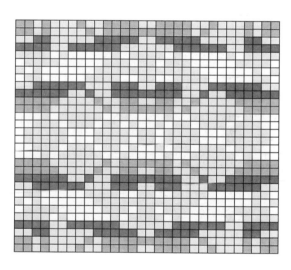

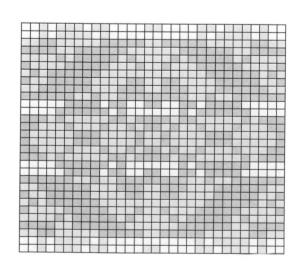

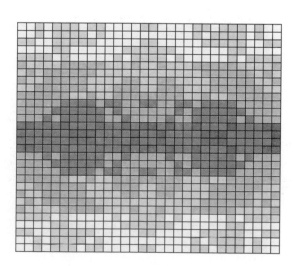

30 Row Motifs

30.3

30
29
28
27
26
25
24
23
22
21
20
19
18
17
16
15
14
13
12
11
10
9
8
7
6
5
4
3
2
1

Rep these 30 sts

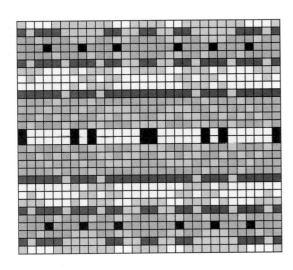

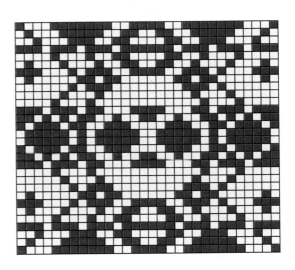

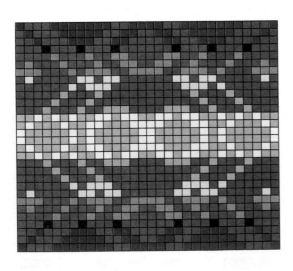

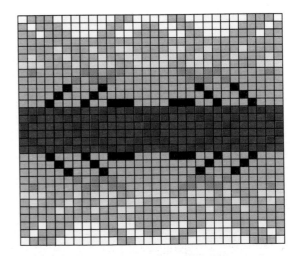

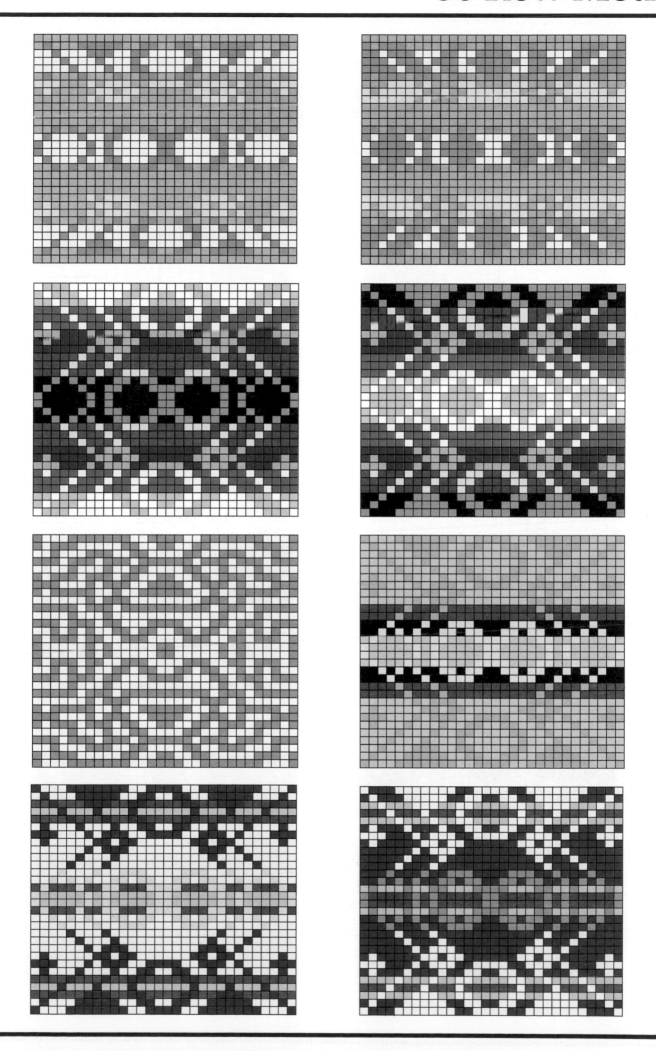

33 Row Motifs

33.1

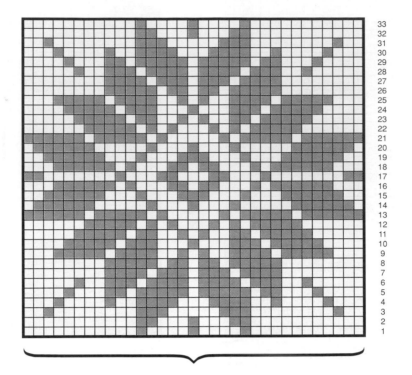

33
32
31
30
29
28
27
26
25
24
23
22
21
20
19
18
17
16
15
14
13
12
11
10
9
8
7
6
5
4
3
2
1

Rep these 33 sts

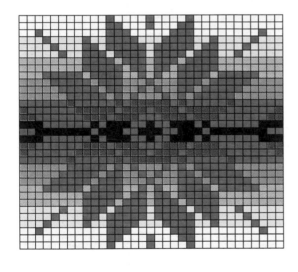

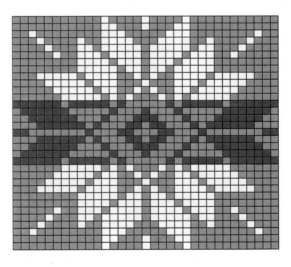

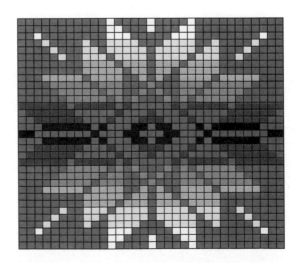

33.2

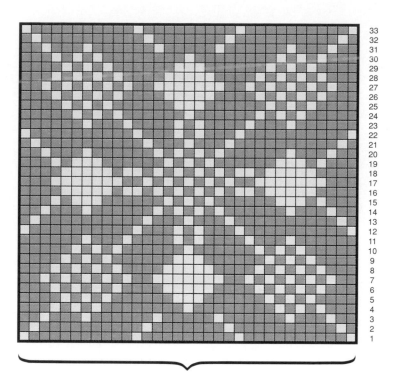

Rep these 33 sts

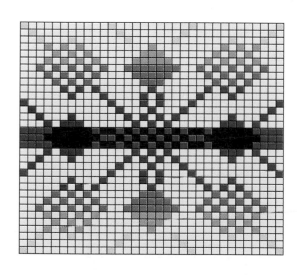

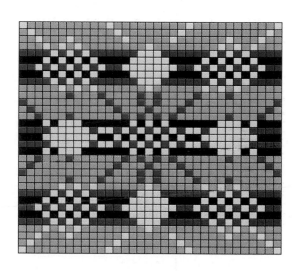

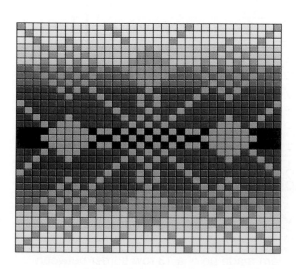

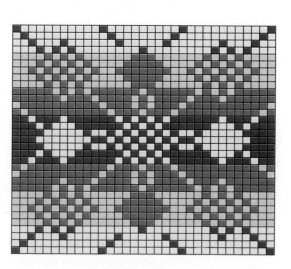

Fair Isle Combinations

I

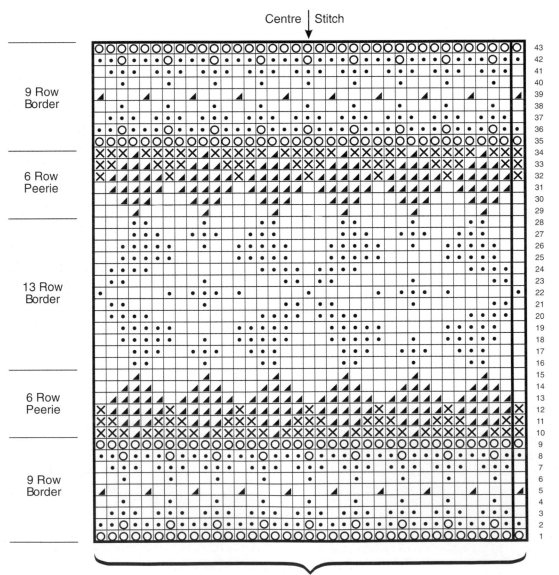

Centre | Stitch

9 Row
Border

6 Row
Peerie

13 Row
Border

6 Row
Peerie

9 Row
Border

43
42
41
40
39
38
37
36
35
34
33
32
31
30
29
28
27
26
25
24
23
22
21
20
19
18
17
16
15
14
13
12
11
10
9
8
7
6
5
4
3
2
1

Rep these 36 sts

The above chart is a 43 row band of pattern made up of a 13 row border between two 9 row borders, and two 6 row peeries. See Fair Isle Top on page 152.

II

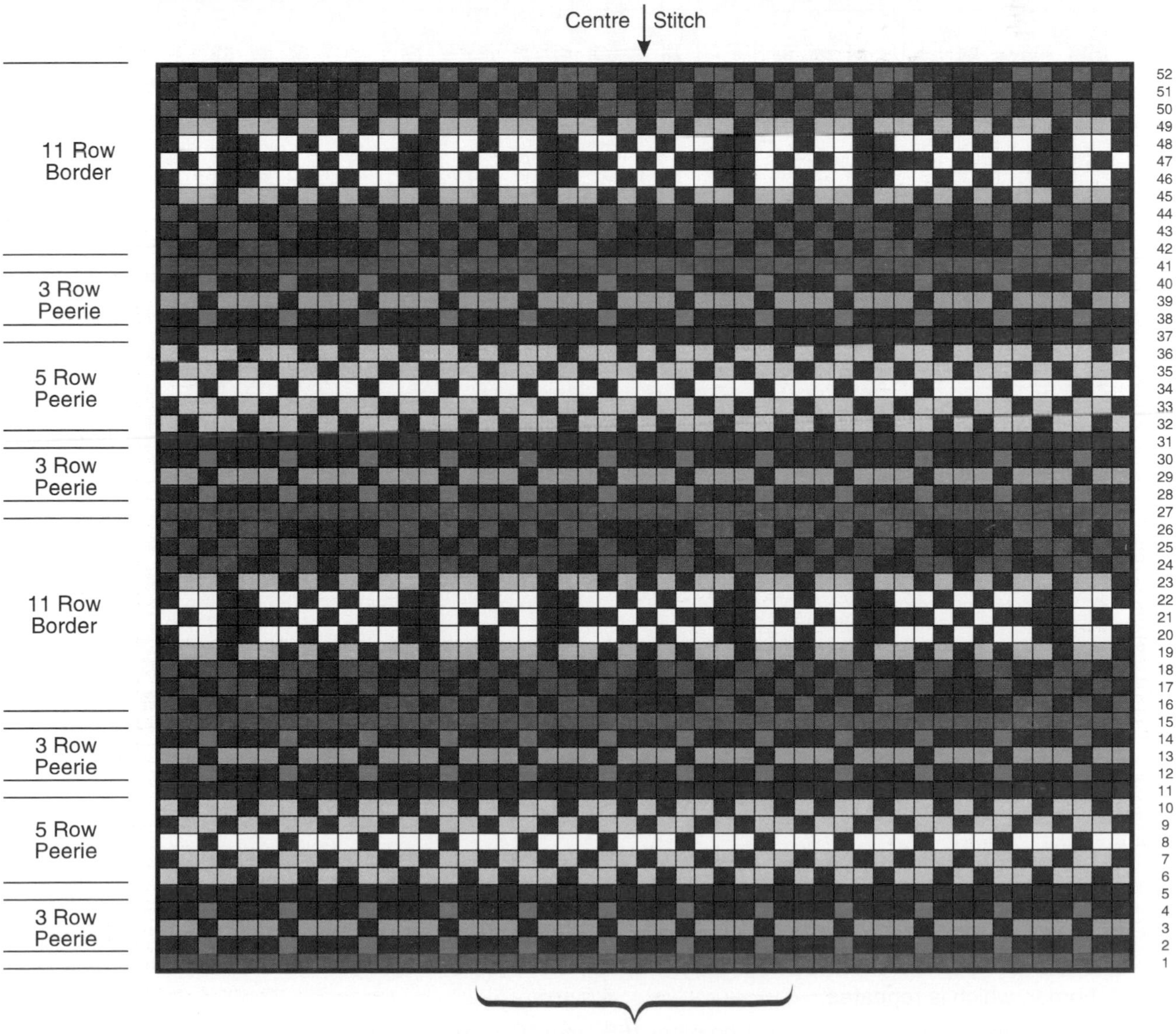

Centre | Stitch

11 Row Border		52
		51
		50
		49
		48
		47
		46
		45
		44
		43
		42
3 Row Peerie		41
		40
		39
		38
5 Row Peerie		37
		36
		35
		34
		33
3 Row Peerie		32
		31
		30
		29
		28
11 Row Border		27
		26
		25
		24
		23
		22
		21
		20
		19
		18
		17
3 Row Peerie		16
		15
		14
		13
5 Row Peerie		12
		11
		10
		9
		8
3 Row Peerie		7
		6
		5
		4
		3
		2
		1

Rep these 16 sts

The above chart is a 26 row repeat made up of a 11 row border, a 5 row peerie and two 3 row peeries.

Fair Isle Combinations

III

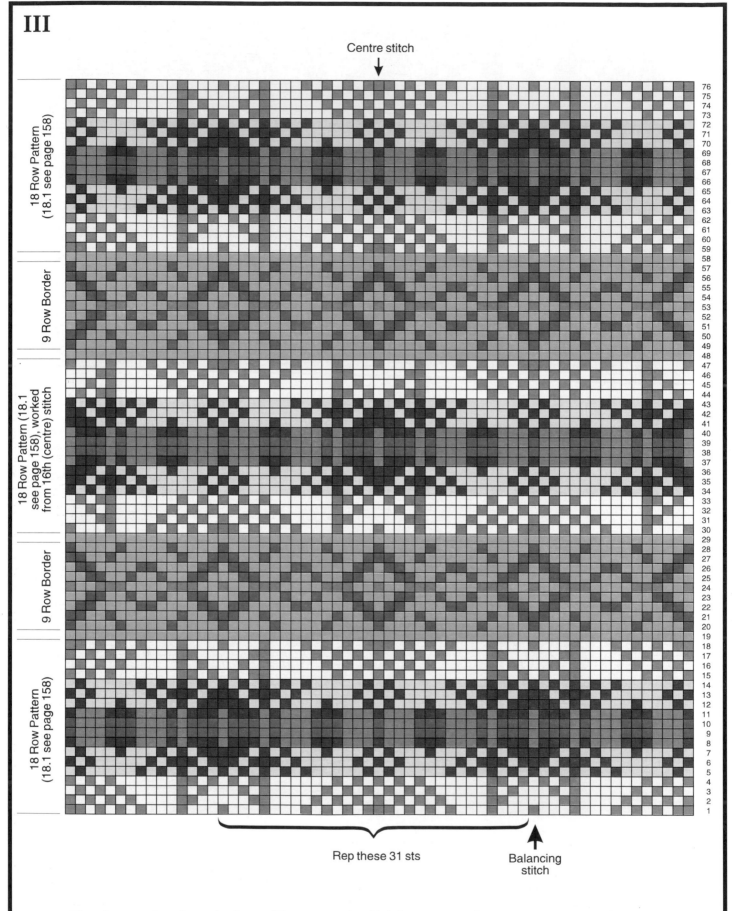

Centre stitch

18 Row Pattern (18.1 see page 158)

9 Row Border

18 Row Pattern (18.1 see page 158), worked from 16th (centre) stitch

9 Row Border

18 Row Pattern (18.1 see page 158)

Rep these 31 sts

Balancing stitch

The above pattern is worked as a 58 row repeat, which is made up of 2 18 row patterns and a 9 row border, which is repeated.

Rows 1 to 18 are as Pattern 18.1 on page 158, row 19 is knitted in one colour, rows 20 to 28 are a 9 row border, row 29 is knitted in one colour, rows 30-47 as chart 18.1 but worked from 16th (centre) stitch -see page 121, then rows 19 to 29 are repeated.

Index

Index